SEARCHING FOR HIDDEN ANIMALS

"Agunalaksh"—the shores where the sea breaks its back.

SEARCHING
FOR HIDDEN
ANIMALS

ROY P. MACKAL

DOUBLEDAY & COMPANY, INC.
GARDEN CITY, NEW YORK
1980

Library of Congress Cataloging in Publication Data
Mackal, Roy P
    Searching for Hidden Animals
    Bibliography: p.
    Includes index.
    1. Animal lore. 2. Monsters. 3. Animals,
Legends and stories of.   I. Title.
QL89.M22   001.9′44
ISBN: 0-385-14897-6
Library of Congress Catalog Card Number 79-6599

301125

The following are the sources of the drawings, photographs, and other illustrations used in this book:

Frontispiece, from *Thiergeschichte der Nördlichen Polarländer* by Thomas Pennant, 1787; 1 (after Edwin H. Colbert), 2, 5, 6, 8, 10, 21, 24, 30, 79, 80 (after Metcalf), 81 (after Ellis L. Michael), 85 (after Henrietta Hyman, *The Invertebrates*, Vol. V), drawn by Kathy Hirsch; 3 (after an American Geographical Society map), 14, 19 (after Gary S. Mangiacopra), 25 (after James Powell), 26 (after James Powell and Ivan Sanderson), 34 (after W. Douglas Burden), 66 (after *Humboldt and the Cosmos* by Douglas Botting), 74, 77 (after a map in *In Patagonia* by Bruce Chatwin, 1977), 78, 86, 88, 90, drawn by Mary Wall; 4, reprinted from *Bering's Voyages*, F. A. Golder, editor, courtesy American Geographical Society; 7, from *A Review of Archaeoceti* by Remington Kellogg, courtesy Carnegie Institution of Washington Press; 11, photo by John Warham, courtesy of Zoology Department, University of Canterbury, Christchurch, N.Z.; 15, courtesy St. Augustine Historical Society and the Smithsonian Institution; 16, courtesy St. Augustine Historical Society; 17, courtesy Smithsonian Institution; 18, courtesy Dr. Joseph F. Gennaro, Jr.; 22, from *Prehistoric Reptiles and Birds* by Josef Augusta and Zdneěk Burian; 23, from *In Witch-bound Africa* by Frank H. Melland, courtesy Seeley, Service & Co.; 24, 27, 28, 29, 29A, courtesy James Powell; 31, 32, courtesy Charles Stonor; 33, courtesy *Illustrated London News*; 35, courtesy American Museum of Natural History; 36, from *Madagascar, Mauritius and Other East-African Islands* by Dr. C. Keller, courtesy George Allen and Unwin Ltd.; 37, 44, 45, from *The Age of Monsters* by Augusta and Burian, courtesy Artia; 38, 39, 40, 41, 42 from *The Dodo and Kindred Birds* by Masauji Hachisuka; 43, courtesy Defense Mapping Agency, U. S. Naval Oceanographic Office; 46, courtesy Otago Museum, N.Z.; 47, courtesy Canterbury Museum, N.Z.; 48, 51, 56 (specimen loaned by the Smithsonian Institution from the Atlantic Bransfield Straight), 57, courtesy Riccardo Levi-Setti; 49, 52 (after Leif Störmer), 53, from *Treatise on Invertebrate Paleontology*, courtesy the Geological Society of America and the University of Kansas; 50 (after Walcott and Raymond from Störmer), 54 (after Van der Hoever from Fage), 55 (after Versluys and Demoll from Kaestner), courtesy W. B. Saunders Company; 59, courtesy Guy Guthridge, National Science Foundation, Polar Information Services; 58, 60, courtesy Larry Sullivan, Lamont-Doherty Geological Observatory of Columbia University and the P. P. Shirslov Institute of Oceanology, USSR Academy of Science; 61, Warren Hamilton and David Krinsley, Bulletin, Geological Society of America, Vol. 78, 1967, courtesy Geological Society of America; 62, from D. Van Hilten, *Tectonophysics*, Vol. 1, 1964, courtesy Dr. D. Van Hilten and Elsevier Publishing Company; 63, 64 (after Chaloner and Lacey, 1973), from original maps in Special Papers in Paleontology, No. 12, courtesy authors and the Paleontological Association; 65, 72, 75, 84, courtesy Grzimek's Tierleben, Kindler Verlag, Zurich; 67, 69 (restored by C. Knight from a skeleton in Princeton University Museum), 68 and 70 (restored from skeletons in La Plata Museum, Buenos Aires), 71 (restored from Sir R. Owen's figure of the skeleton), 76 (from J. Murie), from A *History of Land Mammals in the Western Hemisphere* by William Berryman Scott, 1937, courtesy Sarah P. Scott; 82, from "Medusae from the Maldive Islands" by Henry S. Bigelow, *Bulletin of the Museum of Comparative Zoology*, Vol. XXXIX, No. 9, 1904, courtesy Museum of Comparative Zoology, Harvard; 87, courtesy Coward, McCann & Geoghegan, Inc.; 89, courtesy Associated Press; 91, from The Webster Collection, courtesy New Brunswick Museum; 92, 93, 94, courtesy Milwaukee *Sentinel*; 95, courtesy of the Natural History Museum, Los Angeles, California; 96, courtesy Field Museum of Natural History, Chicago; 97, from *Carnivorous Plants* by Yolande Heslop-Harrison, © 1978 by Scientific American, Inc., all rights reserved. Chart of Geological Time Periods, based on information contained in The Mitchell Beazley Atlas of World Wildlife. Copyright © 1973 Mitchell Beazley Limited. Published in the United States by Rand McNally & Company, Chicago.

Acknowledgments

I wish to expess my indebtedness to the explorers, zoologists, animal collectors, writers, and romantic souls of the past who have in lesser or greater degree laid the groundwork for cryptozoology. I am grateful to a large number of contemporary colleagues who are presently engaged in cryptozoological studies, often in spite of controversy.

I wish to thank my son, Paul Karl, for his helpful suggestions regarding the Preface and Introduction and Professor Riccardo Levi-Setti for his critical editing of Chapter VII and for his contribution of superb trilobite photographs.

I further wish to acknowledge colleagues, specialists in various disciplines, and others not engaged in cryptozoology as such, too numerous to name, but who have so generously contributed their knowledge and encouragement.

A special note of thanks is due my artists, Kathy Hirsch and Mary Wall, who have worked so hard to illustrate my concepts and to my typists, Adelaide Jaffe and Valerie Heim.

I am most grateful for the illustrative material already acknowledged in the text.

In addition, I wish to thank Dodd, Mead & Company for permission to reprint the poem *Story by Lalli-ji, the Priest* from *India's Love Lyrics* by Lawrence Hope, and the Asheville *Citizen Times* for permission to reprint the article by John Parris entitled "Cherokees Have Own Loch Ness Monster."

Lastly, I wish to thank the late Mary Moon and the executors of her estate for allowing me to draw heavily on her compilation of "Ogopogo" data.

Contents

Preface

Officially, "cryptozoology"—that is, an area of study within the main corpus of zoology that is recognized by all and sundry as a legitimate concern of professional zoologists, specifically dealing with the study and search for unidentified living animals—does not exist.

To my knowledge the first use of the term "cryptozoology" was made by Belgian zoologist Bernard Heuvelmans in 1965 in his book *Le Grande Serpent-de-Mer*. Yet the term "cryptozoology" seems to me particularly appropriate, coming as it does from the Greek word *kryptos*, meaning "hidden," "unknown," "secret," "enigmatic," "mysterious"; hence literally the study of hidden animals.

While this area of study is not yet formally recognized, it has existed as a somewhat less than respectable branch of zoology for a long time. More often than not it has been practiced by circus entrepreneurs, commercial animal collectors, and dilettantes. Perhaps the reason for this conjunction is that cryptozoology must be separated from the pure and simple search for new species, which is and always has been a perfectly respectable zoological activity. The animals that fall within our definition of cryptozoology have associated with them some unusually strange or bizarre aspect.

They may have been described or known only as myth or native superstition—for example, the Kraken. They may be reported to be unusually large or diminutive varieties of known species—for example, the pygmy hippopotamus. Or they may be a relict species persisting from the dim prehistoric past, as in the case of the coelacanth, which was thought to be extinct for sixty-five million years, but was found alive and well in 1939 in African coastal seas.

In most instances the existence of this sort of animal was originally discounted entirely or simply dismissed as the mistaken identification of an ordinary animal—for example, the okapi—or even labeled an out-and-out fraud or hoax. Professional zoological skepticism, often faced with fragmentary or inadequate evidence, is justified, and it is precisely the concern of the cryptozoologist to investigate, study, and determine whether or not a particular case represents something solid, real, and, perhaps, unique.

Intimately associated with this endeavor is zoological sleuthing—that is, finding the true explanation for what appears to be zoologically bizarre but in reality may be fantastic and/or trivial.

I expect and hope that cryptozoology will eventually be accepted as a legitimate and recognized scientific activity in a manner analogous to rocketry and space exploratory science. Even though we do not as yet have in hand a single extraterrestrial life form, exobiology is funded and accepted. Why not cryptozoology?

It is toward this end that this book is directed. It is designed to open doors and to engage readers and students. Ultimately, I hope it will prompt those who have the requisite resources to mount searches and expeditions that may, in some cases, lead to new and exciting zoological discoveries and contribute toward the development of science.

ROY P. MACKAL

June 1979

Introduction to the Skeptic

In the view of many people, including professionals, the idea that large undiscovered varieties of animals exist in our atmosphere, our seas and lakes, and on the land masses of our planet seems at least slightly absurd. After all, the last new continent was discovered almost five hundred years ago. Certainly five hundred years is a long time, especially when we note the exponential rise of science, technology, and exploration. It does, therefore, at first glance appear reasonable to conclude that all existing life forms except perhaps a few small obscure creatures have already found their way into zoos, aquaria, museums, or at least zoological and botanical archives and textbooks.

This zoological world view is not of recent origin. Back in 1812 Georges Cuvier, the father of paleontology, stated: "There is little hope of discovering new species of large quadrapeds." Many have come after Cuvier with similar pronouncements, and all have been proved wrong repeatedly. Now it is true that somewhere discovery must end, sometime everything will be numbered, measured, and cataloged. But the question really boils down to whether or not we have reached that point now, granting it had not been reached in 1812 or even in 1900. The chapters that follow, I believe, establish that we are quite a long way from scraping the bottom of the barrel of zoological unknowns. The fact is that there are quite a number of areas, some large, some small, some water, and some land, where the probability is quite high that large unidentified animals still exist waiting for our curious eyes.

The northern Pacific and Arctic Oceans harbor, exclusive of the supposedly extinct northern sea cow, at least one and perhaps as many as three types of unknown aquatic creatures. The depths of the Atlantic Ocean in the vicinity of the Bahama Islands probably are the lair or playground (depending on viewpoint, yours or that of the animal in question) of gigantic octopuses up to 60 meters (200 feet) long, tentacle tip to tentacle tip. Doubters must reckon with documentation and an actual piece of flesh of such a monster preserved in a jar of formaldehyde at the Smithsonian Institution.

Dr. Challenger, in Conan Doyle's novel *The Lost World*, brought back to London a live pterodactyl in order to confound his critics. That of course was fiction, but we shall describe investigations in a remote part of South Africa made by M. Coutenay-Latimer, the discoverer of the coelacanth, which might involve such creatures.

Asia also provides areas with promise of still unknown animals. We all remember the wonder as children of seeing reconstructions of extinct primeval giants, such as the carnivorous reptile *Tyrannosaurus rex*, and the formidable large herbivore with a minuscule brain, *Brontosaurus*. Do such giants still exist in some remote part of Africa or Asia? Most probably not, but giant lizards are still with us, and we shall explore the reports of unidentified giant lizardlike reptiles in northeastern India, possibly related to the famous Komodo dragon found on certain Indonesian islands.

In addition to Asia and Africa, South America is rife with rumors of strange animals. The vast unexplored jungles of the Mato Grosso have intrigued explorers from the very beginning of the discovery of the New World. Today this vast area is succumbing to the bulldozer, and the ancient relict civilization, sought by the great early-twentieth-century explorer Colonel Percy Fawcett, has not been found. Nevertheless, there are still localities that may hide some zoological surprises.

We shall explore the depths of the seas for evidence of animals with external skeletons, born perhaps in the Precambrian Age one hundred million years before the earliest Paleozoic Era, six hundred million years ago. These animals were confined to salt water, but certain fresh-water lakes in Canada and even in the United States may conceal other types of interesting and perhaps new animal species. These lakes offer an opportunity for the low-budgeted amateur zoological sleuth to carry on his own investigations.

Returning to the middle and upper depths of the oceans we shall encounter little-known backboneless animals that form large snakelike colonies up to 23 meters (75 feet) in length. These colonial animals foreshadow the development of higher forms, since not only do they act in concert to provide propulsion, but also they actually become differentiated for specialized functions. Certainly some of the so-called sea serpent reports must have resulted from the observations of such colonies of smaller creatures.

Most nonbiologists intuitively classify life forms as animals if they move about and as plants if they do not move. When we find plants that not only can move rapidly but also are meat-eating, actively trapping animals for food, one experiences a crawling feeling that here is something monstrous. We shall explore and assess legends that describe such giant man-eating plants.

Aside from large continents, are there smaller land masses, islands perhaps, that have escaped man's probing eyes? Again the answer is yes! New Zealand and even tiny coral islands east of the Malagasy Republic may yet yield something quite unusual in birdlife. Perhaps the dodo and giant moa still persist.

Well, you may say, this all sounds very romantic and exciting, but isn't this all part of a "goblin world" of unreality, or at the very best just wishful thinking? As Don Quixote longed for the vanishing days of knights, fair ladies, and noble quests, am I a zoological Don Quixote deluding myself with fanciful tales of monsters long extinct or strange new creatures from the fantasy of dreams?

A fair question, which deserves an answer. First, I must admit that a strain of romance certainly runs through most of us and does indeed contribute toward a wish to believe in the strange, bizarre, unknown, or terrible. However, recognizing that this emotional trait may contribute greatly to the avidity with which some of us pursue the unknown, it should not be allowed to obscure the fact that new and bizarre animals have been discovered in the past and continue to come to light.

I have noted that there is a general feeling afoot, both in the minds of the general public and of noninvolved colleagues, that admits that while discoveries of strange objects or animals have occurred in the past, in this day and age "miracles" no longer happen.

Examination of literature and records of past discoveries reveal, however, that this attitude was always present. This penchant for unreasonable skepticism is well illustrated by the circumstances and events surrounding the discovery of *Octopus giganteus Verrill*, which is not officially accepted to this day (discussed in Chapter 3).

There is also a sense of despair of long standing, having to do with long-drawn-out research, especially when beset by a high proportion of failures relative to successes, and many inconclusive results. Such an atmosphere, which incidentally has been the rule rather than the exception with most difficult projects, not only in zoological sleuthing, tends to discourage and ultimately may produce a negative psychological state antagonistic to the further pursuit of a project or the subject in general. Most of us have had such experiences in varying degrees. This, of course, is part of the reason why ultimate successes in the face of great difficulties are rare. I am not suggesting that one should continue futile pursuits when all or most substantial evidence is negative. As this book shows, evidence relative to such efforts exists in abundance. The effort clearly is justified, in my opinion.

To illustrate my contention, let us consider the case of the okapi, now recognized as virtually a living, breathing "paleotragus" that is alive and well in many zoos in addition to its home in the Congo rain forest—and according to the fossil record extinct since the Miocene Age, twenty to forty million years ago.

Early rock and cave paintings in Africa and elsewhere depict many kinds of animals, some of which can be clearly related to known animals, while others cannot. There are also paintings and carvings on Egyptian, Sumerian, and Assyrian arti-

1. *Palaeotragus.*

facts depicting known and unknown animals, including some perhaps representing nothing more than the artist's imagination or mythical composite creatures. These renderings include some that in hindsight look very much like the okapi, now known to all of us. Dr. Edwin H. Colbert, an eminent paleontologist, published a paper in 1936 in which he made a very convincing case that sivatherium, an extinct giraffid, was represented by a Sumerian chariot rein ring sculpture dating from 2500 B.C. We probably will never know with certainty whether the okapi (or paleotragus) was more widely spread than it is today and so was known to the early Egyptians and Sumerians.

In any case, we know that rumors about a strange horselike animal of striking black and white markings with a horn or horns surfaced from the very depths of the African equatorial forests in the early 1800s. "Ah," you may say, "obviously a zebra!" The problem with that identification is that all types of horses, including zebras, are plains and savanna animals. Historically there have been few if any forest-dwelling species.

These rumors found their way into a book encountered by Sir Harry H. Johnston, explorer and eventual discoverer of the okapi, as a child in the 1860s. He describes in his report of the okapi how the contents of this book* lingered in his consciousness, and were revived when he came upon a reference to reports of asslike animals in the Congo, in H. M. Stanley's *In Darkest Africa*. In Volume II, Appendix B, under Notes we read, "The Wambutti knew a donkey and called it 'atti.' They say that they sometimes catch them in pits. What they can find to eat is a wonder. They eat leaves."

This report from Wambutti pygmies appears to have had little effect on Stanley, but it interested Johnston greatly. When Johnston became the special commissioner for Uganda, British East Africa, in 1899, he determined to make further inquiries.

A lucky circumstance led Johnston in the right direction. Shortly after arriving in Uganda, he was obliged to intervene to prevent, as he put it, "a too-enterprising German carrying off by force a troop of Konga dwarfs [pygmies] to perform at the Paris Exhibition. These little men had been kidnaped on Congo Free State territory. The Belgian authorities very properly objected, and as the German impresario had fled with his dwarfs to British territory, they asked me to rescue the little men from his clutches and send them back to their homes." This he did and discussed with them the strange

* *The Romance of Natural History* by Phillip Gosse, 1860.

horselike creature rumored to inhabit their homeland. The pygmies called the animal "okapi," saying it had stripes like a zebra but only on the legs and lower part of the body, the upper part being brown without stripes. The most exciting part of their description was that feet of the animals consisted of more than a single part—in other words, had several sections or toes.

Johnston's heart must have skipped a beat. Multitoed horses existed in the prehistoric past, but they have been extinct for millions of years. Could this be the three-toed horse known as hipparion?

Unknown to Johnston there had been other reports of this strange animal, some of which today appear to be spurious, and they were only made public after the okapi actually was made known in 1900.

According to C. A. Spinage, a leading authority on the giraffe and okapi, there were at least two authentic reports about okapis aside from Stanley's reference. In 1897 an official of the Congo Free State, under Belgian rule, provided his superiors with a description of a strange animal, assumed to be some sort of antelope, which the Momvus tribe called "Ndumbe." This report, based on descriptions from natives inhabiting the northeastern Congo, escaped notice, but we now know that it clearly referred to the okapi. The report reads: "Of a height superior to the buffalo, with a black head, the neck and body maroon brown; the rump striped with black and white rays. These rays form rings on the four legs. The tail is twenty inches long and terminates in a tuft of hair. It has the graceful form and finish of the zebra. Its flesh is excellent."

Two years later, in 1899, a strip of okapi skin in the form of a strap came into the hands of Lieutenant M. E. Vincait, also a Belgian official. The skin was sent to Belgium, but there it was regarded only as one of many curiosities, perhaps the skin of a mutant zebra.

Johnston, unaware of these and other reports, obtained confirmation of the pygmies' stories from Archdeacon Lloyd of the Moboga Mission, who claimed to have observed live okapis. A Lieutenant Meura at Fort Mbeni in the Congo provided further information in response to Johnston's inquiries. He told Johnston that the natives often brought in carcasses, which apparently seemed hardly extraordinary or significant to Lieutenant Meura. (I might interject at this point that in our own discussions with individuals regarding unknown animals common to their experience, we frequently encountered a similar lack of appreciation of the importance of what to them must be quite mundane.)

Meura agreed to provide guidance to an area where a specimen might be shot. For a short time Johnston thought he had hard evidence without going further since a rumor developed that an actual skin was lying somewhere in the military camp. A search was made, but no skin was found. Instead, two bandoliers apparently made from the skin of a strange animal, probably cut from the okapi hide, were recovered. Johnston acquired these bandoliers and later forwarded them to Dr. Sclater, Secretary of the Zoological Society of London.

Johnston talked further with the natives, who confirmed the horse-like description. But they also said that it had large asses' ears and a slender muzzle and that its foot was divided into more than one hoof. The three-toed hipparion indeed!

Johnston, accompanied by guides, mounted an expedition to search in earnest. Tracks were discovered, but no okapi. The tracks were indeed of a cloven-hoofed animal, but Johnston, now disappointed and believing he might be on a wild-goose chase, refused to follow the tracks, thinking they were only tracks of some forest eland.

The native guides were also discouraged at the doubts and disbelief of the "mad white man," and Johnston never had a chance to change his mind as his entire party became severely ill with malaria and the expedition had to be terminated in failure. In fact, if the Belgians had not sent troops after Johnston to help him back to Uganda, the ill-fated expedition might have ended in tragedy. Lieutenant Meura still promised the now skeptical Johnston a complete skin as soon as possible.

However, Meura died shortly thereafter of blackwater fever without making good on his promise.

This could easily have ended the matter. But Dr. Sclater in London, having received the two bandoliers, concluded significantly that they could *not* belong to any known species of zebra. Sclater named the animal, based on the bandolier skin specimen, *Equus johnstoni*. The assignment to the horse family was based on microscopic examination of the hair, which was similar to that of the zebra and the giraffe, but not like antelopes.

Another officer, Lieutenant Karl Eriksson, originally under Lieutenant Meura's command, remembered his now dead superior's promise, and when in February 1901 a skin complete with skull and a second skull became available, he promptly shipped these to Johnston. Johnston prepared a painting of what the animal might look like based on the skin and shipped everything to the British Museum.

Johnston, being a man of many parts, though not an expert paleontologist, realized that the skulls represented a giraffelike animal much like an ancient Greek fossil known as *Helladotherium*. In fact, based on his examination, Johnston named it *Helladotherium tigrinium*. Almost instantly the zoological world was electrified by the possibility that an extinct Miocene giraffid had been discovered still alive.

Sir E. Ray Lankester, director of the British Museum, noting that there were some differences from *Helladotherium*, called it *Okapi johnstoni*.

Further study of the okapi material revealed that it was a form even more primitive than the *Helladotherium*, almost identical to paleotragus, the Miocene and Pliocene ancestors of modern giraffes. At this point Dr. Colber's conclusion, as published in the *Journal of Mammalogy*, is apt: "A detailed osteological study of Okapia, whereby it is compared with all the other genera of Giraffidae, both living and fossil, and with other types of pecorans, shows that it is a truly primitive giraffid, in many ways more primitive than the earliest of the fossil giraffes. Generally speaking, the okapi may be considered

2. Modern *Paleotragus* or Okapi, drawn from life.

as a 'living fossil' that has persisted with but relatively few changes from the Upper Miocene period to the present day." Colbert concludes by stating that "the minor differences are not of sufficient importance to exclude the genus from the *paleotragine* group of giraffes."

After reaching this high point of zoological discovery and romance it is certainly anticlimactic to finish our okapi story by noting that many expeditions followed and false claims were made as to priority of discovery. The first live okapi was captured by Lieutenant Sillye in 1903 but escaped soon after capture. Thus it was the Alexander-Gossling Scientific Mission that was the first to obtain and retain a live specimen, in 1906.

The okapi story thus has a happy conclusion, realizing more than the wildest dreams of our romantic explorer-zoologist Sir Harry H. Johnston. For us, however, its importance lies in the fact that this episode is not an isolated case. Many more such stories could be related, and some will be described in the chapters of this book. Moreover, if just one comparable discovery were to be made by investigations based on evidence presented in the pages that follow, it would all have been worthwhile. Moreover, Johnston's story should convince everyone that no one, whether amateur or professional, need apologize for his or her romanticism, provided that it is accompanied by a reasoned and balanced credulity. After all, Johnston's boyhood experience and his romantic curiosity resulted in the marvelous discovery of a relict species, persisting far beyond its supposed extinction.

I hope the reader will join me and my colleagues, at least in spirit, in the search for unknown forms of animal life.

"The most beautiful thing we can experience is the mysterious. It is the source of all true art and science."

—Albert Einstein

SEARCHING FOR HIDDEN ANIMALS

I

Sea Apes and Northern Sea Cows

"Where the sea breaks its back" epitomizes that vast mysterious area encompassing the northern Pacific Ocean and part of the Arctic seas. And indeed it is mysterious, if only because remoteness and inhospitable natural conditions have prevented thorough exploration.

In the northernmost part for the summer months of the year the sun never disappears; even at midnight the orange orb rides the edge of the horizon. For the winter months there is perpetual night and the heavens are lit by the kaleidoscopic play of the aurora borealis, a magnificent, ever-changing panoply of varicolored light, emitted as a result of ionization high in the upper atmosphere. For some of the sparsely distributed inhabitants these displays represent portents of doom; for others, omens of good hunting—perhaps a sign that a seal will be killed soon, driving the specter of starvation back among the ice floes.

As the ocean currents from the South rush northward, they encounter the fogbound, forbidding Aleutian chain of islands. The word *Unalaska*, the name given the area by the natives, is derived from the original Aleut term *Agunalaksh*, which literally translates to "the shores where the sea breaks its back."

All the islands of the Aleutian chain were once mountain peaks, in many cases volcanic craters. In the distant past this mountain range connected the Asian and American continents; later it sank in some catastrophic dislocation of the earth's crust. The seas rose, covering whole valleys and plains, leaving only a few peaks and smoking craters.

In this region there is a high probability that one or more zoological enigmas remain to be resolved. In contrast to the Antarctic, where many nations have established research stations, this vast area has been largely neglected since the epic investigations of great explorer naturalists such as Georg Wilhelm Steller, Baron A. E. Nordenskjöld, and Leonhard Stejneger of the United States National Museum, this last taking place in 1940.

There are at least three zoological mysteries in this loneliest and least-known area of the earth. The first involves the earliest of Arctic explorers, Georg Wilhelm Steller. Steller's voyage, commanded by Vitus Bering, resulted in marvelous discoveries, including many theretofore unknown plants and animals. This great voyage culminated in disaster when Steller and Bering were finally shipwrecked on Bering Island on November 28, 1741 (see Illustration 3), but a detailed record of this adventure has been preserved for us in Steller's journal, first published in German in 1793, some fifty-two years after his death. The original manuscript lay buried in the ancient archives of the Russian Academy of Sciences in Leningrad until it was discovered by Dr. F. A. Golder and was translated into English by Dr. Leonhard Stejneger. Stejneger's translation is very important for anyone interested, since the earlier translation into German by P. S. Pallas, a contemporary and admirer of Steller, was much abridged and censored, in that sections that seemed controversial at the time were expurgated. The number of new plants and animals described by Steller are far too numerous to recount here, nor is such a catalogue necessary. But what is important is the fact that with *only* one exception every single description of a new species has been corroborated. With such a record of reliability we must attach

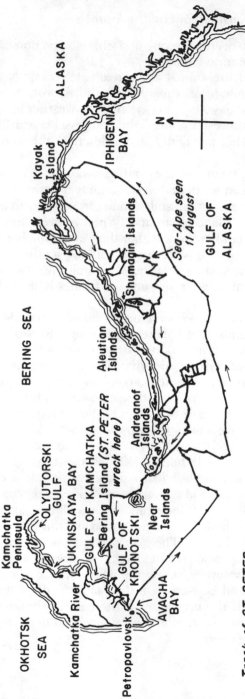

OKHOTSK
SEA

Kamchatka
Peninsula

Kamchatka River

BERING SEA

OLYUTORSKI
GULF

UKINSKAYA BAY

GULF OF KAMCHATKA

Bering Island (ST. PETER wreck here)

GULF OF KRONOTSKI

Petropavlovsk

AVACHA BAY

Near Islands

Andreanof Islands

Aleutian Islands

Shumagin Islands

Sea-Ape seen 11 August

GULF OF ALASKA

IPHIGENIA BAY

Kayak Island

ALASKA

N

Track of ST. PETER

3. Chart of the voyage of the *St. Peter* showing her position when Steller reported seeing the "sea ape."

considerable credence to the one and only observation of an as yet unknown marine animal.

Steller observed the animal at approximately 52½° N latitude, 155° W longitude on the afternoon of August 10, civil time (astronomical day August 11, 1741). The weather was fair and the wind southwesterly and light; the vessel was drifting at less than one knot per hour. Steller describes the sighting thus:

"On August 4, going on the southerly course, we finally sighted also between south and west, about two or three miles from us, many high, large, and wooded islands, so that we were hemmed in by land all around. Wherever we wanted to get out there was land in the way, but the winds, which at this time and until August 9 were mostly east or southeast and could have advanced us several hundred miles on a straight course to Kamchatka, were not utilized fruitlessly in tacking up and down.

"During this time that we were near land or surrounded by it we saw large numbers of hair seals, sea otters, fur seals, sea lions, and porpoises. On this occasion as well as later on I learned from repeated experience that whenever these animals were to be seen unusually often in a quiet sea, a storm followed soon after, and that the oftener they came up and the more active they were, the more furious was the subsequent gale.

"On August 10 we saw a very unusual and unknown sea animal, of which I am going to give a brief account since I observed it for two whole hours. —It was about two Russian ells* in length; the head was like a dog's, with pointed erect ears. From the upper and lower lips on both sides whiskers hung down which made it look almost like a Chinaman. The eyes were large; the body was longish round and thick, tapering gradually towards the tail. The skin seemed thickly covered with hair, of a gray color on the back, but reddish white on the belly; in the water, however, the whole animal appeared entirely reddish and cow-colored. The tail was divided into two fins, of which the upper, as in the case of sharks, was twice as large as the lower. Nothing struck me more surprising

* About 1.5 meters (5 feet).

than the fact that neither forefeet as in the marine amphibians nor, in their stead, fins were to seen. In default of a more detailed description one can do no better than compare the shape of this animal with the picture which Gesner received from a friend and which he has published under the name of *Simia marina danica* in his book on animals. At any rate our sea animal deserved this name because of its resemblance to Gesner's sea monkey as well as on account of its wonderful actions, jumps, and gracefulness. For over two hours it swam around our ship, looking, as with admiration, first at the one and then at the other of us. At times it came so near to the ship that it could have been touched with a pole, but as soon as anybody stirred it moved away a little further. It could raise itself one-third of its length out of the water exactly like a man, and sometimes it remained in this position for several minutes. After it had observed us for about half an hour, it shot like an arrow under our vessel and came up again on the other side; shortly after, it dived again and reappeared in the old place; and in this way it dived perhaps thirty times. There drifted by a large American seaweed 3 to 4 fathoms long, club-shaped and hollow at one end like a bottle and gradually tapering at the other, towards which, as soon as it was sighted, the animal darted, seized it in its mouth, and swam with it to the ship, making such motions and monkey tricks that nothing more laughable can be imagined, once in a while biting a piece off and eating it. Having now observed it for quite a while I had a gun loaded and fired at this animal in order to get possession of it for a more accurate description, but the shot missed. Though somewhat frightened it reappeared at once and gradually approached our vessel. However, it went off to sea as a second shot was fired at it without effect or perhaps only slightly wounding it and did not appear again. It was seen later, however, several times at different places of the sea."

What are we to make of this description? First it should be clear that there is no known animal, in the sea or, for that matter, on land, that corresponds to Steller's description. The debate as to the nature of the sea ape has been going on for two hundred years. Steller referred to Konrad von Gesner's account in his *Historia Animalium* (1551–58) of a *Simia marina danica*, or Danish sea monkey, but when Golder made a search through Gesner's work, no description or illustration was found that even remotely resembles Steller's observation. However, Golder states that while no single picture corresponds to Steller's description, several of the most prominent features are recognizable in various woodcuts.

Are we to believe, then, as some do, that Steller had a fantastic vision at dusk? That really he saw some known animal, a sea otter, perhaps, or the fur seal *Callotaria ursina cynocephala?* This is what Stejneger and Tilesius argue. Yet this is hardly an acceptable solution. As the naturalist and historian Corey Ford wrote, this would be highly unlikely; after all, Steller "studied the animal for two hours, sometimes at close enough range to have 'touched it with a pole.' As trained and exact a scientist as Steller could scarcely have confused it with an otter or seal, particularly since his journal mentions that he had seen both of them previously; nor was he given to erratic flights of fancy. The simplest explanation is that the 'sea monkey' actually existed, and that Steller saw it for the first and last time before it became extinct, like the northern sea cow which he was the only naturalist ever to observe."

I agree with Ford with respect to his opinion of Steller, but I do not believe that this was the first and last time this animal was seen, as will become clear as we explore the possible nature and identity of this animal.

One suggestion is that this creature was a single example of a congenital anomaly—for example, a seal born without its forelimbs. The conjecture is possible. However, statistically it is extremely unlikely that Steller would have seen such an aberrant form—one of a kind in the huge expanse of the northern Pacific Ocean. Then, too, there is at least one cogent reason for rejecting this idea. Steller's description establishes that the animal was a marvelously accomplished swimmer, for he writes, "After it had observed us for about half an hour, it *shot like* an arrow under our vessel and came up again on the other side" (my emphasis). A congenitally deformed fur seal, anatomically designed to function with a pair of pectoral flippers, would hardly be able to perform in such a fashion if it were deprived of its forelimbs and in addition possessed anomalous hind limbs, one larger than the other—features described as an asymmetrical tail by Steller. Steller's precise statement was that the tail was divided in two parts, of which the upper was *longer*. If the tail was a pair of hind flippers turned back, one would expect them to be of equal size, while, on the other hand, asymmetry of the tail fin is a feature found in a number of aquatic animals—sharks in particular—and there is no reason to doubt Steller's accuracy in describing this characteristic.

Steller was, as we have seen, a most careful observer in the context of his viewing this creature. A measure of his accuracy in observation is his description of the seaweed with which the animal amused itself for a time. The seaweed described conforms *exactly* with the now well-known species *Nereocystis priapus*.

Rational observers are forced to conclude that Steller must have observed a real animal, one that is unidentified to this day.

The debate as to what Steller's sea ape was is no longer a burning issue in the minds of modern zoologists. In fact, most know little if anything about Steller's strange observations, nor do they care.

In the last decade and even as recently as 1977 new data have come to my attention that may contain clues as to the sea ape's true nature. This information comes to us from an analysis of observations of strange aquatic creatures along the western coast of Canada on the one hand and from information gleaned from Eskimos inhabiting King Island, located to the west of the Alaskan mainland, on the other. However, before we attempt to pursue the matter further, let us finish with Steller and his zoological adventures; we will follow the leads provided by new evidence, which may provide a clue as to the nature of the sea ape, in the next chapter.

Early on in the expedition, on June 20, 1741, the companion

vessel, the *St. Paul*, under the command of Captain Chirikov, had become permanently separated from the *St. Peter*, each vessel proceeding from the point as a separate expedition. Steller's greatest discovery, the northern sea cow, was still in the future, as was a great misfortune, the wreck of the *St. Peter* on an uncharted island (later named Bering Island). As a result of this wreck, all the specimens so painstakingly collected by Steller, at great hardship and cost even of human life, had eventually to be abandoned: an inestimable loss to science. Vitus Bering, the commander of the expedition, would make an even greater sacrifice: his own life.

Steller records how after the episode with the sea ape, conditions of the men, the ship, and the weather steadily worsened. Storms became more violent, and scurvy and exposure were beginning to take their toll among the crew. Finally, it was decided to cut the voyage short and return forthwith to Avacha Bay on Kamchatka. However, the shortest way became the longest way. Buffeted by gales and storms, the *St. Peter* was on November 1 far to the north, at 55° N latitude, about three hundred nautical miles north of Attu Island, the most westerly part of the Aleutian chain. Bering was extremely ill, and hardly a day passed without a death among the crew.

On November 4, although Steller believed it was November 5, land was sighted. A low range of jagged terrain rose out of the sea toward the north. Everyone was convinced that the coastline of Avacha Bay was before them, but joy was short, as no familiar landmarks came into view. However, since the ship was more like a wreck than a seaworthy vessel, with rotten sails and weakened shrouds parted by wind and ice, and only six barrels of water in the hold and a handful of able-bodied men to sail her, it was decided to land regardless of whether it might be Kamchatka or some unknown land.

Bering himself was dying, his hope of being buried at home never to be realized. The entire crew was now in such bad shape that the vessel, after having snapped her anchor cable twice, was left at the mercy of the raging waters. Two times her keel struck submerged rocks; a third blow would surely have split the vessel. But a mighty wave lifted the vessel, carrying her over a reef and miraculously depositing the ship in a placid bay. The battered hulk would never sail again. Steller and those of the crew still alive decided to winter on this strange island until spring when, it was hoped, a smaller vessel could be fabricated from the wreck of the *St. Peter*.

The behavior of the otters, blue foxes, and other animals soon convinced Steller that Kamchatka had not been reached. Animals showed a complete fearlessness of man, indicating that this land mass had probably never been visited by man, the greatest predator of all.

Then Steller noticed strange, enormous, dark-colored hulks resembling overturned boats drifting or moving about the reefs. Periodically something like a snout would be raised, expelling air with a snort. Steller wondered whether these strange creatures could be whales or some kind of giant shark, but soon it became clear that these creatures, reaching lengths of up to 11 meters (thirty-five feet), were like nothing ever seen before.

Subsequently, Steller was able to study and dissect these strange new creatures, and his findings were published in his *De Bestiis Marinis*. Steller was a very poor artist, so the original drawings were executed by another more talented expedition member, Frederick Plenisner, but, unfortunately, these were lost en route to St. Petersburg. Even the complete skeleton of this animal, which had been prepared by Steller, never left Bering Island, as the vessel constructed from the timbers of the wreck of the *St. Peter* was too small to carry it. As a result no accurate illustrations of *Rhytina stelleri* survived, and the fragmentary skeletal material in museums today was procured by later expeditions. To this day adequate skeletal material does not exist anywhere.

A succinct description of this giant relative of dugongs and manatees is provided by A. E. Nordenskjöld, who visited Bering and Copper islands a century later to determine if these creatures really had become extinct in 1768, as most believed. "Steller's sea cow held in a way the place of the cloven-footed animals among the marine mammalia. The sea cow was of a

4. Reconstruction of Steller's sea cow showing Steller taking measurements by L. Stejneger. The reconstruction is based on measurements given by Steller in *De Bestiis Marinis*, pp. 294–96.

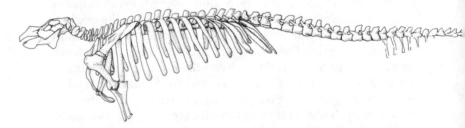

5. Drawing of skeleton of Steller's sea cow made under the direction of the author. The drawing is based in part on partial skeleton shown at the *Vega* exhibition at the Royal Palace, Stockholm.

dark-brown color, sometimes varied with white spots or streaks. The thick leathery skin was covered with hair which grew together so as to form an exterior skin, which was full of vermin and resembled the bark of an old oak. The full grown animal was from twenty-eight to thirty-five English feet in

6.

length, and weighed about sixty-seven cwt. The head was small in proportion to the large thick body, the neck short, the body diminishing rapidly behind the short fore-leg terminated abruptly without fingers or nails, but was overgrown with a number of short thickly placed brush-hairs; the hind-leg was replaced by a tail-fin resembling a whale's. The animal wanted teeth, but was instead provided with two masticating plates, one in the gum, the other in the under jaw. The udders of the female, which abounded in milk, were placed between the fore-limbs. The flesh and milk resembled those of horned cattle, indeed in Steller's opinion surpassed them. The sea cows were almost constantly employed in pasturing on the seaweed which grew luxuriantly over the coast, moving the head and neck while so doing much in the same way as an ox. While they pastured they showed great voracity, and did not allow themselves to be disturbed in the least by the presence of man. One might even touch them without their being frightened or disturbed. They entertained great attachment to each other, and when one was harpooned the others made incredible attempts to rescue it."

Nordenskjöld, who was very interested in Steller's sea cow, *Rhytina stelleri*, searched the records for information regarding its fate. He found that sea cows were caught in 1754, 1757, 1756, and 1762.

In 1772 Dmitri Bragin, a hunter, wintered on Bering Island. A journal was kept and although the large marine animals occurring in the vicinity of the island are enumerated, nothing was said about sea cows. Subsequent visitors to Bering and Copper islands made no mention of the sea cow. Even so, Nordenskjöld questioned the validity of the date 1768 for the total extermination of the sea cow. During the latter part of his 1878–80 voyage of polar research and exploration, he visited Bering Island to investigate this matter and to acquire further skeletal materials of *Rhytina*. On the basis of rather extensive interviews with residents on the island he concluded that the *Rhytina* did not become extinct until at least 1854.

One native of mixed Russian and Aleutian parentage reported that his father, who had died in 1847 at the age of eighty-eight, had first come to Bering Island at the age of eighteen from Volhynia in 1777. During the first two or three years of his father's stay (1779–80) he had affirmed that sea cows were still being killed as they pastured on seaweed. The heart only was eaten, and the hide used to make *baydars* (native boats). A more wanton and pointless destruction of a most rare animal species can hardly be imagined.

Two other natives, Feodor Merchenin and Stepnoff, were also interrogated. Stepnoff stated that about twenty-five years ago, at the east side of the island, they had seen an animal unknown to them. Nordenskjöld, from the details extracted during this interview, was convinced that the unknown animal was a sea cow.

For us, however, the questions really are: Are the animals really extinct? Do some persist? Isolated reports of sightings are still made, the most recent being a Russian report in 1962.

Russian scientists A. A. Berzin, E. A. Tikhomirov, and V. I. Troinin published a report of what may have been a whole herd of sea cows in the Russian journal *Priroda* in 1963. The episode involved the whaler *Buran* in the vicinity of Cape Navarin, south of the Gulf of Anadyr. Early on a July day in 1962 a small number of strange animals, neither seals nor whales, were observed close in-shore. These observers were experienced hunters and whalers making observations at less than 100 meters (a hundred yards); certainly they were likely to identify known marine life. The same kinds of animals were seen again the following day in a shallow lagoon where plenty of aquatic vegetable matter, including the known types of seaweed and sea cabbage favored by Steller's sea cow, was flourishing. The lagoon did not freeze over even in winter and therefore would be a likely place for sea cows to find food and shelter. According to the report of the crew of the *Buran*, the animals were 6 meters (twenty feet) to 8 meters (twenty-six feet) in length, dark in color, with a small head. They appeared to have a harelip, and their heads were differentiated from the bodies or necks. The tail resembled the bilobate tail of Steller's sea cow and sprouted a sort of fringe along the edge. The animals moved about slowly, submerging and surfacing regularly.

Most of these reports have been dismissed as mistaken identification of a narwhal as Steller's sea cow. That sea cows are no longer present around Bering and Copper islands cannot be disputed. Nordenskjöld, however, pointed out that extinction, if it has occurred, probably was due both to overkilling and to the driving of the herds to areas where conditions were not suitable for survival. Of prime importance is the food supply, which in the case of *Rhytina* was the seaweed, particularly the twenty-meter-long (hundred-foot-long) *laminarias*. Steller recorded that they favored certain types including *Nereocystis*.

Now these types of seaweed are found in other areas, including the Aleutian chain of islands. It is generally believed that the sea cows once were much more widespread, ranging perhaps even into the Sea of Japan and along the Aleutians proper. Nordenskjöld ruled out the Aleutians as a locale for sea cows on grounds that no fossil remains were found among bone assemblages collected from the islands. Yet there have been occasional sea-cow reports from Aleutian natives, particularly from Attu and the Kamchatkan coast, although the reports are too vague to be of much value. Whether these reports refer to narwhals mistaken for sea cows, to *Rhytina*, or even to a subspecies can only be settled by a firsthand investigation of Attu and adjacent areas and islands. Such an investigation should certainly include a search for skeletal material, either fossil or green or both.

Naturalist Leonhard Stejneger also investigated the matter of the extinction or possible persistence of the northern sea cow, visiting Bering Island in 1882 and collecting additional although fragmentary *Rhytina* skeletal material. Stejneger checked on Nordenskjöld, interviewing some of the identical witnesses, and reported these interviews verbatim in the *Proceedings of the U. S. National Museum*, 1884, Volume VII.

It took considerable intestinal fortitude on the part of Stejneger to publish this critical refutation of Nordenskjöld's claim that *Rhytina* persisted till at least 1854. As one reads Stejneger's demolition of a senior colleague, not only a professor of great stature in the scientific community but also a noble, one understands the almost apologetic tone in parts of his article.

With these published interviews Stejneger demonstrated rather conclusively that Nordenskjöld was at the very least wrong, and that he had perhaps been professionally incompetent. In the process Stejneger concluded that the unknown animal observed in 1854 by the Bering Island natives Stepnoff and Merchenin was a female narwhal that had strayed south from its normal locale in the Arctic Ocean.

Looking at all of the relevant data, it seems probable that Stejneger was only partially right and that the *Rhytina stelleri* may have survived in remote regions other than Copper and Bering islands.

However, although the matter cannot be settled without an extensive exploration of islands in the vicinity of Bering Island, it appears that Nordenskjöld was right in one respect: The sea cows were not exterminated at Bering and Copper islands but were driven away. He believed they then became extinct in other areas. But which areas? In a search for these animals particular attention should be given to those land masses where seaweed such as *laminaria* and *nereocystis* is abundant. Skeletal remains of *Rhytina* also would be welcomed by most museums, even if a living, breathing sea cow can no longer be procured.

There are additional rumors and undocumented statements, which I have not been able to substantiate, that an animal very much like *Rhytina stelleri* but somewhat smaller is still sometimes observed in the vicinity of the western Aleutians. In support of these rumors we have the 1777 writings of Peter Simon Pallas, German naturalist and professor of natural history. In his seven-volume report as the leader of a scientific expedition to Siberia under Catherine the Great, he discusses the numerous islands of the western Aleutian chain including Attu (called Attak), Stemiya, and Semichi. First he touches on the inhabitants, and then he describes the animal life. He states: "Sea otters come only in small numbers to these islands and almost never to Bering Island, though the shipwrecked discoverers of that island and the first hunters who tried their luck there were able to kill as many as they wanted. But plenty of sea lions, sea bears, manatees (sea cows), and other sea animals are still to be found about all these islands."

Later when discussing the eastern Aleutians, including Umiak and Kodiak, he states: "In the adjacent ocean there are also all kinds of seals, dolphins, and whales; but sea lions and lakhtaken (largest seals), whose hides are used chiefly for canoes, are seldom found there, and sea cows are never seen."

Was this information regarding the presence of some form of sea cow in the western Aleutians correct, or is Pallas using obsolete or faulty information? Again only a careful island-to-island check of the area can establish whether there is any substance to these reports.

While this chapter was in preparation, an article by Delphine Haley entitled "Saga of Steller's Sea Cow" appeared in *Natural*

History magazine. In this article, Haley reported that an alleged sighting of Steller's sea cow had been published in a Russian newspaper, *Kamchatsky Komsomolets*, in Petropavlovsk. The observations were made by fishermen at Anapkinskaya Bay, just south of Cape Navarin, located approximately 179° W longitude, 62° N latitude. According to Haley, the fishermen were questioned by Vladimir Malukovich of the Kamchatka Museum of Local Lore. The description in translation from the Russian reads: "Its skin was dark, its extremities were flippers, its tail forked like a whale. A slight outline of round ribs was noticeable. We approached the animal, touched it, and were surprised as its head bore an unusual form and its snout was long." Confronted with an illustration of Steller's sea cow, he said that this was the animal in question. As usual there was speculation as to which aquatic mammal may have been mistaken for the sea cow. At least one expert, Edward Mitchell, research biologist for the Canadian Department of Fisheries, stated that the extinct status of Steller's sea cow is a presumption. "There simply haven't been exhaustive inventories of marine vertebrates so that one could state unequivocally that this or any species does not survive." He goes on to suggest that the area should be surveyed by ship. I could not agree with him more.

Realistically it would in my opinion be hasty and unwarranted to conclude that the northern sea cow, or a closely related form, has been lost to us forever. Often enough conservationists and zoologists have been absolutely convinced that this or that species has passed into oblivion, only to find years later that survival has occurred in the face of almost impossible circumstances, not the least of which have been the predations of man himself.

I for one am not prepared to dismiss lightly the observations of knowledgeable seagoing observers, such as the Russian crew of the *Buran* or the fishermen of Anapkinskaya Bay, as mistaken observations of female narwhals.

II

Aleutian Dinosaurs and Canadian Sea Serpents

Aside from Steller's mysterious sea ape and sea cow, at least two other zoological mysteries in the northern Pacific require a solution. Reports of strange aquatic animals continue to be received from Canadian coasts between Vancouver and Alaska. These reports are taken seriously by more than one established scientist, including Dr. Paul H. Leblond of the Institute of Oceanography, University of British Columbia, who, with Dr. John Sibert, is engaged in serious studies of these sightings. Together, Leblond and Sibert have published a report entitled *Observations of Large Unidentified Marine Animals in British Columbia and Adjacent Waters*. This excellent study consists of twenty-three new firsthand reports and an additional seven new secondhand observations. They also include some twenty-seven reports recorded by zoologist B. Heuvelmans from the same area by way of comparison.

The most important step in dealing with data of this kind is to separate the "wheat from the chaff." Leblond and Sibert began by separating two classes:

1. Sightings of animals that are already known but are not recognized by the observer, or that *might* be accounted for by

animals already known.* The animals falling into this category identified by Leblond and Sibert include giant squids, elephant seals, nudibranch (a species of sea slug), and oar fish.

2. The second category involves those observations that cannot be accounted for by any known creature.

Leblond and Sibert then proceeded to further classify and compare their unknowns. At first they tried to follow Heuvelmans' classification as given in his book *Le Grande Serpent-de-Mer*, but they found this part to be impossible, probably because Heuvelmans was dealing with "sea serpent" reports covering the seas and oceans from the entire globe, whereas they were dealing here with a restricted area of the northern Pacific Ocean. Abandoning Heuvelmans' more extensive classification, Leblond and Sibert picked three characteristics to use as sorting criteria: (a) big eyes, (b) small eyes, and (c) vertical loops. These characteristics are not necessarily the best ones, although one of course has to begin somewhere when attempting to classify unknowns. Further, it should be noted that "big eyes," "small eyes," and "vertical loops" are not mutually exclusive when applied to a population of animals, even of the same species. For example, all of the animals might flex vertically and the females might have small eyes and the males big eyes.

The reader should therefore bear in mind that these characteristics do not necessarily provide bases for ironclad, mutually exclusive classification. Of course, it seems unlikely that a single specimen could have one pair of eyes that are both big and small, unless they expand and contract, an unlikely if not impossible anatomical feature.

In summary, Leblond and Sibert believe their data indicate the existence of three types of relatively large, 2-meter (6 foot) to 20-meter (65 foot) unidentified animals. Please remember that in light of the foregoing discussion this *may* or *may not* mean that there are three distinct species involved.

---

* This part of an analysis of reports of unknown animals is far from a waste of time. To a great extent the analyst must rely on these data as a control for comparing and making judgments of the balance of his data. In 1967 I used exactly this approach to analyze the "Loch Ness Monster" data.

1. A creature with large eyes set laterally on a horse- or camel-shaped head mounted at the end of a long neck. This animal is a fast swimmer, has short, dark-brown fur, and no mane. It is probably a mammal and may be related to seals.

2. An animal similar to the first type but with small eyes, sometimes described with horns or mane. Both types are not only fast, but also smooth swimmers, submerging vertically as if pulled under.

These two types might be the females and males of the same species, showing sexual differences technically termed "sexual dimorphism."

3. A long, serpentine animal, showing loops of its body above water and swimming fast, with much thrashing. Its head is described as sheeplike with small eyes, and it has a dorsal fin running along part of its back.

We can supplement the findings of the University of British Columbia Institute of Oceanography's study somewhat before we suggest what these animals might be and what, if any, relation exists between them and Steller's sea ape. First, all of the animals, Steller's sea ape and the three types established by Leblond and Sibert are most certainly mammals. Vertical coils—that is, vertical flexure when established, bending the body top to bottom—almost always belong to mammals; horizontal flexure—bending side to side—is the rule in practically all other classes of marine animals. The only realistic exceptions might be the tentacles of giant sea squids, giant octopuses (see Chapter III), or colonies of oceanic tunicates called "salps," which hang together in long chains. A few cases of giant "venus girdles" 9 to 12 meters (thirty to forty feet) long—that is, tenophores related to jellyfish—that could be bent in any direction have been reported, but they are less likely to be mistaken by an observer since they cannot normally form vertical arches protruding from the water.

Relevant to the possible identity of the large animals reported to flex vertically is the experience of two hunters, Cyril H. Andrews and Norman Georgeson. Their observations were close at hand and corroborated later by other observers. After the episode both duck hunters made an affidavit that was placed on record with Justice of the Peace G. F. Parkyn of Bedwell Harbor, Vancouver.

On the morning of Sunday, February 4, 1934, at about 11 A.M., Andrews and Georgeson found themselves on the rocks near Gowland Head, South Pender Island. Andrews looked down into the water and was astounded to see a long, snakelike object just below the surface. Apparently this experience did not deter the hunters, for shortly thereafter they brought down a duck close by. The duck was not dead, but it was wounded severely, and the hunters attempted to retrieve the wounded animal by means of a small boat. Just as they approached the duck a head and two loops or segments came clear of the water. Georgeson observed one loop and the head well clear of the water. Then the whole thing except the head, which remained just out of the water, sank. The monster then opened its large mouth, seized the duck, and swallowed it. Numbers of sea gulls swooped down at the creature, which snapped at them when they came too close. Shortly after this it sank below the surface.

The head of the creature resembled a horse without ears or nostrils. The tongue came to a point, and its teeth were fishlike. In color it was a gray-brown with a darker brown stripe running along the body slightly to one side. (Presumably, there was a corresponding stripe on the other side.)

Immediately after the episode Andrews phoned the local justice of the peace, G. F. Parkyn, who came along some fifteen minutes later. About ten minutes after Parkyn arrived, the creature's head and part of the body broke the water about 18 meters (twenty yards) from shore, swimming in an undulating manner away from it. The head did not appear to come clear of the water; it seemed to rest on the surface; about 4 meters (twelve feet) of the body behind the head showed, and the body had an estimated diameter of ⅔ meter (two feet.) On this occasion the creature was seen by twelve residents of South Pender Island.

Andrews, who was only 3 meters (ten feet) from the animal when it gulped down the duck, estimated the overall length of the animal at 12 meters (forty feet) and its diameter at the thickest part about ⅔ to 1 meter (two to three feet). The body gradually tapered toward the tail. He estimated the head to be about 1 meter (three feet) long and ⅔ meter (two feet) wide.

One could hardly ask for a better set of anecdotal observations, in laymen's terms, of the primitive snakelike whales known as zeuglodons, which were mistakenly first identified in the fossil record as marine reptiles and named *Basilosaurus.* A variety of related forms roamed the seas as recently as the Miocene, twenty-five million years ago, reaching lengths up to 21 meters (seventy feet). Even a casual comparison of the skeletons of these creatures (Illustration 6) reveals the striking agreement with the description of the observed animal. A reconstruction of one of these primitive toothed whales is shown in Illustration 8. The range of these animals was once quite wide, remains having been found in New Zealand, the Ukraine, France, the United States bordering the Gulf of Mexico and the Atlantic Ocean, England, Nigeria, Egypt, and, interestingly, on Vancouver Island not far from our reported episode. The distribution of the fossil remains with other shallow-water fauna suggests that these animals frequented shallow water, which is consistent with the experience of our duck hunters.

7. Zeuglodons: *Basilosaurus cetoides* skeleton top, and *Zygorhiza kochii* below.

8. Reconstruction of *Basilosaurus cetoides* according to the author.

The story of the discovery of the first zeuglodon remains is a bizarre story in itself and warrants recounting.

Almost 150 years ago, the remains of an extinct whale were found washed up out of a marl bank belonging to the Upper Eocene Jackson formation in the state of Louisiana, a deposit at least 60,000,000 years of age. Twenty-eight vertebrae had been exposed, after continued rains, by the slump of a hill near the Ouachita River in southern Caldwell Parish. In 1832 one of the vertebrae was sent to P. S. Du Ponceau, president of the American Philosophical Society, who asked Dr. Richard Harlan to publish an account of the discovery.

At first the elongated snakelike configuration led everyone to believe that the remains of a true sea serpent or marine reptile had been discovered, and perhaps these early conclusions will turn out to be correct after all, not because the remains of this ancient archaeocete are reptilian, but because their modern-day descendants continue to be reported as sea serpents. In any case, based upon the mistaken supposition that the remains represented a reptile, it was christened *Basilosaurus*, "the king of lizards."

The affinities of *Basilosaurus* were immediately questioned and aroused worldwide controversy. Shortly after the original find, in 1834 and 1835, additional fossil material was found on the plantation of Judge John G. Creagh in Clark County,

Alabama. On the basis of this additional material, brought by Dr. Harlan to London in 1839, the true relationship of *Basilosaurus* was established. Harlan provided Professor Richard Owen with teeth, which were sectioned and studied. Microscopic examination of these teeth allowed the great scientist to establish conclusively that this animal was a mammal. As a result, Owen proposed to rename *Basilosaurus*, *Zeuglodon cetoides*, in allusion to the yokelike appearance of the cheek teeth and the whalelike structure of the vertebrae. As more and more remains were recovered, an association with the reports of sea serpent sightings was inevitable.

The interest and in some cases the notoriety aroused by these discoveries induced Dr. Albert Koch, a German collector, to visit Alabama. Koch was able to collect remains from various sites in Alabama, and from these bones, representing at least five different individuals, he assembled an animal measuring 35 meters (114 feet) in length. This composite was exhibited by Koch in 1845 as a sea serpent, which he called *Hydrargos sillimanii*. In spite of Owen's published results that these remains represented mammals, not reptiles, Koch continued to exhibit his monstrosity in the principal cities of Europe.

Eventually the materials came into the possession of the Royal Anatomical Museum of Berlin, where they were properly sorted and prepared for study.

Studies by Müller in 1849 and others corroborated the contention that Koch's skeleton was a composite, although this was vehemently denied by Koch himself. Koch's archaeocete collection was purchased in 1847 by the King of Prussia, the proceeds enabling Koch to return to Alabama to search for further material. Again he was successful, acquiring an almost complete skeleton from the vicinity of the Washington Old Court House. This second collection was prepared in Dresden, Germany, and displayed in various European cities, eventually returning to the United States, where it went on display in New Orleans, in St. Louis, and finally in Wood's Museum in Chicago, where it was destroyed by the great Chicago fire of October 9, 1871.

Many other finds have been made since, giving us a rather complete picture of this interesting and controversial animal. However, no soft parts have been preserved, so there are differences of opinion as to the actual details of the fleshy parts of these animals.

In order to infer accurately the fleshy parts of an animal of which only bones are available, we must rely on an accurate reconstruction of the skeleton, and the more we know of the behavior of the animal, the more reliable the inferences. In the case of zeuglodons quite a bit of skeletal material has been assembled, with reasonable accuracy. Moreover, while paleontology has experienced many blunders of reconstruction of extinct animals, because of the controversy and notoriety attending Dr. Koch's early composite and incorrect reconstruction, the material has been thoroughly worked over.

Measurement of the skeleton shown in Illustration 7 reveals that the head represents about 8 per cent of the overall length. The duck hunter Andrews estimated the overall length of his unknown animal at about 12 meters (40 feet) and the head length at about 1 meter (3 feet): 7½ per cent, a close approximation for the zeuglodon hypothesis.

According to Andrews, the thickest portion of the animal was estimated at ⅔ to 1 meter (2 to 3 feet) and located toward the anterior (he described the animal as snakelike and tapering toward the tail). Again referring to the illustration, we see that the head measures 1 meter (3 feet) and the body thickness of the skeleton measures about the same—1 meter (3 feet) at the thickest or front part of the rib cage. Once again: excellent agreement.

The characteristic "pushing" of the head out of the water is decidely cetacean, and the general description of the head, by Andrews and others, as resembling the head of a horse, a camel, or a cow is not unreasonable. The definite description of separate teeth fits especially well with zeuglodon jaws and teeth, whereas the absence of visible ears is again expected from such a cetacean. The failure to note eyes is also expected; eyesight was poor in these animals, which probably relied on a highly developed tactile sense to obtain information concerning food and enemies, and the eyes were, therefore, very small. Casts of the interior of the skull indicate a relative loss of sight as contrasted with a considerable development of the fifth pair of cranial nerves and olfactory parts of the brain as described by paleontologists. Dr. Raymond Dart, a noted paleontologist and discoverer of African man apes, further contends that the development of the fifth pair of cranial nerves in these primitive whale brains is correlated with an increased sense of touch: another reason to believe that the animals frequented shallow water, although this does not necessarily follow, as food gathering may be the relevant reason for the tactile sense development. Heuvelmans disagrees with Dart's opinion and believes that zeuglodons were deep-sea creatures, but there is not necessarily a contradiction: Deep-sea cetaceans certainly can approach shallow areas, possibly to get food. The snatching of a live wounded duck at the surface is perfectly compatible with known behavior of certain species of cetaceans, a case in point being the killer whale, which feeds on warm-blooded prey, including penguins.

The absence of any sort of conspicuous dorsal fin along the forepart of the snakelike body reported by Andrews is also compatible with at least one expert opinion. The Dutch expert on cetaceans, Professor E. J. Slijper, believes that zeuglodons possessed a small horizontal caudal tail fin. He based his view on the atrophy of the last eight vertebrae in the tail and the presence of artery traces, which betray a considerable blood supply. Others, however, believe that the anatomy of the tail suggests that the muscles surrounding the backbone were not developed sufficiently to drive the large tail flukes of recent whales.

Even granting small flukes, the zeuglodons must have had a more adequate means of propulsion. The structure of the vertebrae suggest great mobility for vertical undulatory movement. Heuvelmans believes that the propulsive mechanism was in the nature of a pair of symmetrical and continuous lateral fin folds extending in a fore-and-aft direction along most of the length of the tail. This idea is compatible both with the duck hunters' description and with a low posterior dorsal ridge or fin of the sort required for complete stability in three planes. It would leave the forward portion of the back smooth, as so often reported.

Confirmation of the idea that zeuglodons still exist is provided perhaps in the observations of creatures popularly called "cadborosaurus." Observations of such animals have been reported for decades in the waters of the Juan de Fuca Strait and the Georgia Strait, which border the lower end of Vancouver Island. The first modern report was made on October 5, 1933, in Cadboro Bay by Frederick Kemp, a provincial architect, and Major W. Langley, a clerk of the British Columbia legislature. Since then the newspaper files are full of similar reports, from both residents and nonresidents alike. The popular term for these animals is "Caddy," and the general descriptions (allowing for a reasonable degree of latitude for error in anecdotal reports of this type) agree remarkably well with our conception of zeuglodons. Thus it seems reasonable to accept as a working hypothesis the identification of large, vertically undulating sea serpents as zeuglodons—if you are willing, that is, to accept the persistence of some archaic forms.

What about the other two types of animals sorted out by Leblond and Sibert, and Steller's sea ape? At this stage of our inadequate knowledge I believe it is better to be a "lumper" rather than a "splitter" and not to pay too much attention to what appear to be minor differences. Leblond and Sibert themselves state that their two types of animal are very similar in general body build except for a difference in eye size. Some specimens are reported to have a long floppy mane at the back of the neck and short protuberances (horns? ears?). They are fast swimmers, dive smoothly, and have short fur and a long neck 1½ to 3 meters (five to ten feet).

As was pointed out earlier, these animals, whether one species with male and female differences (sexual dimorphism) or separate forms, must certainly be mammals. Most probably they are pinnipeds (seals).

Seals, however, have front flippers, and Steller's sea ape, clearly observed for two hours and also most probably a seal, did not have them. A large species of seal, serpentine in form with no front flippers, or with front flippers tightly folded against the body when rearing out of the water, would fit the bill. Does such an animal exist? The answer is yes, but not in the Northern Hemisphere, only in the lower latitudes of the Antarctic.

In general, there is much symmetry in animal species found in the Arctic and those of the Antarctic: penguins and auks, southern sea-elephants and northern sea-elephants, etc. However, in the case of the leopard seal, *Hydrurga leptonyx*, no

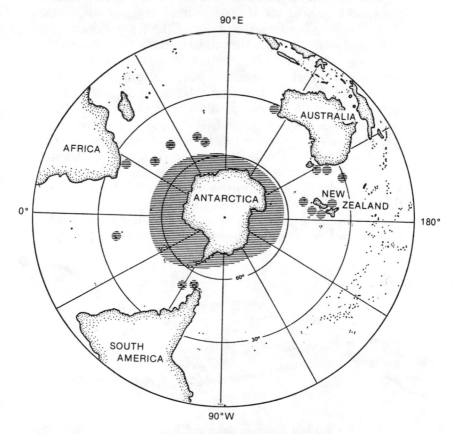

9. Distribution of the leopard seal.

northern counterpart is known. The center of the breeding range of this animal lies in Antarctica, never going beyond 30° S latitude. This seal is thus widely distributed (see Illustration 9) but nowhere abundant, recorded from scattered points around Antarctica, occasionally from southern tips of the southern continents. The animals tend to be solitary, eating a variety of foods—penguins, fish, squid, seals, and carrion. The animals are remarkably snakelike and reptilian in appearance (see Illustrations 10 and 11). The long, slim body— 3.7-meter (12-foot) females, 3-meter (10-foot) males—large head and long neck about equal in diameter, give the appearance of a long head-neck in front of the front flippers. The wide gape of its jaws and formidable teeth contribute to its terrifying appearance. Its method of moving over land by wriggling at remarkable speeds contributes further to its snakelike resemblance. L. Harrison Matthews, in his *The Sea Elephant*, aptly describes the movement of the sea leopard, as observed on South Georgia Island: "And when it moves the resemblance [to a snake] is heightened for, unlike every other sort of seal, it holds the foreflippers closely pressed to the body and makes no use of them to help itself along—it wriggles with an up-and-down looping movement, pressing the chest and the pelvic region to the ground alternately."

The swimming ability as observed and described by Matthews corresponds remarkably with Steller's observation. Mat-

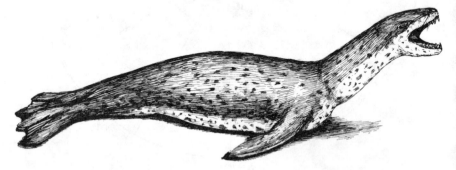

10. The leopard seal *Hydrurga leptonyx*, showing its snakelike characteristics.

11. The head of a leopard seal.

thews states: "I was watching a leopard one day—he had been fishing for some time and was ready for a nap; he swam up to a large floe and had a look at it, treading water and stretching his head far out to get a good view. Then he dived and swam away under the water, turned and came back at full speed, broke surface and shot out of the water like a rocket, landing neatly six feet up on the spot he had chosen for his bed."

For all the similarities among Steller's sea ape, Leblond's first and second categories, and southern sea leopards, there is at least one problem with the hypothesis that the unidentified animals all are northern sea leopards. Leopard seals belong to the *Phocidae* or earless seals. The head is smooth without external ear flaps, which could be interpreted as protrusions.

Steller described protuberances, possibly ears, and the same is true for Leblond's animals. Is it possible that a particular species of the *Phocidae* has evolved without losing the external ear that must have been present in more primitive forms? It could be that this species has achieved sufficient streamlining of the head by folding the ears into depressions in the skull and retaining the ear flaps for more acute hearing. A somewhat analogous condition exists with regard to the front flippers of these animals, which, when they swim, are usually flattened to the body in depressions corresponding to armpits, so that they do not interfere with streamlining. The main propulsive force comes from the hind flippers, the front ones being used only for steering and maneuvering. What is possible, then, is that an unknown species of seal evolved characteristics similar to the leopard seal and fills a northern ecological niche comparable to that occupied in the South by the leopard seal. Such animals could have remained obscure because the center of their range is so far north, out of the purview of man.

However, if natives (Eskimos) live in their range, one should expect to have had reports from them, and, as a matter of fact, we have. The native inhabitants of King Island, located at 65° N latitude, 168° W longitude, talk about the strange creatures, resembling dinosaurs, but only with great reluctance. They apparently associate a great taboo with these unusual animals. Dr. John White, formerly of the Field Museum of Natural History, met with and talked with the King Island natives at great length. He provided the following information:

The natives describe an animal unknown to science called Tizheruk on King Island and Pal Rai Yuk on Nunivak Island. Usually only the head and neck are observed, and they rear 2 to 3 meters (seven to eight feet) out of the water. The head looks like that of a snake. The tail, when seen, has a flipper on the end. Animals are usually seen in bay areas, less frequently in the open ocean. With the ear placed against the inside of the boat, the natives say, they can hear the animals come up for air, and they claim they are able to call them by tapping on the inside of the boat.

The natives further claim that the animals will attack humans. They relate numerous episodes in which hunters were killed by these animals, including an attack on a lone hunter in a kayak.

In one story it is related how a mother was always bragging about her son, a young hunter. Apparently the community got sick of her constant bragging and suggested that if her son were such a great hunter he should have killed the Pal Rai Yuk. To live up to the reputation created by his mother, the hunter set out to hunt the dreaded beast. The hunt was not successful: The hunter was killed by the hunted. Another story relates how a man on a pier called a Pal Rai Yuk, presumably by tapping against the pier supports. Shortly, one of the animals appeared and attempted to snatch him from the pier. The man got away and staggered back to his village. In the end, he did not really escape, however, for he died shortly thereafter.

The anecdotal evidence cited, while fragmentary, must relate to a mammal. The natives are totally familiar with all the known animals native to the region, and there can be no question that they are unable correctly to identify commonly encountered animals. However, the data do not permit definite assignment either to the zeuglodon category or to the leopard seallike category, although on balance the latter seems the more probable.

The matter of calling these animals by rapping on a boat in the water or on pier supports is curious and I believe quite correct. Relevant to this point we again rely on L. Harrison Matthews' experience. In *Sea Elephant* he describes the behavior of sea leopards thus:

"Sea leopards are very inquisitive—if there was one about in any bay where we went ashore it was sure to come to see what was going on, poking its head out of the water and nearly getting into the pram, very unlike the indifferent bovine stare you get from a sea elephant. The pram was usually much overloaded when we took the sealers ashore—often enough it had barely an inch of freeboard—and if a leopard followed us, coming alongside like a speedboat while we laboriously pulled the sluggish craft, we had to bail when its wash slopped over the gunwale, everyone shouting and splashing to scare it away and the rowers trying to hit it with an oar. Many a time when I have been fishing with the pram moored to the floating kelp I have brought a leopard right alongside by playing on its curiosity—*if you tap gently and regularly* with a rowlock on the gunwale or thwart you very soon find any leopard that may be near swimming alongside and looking up into your face" (my emphasis).

Clearly, certain pinnipeds are capable of responses comparable to those claimed by the King Island Eskimos. The characteristics of such a long-necked seal would be much like those of an enlarged leopard seal, with perhaps the following differences:

A pair of ears or protuberances that either can be flattened against the head or retracted. The animal apparently has no front appendages; if it does, they can be folded tightly against the body so it appears to be without them when observed out of the water. The animal described by Steller as a sea ape might easily have been a juvenile of this species. While the reduced front flippers tightly folded against the body at times seems more likely, it is also possible that a particular species of seal could have evolved even farther into a snakelike configuration free of front flippers, or at most with only inconspicuous vestiges.

An expedition into the Pacific Northwest and the Arctic Ocean in the vicinity of King Island may well produce the discovery of at least one, possibly two, new large aquatic mammals, certainly of sufficient importance to warrant considerable expenditure and an investment of the necessary time and effort.

III

Octopus
Giganteus Verrill

If you ask a zoologist if giant octopuses exist, he will probably tell you "no." Giant *squid*, yes; *octopus*, no! The giant octopus is supposed to exist only in man's imagination and works of fiction such as Jules Verne's *Twenty Thousand Leagues Under the Sea* and Victor Hugo's *Toilers of the Deep*.

Yet we have in hand *hard* evidence in the form of tissue samples, analyzed by modern biochemical techniques, that indicate the contrary. It is, in fact, probable that the carcass of an octopus measuring 60 meters (200 feet), tentacle tip to tentacle tip, was washed up on the beach of St. Augustine, Florida, in 1896.

Reports of giant octopuses are as old as man's ability to navigate the open sea. They date from Greek and Roman times, and the creatures were termed *kraken* by Norwegian sailors. Most authorities, with less than a handful of exceptions, have concluded that such references are to the giant squid, *Architeuthis*, which is quite well known. Bernard Heuvelmans, in his *In the Wake of the Sea Serpent*, has documented the occurrence and characteristics of these great animals in detail.

However, the octopus, while also a cephalopod (head-footed), is quite a different animal. The octopus, like the squid, is a mollusk with eight sucker-bearing feet (called arms or tentacles) of about equal length. Squids, in contrast, have two additional retractable tentacles, much longer than the other eight and specialized for mating and for grasping prey. The octopus is designed for a relatively sluggish bottom-dwelling life, with a bulbous body and tentacles arranged around the head in a circular fashion. The squid, on the other hand, is streamlined for fast swimming, has some rudimentary internal cartilaginous structural supports, and a pair of horizontal fins; it is an active predator that pursues its prey. Heuvelmans documents the existence of giant squids of over-all length of 74 meters (240 feet) (including the two long tentacles) and makes a strong case for animals even larger. But he also takes the position that all animals referred to as giant octopuses must be giant squids.

In 1957 F. G. Wood, senior scientist and consultant with the Ocean Sciences Department of the Naval Undersea Research and Development Laboratory at San Diego, California, was looking for some notes he had made on the behavior of octopuses in the Marineland Research Laboratory files, collected over twenty years. He came across a clipping, illustrated and yellowed with age, entitled "The Facts About Florida." It contained a drawing of an octopus with the following caption: "In 1897, portions of an octopus, said to have been more gigantic than any ever before seen, were washed up on the beach of St. Augustine. Professor Verrill, of Yale University, an eminent zoologist of the time, examined the remains, which reputedly weighed over 6 tons, calculated that the living creature had a girth of 25 feet and tentacles 72 feet in length."

Thus begins the modern part of the saga of the giant octopus. Wood, knowing something about octopuses, reacted with immediate disbelief, since the largest acceptable size as far as he was concerned was the northern Pacific species, *Octopus dofleini*, 57 kilograms (125 pounds) 6 meters (20 feet) tentacle tip to tentacle tip. However, Wood was intrigued, especially since the supposed site of the stranding of the carcass was only 25 kilometers (16 miles) from where he was working, and he knew that Professor A. E. Verrill of Yale had been a noted authority on cephalopods. He states, "Verrill's name, along with a specific year and place, was enough to set me digging." Unfortunately, neither the date nor the newspaper name was given. The Jacksonville Public Library informed him that the clipping was from the Florida *Times-Union*, Tuesday, December 1, 1896. The article stated that the carcass was a portion of a whale 92 feet long by 6 feet wide; but "President Webb" (president of the St. Augustine Scientific Society) had examined the monster and pronounced it to be an octopus.

Wood continued his sleuthing, uncovering further details, including photographs and articles by both Webb and Verrill. Verrill's last article retracted his earlier identification of octopus, based, he said, on general form and appearance. Verrill's specimens were large masses of exterior skin, three to ten inches thick, firm, elastic, and very tough, and he now thought the animal must be a vertebrate, probably related to whales, but he could not refer the carcass to any part of any known whale or, in fact, to any other known animal.

Wood was not convinced that Verrill's final assessment was correct, especially after Wood obtained a copy of Verrill's article in the *American Naturalist*, April 1897, which was written prior to his final change of heart.

Wood obtained further data through Gilbert L. Voss of the University of Miami Marine Laboratory, including information that the Smithsonian Institution possessed a large jar of preserved tissue bearing the label *Octopus giganteus Verrill*. Things were really getting interesting now! If truly an actual piece of tissue was available for analysis, modern science should be able to settle the matter. Naturally, Wood contacted the Smithsonian posthaste, and was told by the associate curator of mollusks that they indeed had such a specimen! The prime question was of course whether a small sample of tissue could be obtained for analysis.

Wood now turned to a friend, Dr. Joseph F. Gennaro, Jr., of the University of Florida, who had been working on octopus material at the Marineland Laboratory. Dr. Gennaro was most interested, and proceeded to contact Harold A. Rehder, curator of mollusks at the Smithsonian. Gennaro succeeded in obtaining a sample of the tissue plus additional data, including a photograph made from an original glass plate exposed more than sixty years before.

A detailed account of the discovery of the carcass has been published by Gary S. Mangiacopra in the Spring 1975 issue of *Sea and Shore*. Gary Mangiacopra, whom I first met after a lecture I had given describing our researches at Loch Ness, had been doing an exhaustive investigation and collecting data concerning unidentified aquatic creatures. Not only had he been able to collect and locate more historical data about *Octopus giganteus Verrill*, but he also continues to discover heretofore unknown references to unusual or unidentified lake and sea monsters. A former biology student at Yale, Mangiacopra remains a dedicated cryptozoologist.

For our purposes it will suffice to summarize Mangiacopra's account of the discovery of the giant carcass on the St. Augustine beach on November 30, 1896.

Two youngsters, Herbert Coles and Dunham Coretter, while cycling on Anastasia Beach, discovered a huge carcass partially buried in the sand. Their planned excursion to Matazas Inlet was of course forgotten in the excitement of this fantastic discovery. Almost immediately the presence of the carcass was reported to DeWitt Webb, a medical doctor whose hobby was natural history, especially that of the area around St. Augustine. According to Mangiacopra, Dr. Webb was responsible for the founding of the St. Augustine Historical Society and Institute of Science, serving as president of this society for thirty-four years.

Webb recognized the importance of examining and preserving at least part of the creature, presumably a whale. On the next day, December 1, Dr. Webb and others examined the "whale." They concluded that the creature had been beached for a number of days prior to the discovery and was already in a poor state of preservation. The estimated weight was given as five tons, the part visible above the sand twenty-three feet long by four feet high and eighteen feet across the widest part. The outer layer appeared light pink, almost white with a silvery cast. From his examination, Dr. Webb came to the earth-shaking conclusion that the animal was not a whale, but a giant octopus!

Because of bad weather, Webb was not able to study the carcass further until December 5 and December 7, when two photographers accompanying Webb made a number of photographs. The whereabouts of these original photographs are not known at present, but two drawings based on two of the snapshots made by A. Hyatt Verrill, the son of Dr. Verrill who was later to corroborate Webb's identification of "octopus," are in hand. The drawings, even if accurate, do not tell us much (Illustrations 12 and 13); however, Mangiacopra has noted that the most important feature, in Illustration 12 is what looks like the proximal stumps of five tentacles. (An idea of size is given by the inclusion of a human figure.) The second picture is a side view, the right side representing the front portion as shown in Illustration 12.

12. The Florida Monster, end view, drawn by A. Hyatt Verrill, from a photograph taken December 7, 1896.

13. The Florida Monster, side view.

A few days later, a Mr. Wilson reported to Dr. Webb that while digging around the carcass, he had discovered fragments of the tentacles. According to Wilson, "one arm was lying west of the body, twenty-three feet long; one stump of arm, west of body, about four feet; three arms lying south of the body and from appearance attached to same (although I did not dig quite to body, as it lay well down in the sand, and I was very tired), longest measured over thirty-two feet, the other arms were three to five feet shorter." Unfortunately, Wilson was alone, so his statement is uncorroborated. Shortly thereafter a storm washed the carcass back into the sea, but again the remains were beached, now two miles farther south, at Crescent Beach (Illustration 14).

Webb now sent several letters describing the carcass to scientists, one of which eventually reached Professor Verrill of Yale, a zoologist of great standing, having described many new species and recognized for his work on cephalopods, particularly giant squids. Verrill promptly published a short note in the *American Journal of Science*, January 1897, concluding, however, that the creature was a giant squid, not an octopus, but much larger than the specimens he had examined in Newfoundland in 1870.

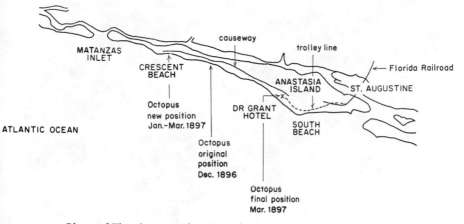

14. Chart of Florida coast showing where octopus carcass was washed ashore.

15. Photograph of the Florida Monster, taken second week of January 1897.

16. Photograph of another view of the Florida Monster, taken second week of January 1897. Note break in tissue exposing muscle tissue.

Webb, meanwhile, forwarded additional data and photographs to Verrill, and these caused him to change his mind. Verrill now published two articles describing the giant octopus, one in the *American Journal of Science*, February 1897, and the other in the New York *Herald*, January 3, 1897. Verrill calculated, by comparing proportions with smaller species, that the tentacles were 20 to 30 meters (75 to 100 feet) by .5 meter (18 inches) at the base. The creature was designated *Octopus giganteus*.

Webb was not able to further pursue his investigation of the carcass until the second week in January, after the carcass had been washed out to sea with further losses and mutilation. But Webb now began to work in earnest, reporting by letter both to Verrill and to Professor William Healey Dall, curator of mollusks at the National Museum in Washington, D.C. (now the Smithsonian). Mangiacopra's investigations revealed that seven letters written by Webb are in existence, although the replies from Verrill and Dall have not been found.

In spite of the continuing flow of information from Webb

17. Carcass of the Florida Monster in the process of being moved up the beach by a team of horses. The man shown in the picture is most probably Dr. DeWitt Webb.

to Verrill and Dall, neither scientist made an effort to inspect the carcass. Neither of these scientists or the institutions they represented was willing to provide the necessary time and money to properly preserve and study the animal. Webb, however, continued his work. Through the efforts of local citizens and companies, he was able to move the carcass farther up the beach, using teams of horses, thus preventing the possible loss of the remains by being permanently washed out to sea. On February 1 Webb prepared separate specimens for shipment to Verrill and Dall. Webb cut two pieces from the mantle and two from the body, preserving them in formaldehyde. If it were not for this action by Webb, no hard evidence would have been preserved for us to study. Webb was interested in preserving all of the carcass, and according to at least one letter, preservatives were forwarded to him for this purpose. Verrill, prior to receiving the tissue samples, continued to write articles about the giant octopus in which he speculated about its habitat and behavior.

On February 23 Verrill received Webb's specimens and began to have second thoughts, shortly thereafter writing letters of retraction, which were published in *Science* on March 5, 1897, and in the *Herald* on the seventh. He described the samples visually and concluded, in spite of the fact that they contained little oil, that they resembled the blubber of some cetaceans and could not be octopus tissue.

Professor Frederic Augustus Lucas, of the National Museum, also examined the specimens sent by Webb and was far less cautious, stating: "The substance looks like blubber, and smells like blubber, and it *is* blubber, nothing more nor less.'

Verrill made additional examinations of the tissue, concluding finally, with some reservations, that the baglike mass was probably the whole upper part of the head and nose of a sperm whale. Dr. Webb apparently received this news with incredulity, which is expressed in his last letter to Professor Dall.

To Professor Verrill's credit, although he officially retracted his original identification, in the April issues of the *American Journal of Science* and the *American Naturalist*, he does not soft-pedal the objections to and problems with his identification of the tissue as coming from a whale. He also pointed out in a footnote that other zoologists had examined the tissue and still believed that it represented an unknown cephalopod related to the octopus.

During the intervening years no further serious work was done on the tissue specimens until Dr. Wood became interested, in 1957. Wood, having involved Dr. Gennaro, now waited to see what Gennaro's analysis of the tissue would show. Gennaro personally made a trip to the Smithsonian to collect the precious specimens. Gennaro writes: "There by the sink was a glass container about the size of a milk can. Inside it was a murky mixture of cheesecloth, formalin (and I think some alcohol), and half a dozen large white masses of tough fibrous material, each about as large as a good-sized roast. We lifted them up with the cheesecloth, then took them out with forceps."

Gennaro noted that the material corresponded closely to Webb's description, containing little oil and looking much like soap. He was permitted to remove what he wanted with a dissecting knife with replaceable blades. It took four fresh blades to cut the two pieces required, each blade being dulled in turn by the tough tissue. The pieces were carefully wrapped in cheesecloth, placed in a jar, and transported by Gennaro himself to his laboratory.

Initial examination proved disappointing in that no recognizable features such as suckers, identifiable skin structures, or muscular masses were apparent. Everything was uniformly tough, white, and fibrous. One small piece dissected out of the material did, however, appear to be from the skin of the animal. The material, because of its natural smoothness, may have come from the outer surface (or, for that matter, from an inner surface). Gennaro noted, "Certainly, there was none of the typical covering layer one would expect from either a mollusk or mammal."

As any good scientist, he now prepared not only his samples for histological analysis but also prepared "control" specimens of known squid and octopus. With considerable excitement he viewed his slides through the microscope. To his dismay no cellular fine structure was observable. He had expected the highly differentiated cells of a mammal (if the sample came from a whale) or a structure typical of a squid or an octopus. Nothing like that at all was apparent. Could the carcass have been dead too long prior to preservation or had the samples been in formaldehyde too long? Now he turned to his known samples of octopus and squid, properly prepared, and found that they also revealed very little if any cellular structure. Differences of connective-tissue patterns were, however, quite striking. Octopus connective tissue could immediately be distinguished from squid tissue, while neither could be mistaken for the pattern found in mammal tissue.

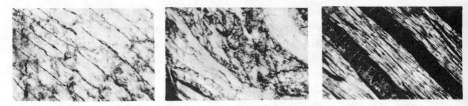

18. Micrographs of tissue samples as seen in polarized light, dark field illumination—squid at left, octopus at middle, Florida Monster at right. The bright portions in each are connective-tissue strands oriented parallel to the plane of the section; dark portions are similar strands oriented perpendicularly. In the octopus, equally broad bands of parallel and perpendicular tissue alternate. In the squid, broad bands of parallel fibers are separated by very thin perpendicular regions. In the monster, fewer bands are visible, but there are two broad bands of parallel fibers with an equally broad band of more or less perpendicular fibers between them. This is proof that it was not a giant squid.

Gennaro now decided to compare connective-tissue patterns rather than looking for cellular structures, employing polarized light. Differentiation between ordered protein fibers aligned in the plane of the polarized light and those aligned at right angles was pronounced, one appearing bright, the other dark.

Again let us quote Gennaro as to his findings: "Now differences between the contemporary squid and octopus samples became very clear. In the octopus, broad bands of fibers passed across the plane of the tissue and were separated by equally broad bands arranged in a perpendicular direction. In the squid there were narrower but also relatively broad bundles arranged in the plane of the section, separated by thin partitions of perpendicular fibers.

"It seemed I had found a means to identify the mystery sample after all. I could distinguish between octopus and squid, and between them and mammals, which display a lacy network of connective-tissue fibers.

"After seventy-five years, the moment of truth was at hand. Viewing section after section of the St. Augustine sample, we decided at once, and beyond any doubt, that the sample was not whale blubber. Further, the connective-tissue pattern was that of broad bands in the plane of the section with equally broad bands arranged perpendicularly, a structure similar to, if not identical with, that in my octopus sample.

"The evidence appears unmistakable that the St. Augustine sea monster was in fact an octopus, but the implications are fantastic."

We can certainly agree with this assessment, but upon reflection perhaps we should not be surprised that giant octopuses have not been verified before. We must remember, as noted earlier, that the octopus is a sluggish deep-sea dweller, not an active predator such as the squid. Perhaps the giant .5-meter- (18-inch-) diameter sucker marks reported by whalers on whales are made not by giant squids but rather by *Octopus giganteus*.

But where are we to look for these giants of the deep? In what ocean depths are they likely to exist? Off the coast of St. Augustine, Florida, perhaps? This question also intrigued Dr. Wood, who has investigated the situation and provides the best clues as to where an expedition might search for this creature. Of necessity, as is so often the case in cryptozoology, we must rely initially on anecdotal reporting for our leads. Such evidence must, of course, be used with caution, but more often than not experience has taught us that if the source and character of the informant are taken into account, such data may indeed lead to important discoveries.

Wood's clues relate mainly to the region surrounding the Bahama Islands, not of course ruling out other ocean deeps in other parts of the world.

In 1956, even before he discovered the newspaper report about the St. Augustine sea monster, Wood was working at West End, Grand Bahama Island, surveying possible collecting areas for Marine Studios. He had working for him a most reliable guide named Duke, who almost without fail provided information as to the location of various species of sought-after marine life. Clearly Duke's knowledge of the marine fauna in the area was at once extensive and accurate.

At one point Wood recounts how he remembered vague references to "giant scuttles" years ago while working around Bimini. "Scuttle" is the Bahamian word for octopus, the small

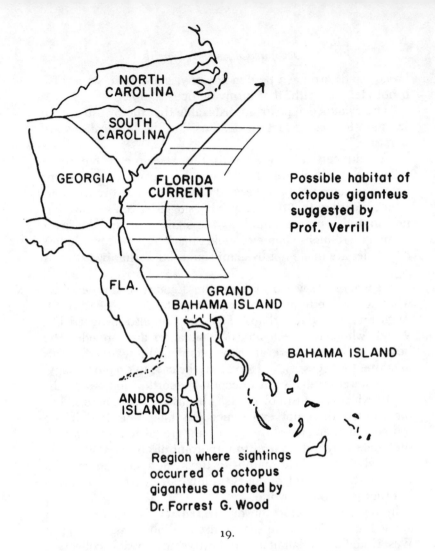

Possible habitat of
octopus giganteus
suggested by
Prof. Verrill

Region where sightings
occurred of octopus
giganteus as noted by
Dr. Forrest G. Wood

19.

varieties of which all natives are familiar with. Wood asked
Duke whether he knew anything about giant scuttles in the
area. Duke stated that he did indeed and provided data as to
when, where, and by whom observations had been made,
indicating that the most recent observations had been made
about ten years ago. Duke maintained that the arms of the
giant scuttles were as long as the distance to a nearby building,
about twenty meters (seventy-five feet) away. He also stated

that they are not dangerous to fishermen unless they can at the same time hold fast to the bottom and grasp the fishing boat with other tentacles.

Wood later discussed the information obtained from Duke with the island commissioner, a native of Andros Island, who proceeded to recount an experience he had undergone as a boy while fishing off Andros Island with his father. They were over a depth of 185 meters (six hundred feet) of water fishing for silk snappers. His father hooked something heavy. At first he thought he had snagged the bottom, but he was able to draw the line up slowly, and when the end came into view, they saw a very large octopus holding fast to the line. The octopus released the line and attached itself to the fishing boat. They were very fearful, but eventually the octopus let go and vanished in the deeps. Questioned by Wood as to estimated size, the commissioner, a well-educated and conservative man, would not venture a guess, since it had happened long ago, but certainly it was a large animal, not of the garden variety of small shallow-water octopuses.

Additional information about the giant octopus tradition around Andros Island has been provided by George J. Benjamin. Benjamin is a research chemist, but his avocation is underwater exploration and photography. He has been intrigued by the great blue holes in the ocean around Andros Island and has spent the past ten years investigating them. These strange holes, over sixty meters (two hundred feet) deep in the seas around Andros, are enigmas from several viewpoints, including the strange movement of water in and out of them and a possible connection of some of them to inland lakes on Andros. Blue holes are not unique to Andros; one, located off the coast of British Honduras (now Belize) and sounded by the British Geodetic Survey in 1931, was deeper than one thousand meters (three thousand feet). However, fascinating as they may be, the strange blue holes per se are beyond the scope of our discussion.

Benjamin and his colleagues have never observed any giant octopuses or squids during their investigations of the blue holes around Andros, none of which has been much more

20.

than sixty meters (two hundred feet) deep. The tradition is so widespread, however, that some credence must be given to these stories. The nature of these traditions is best illustrated by quoting one of Benjamin's native helpers. "You go down dere and Lusca, him of de hahnds, sure to catch you. Once de hahnds get hold of you, you dead, mahn!"

He then described an encounter. "I remind de time one stop a two-master dead in de water. He wrap all around de rudders and wid de free hahnds he feelin' on decks. Once de hahnd feel a mahn, dey was a flunder in de water, and bot' mahn and Lusca gone."

Whatever one may believe about these stories, they give one pause before diving in these waters much deeper than sixty meters (two hundred feet). It seems likely that natives attribute all unexplained disappearances of boats and boatmen to the Lusca, even when they are the result of other accidents. Nevertheless, the greater depths may harbor *Octopus gigan-*

teus, since Benjamin and his team have established only that the upper sixty meters (two hundred feet) of the ocean appear to be free of such creatures, real or imagined.

Bruce Wright, director of the Northeastern Wildlife Station, believes that giant cephalopods do indeed live in the depths of the Bahamian waters, but that they are the giant squids *Architeuthis*. He has published his views in an article for the *Atlantic Advocate* under the title "The Lusca of Andros." He also interviewed natives extensively about the Lusca. According to his informants the creatures had long tentacles that could be shot out to seize a victim, and these tentacles were tipped with strong suckers. Once securely anchored, no man could break the Lusca's grip. They were rare, but still encountered from time to time.

Another interesting aspect is that the natives allege that the Lusca are occasionally found inland in deep holes in lakes and other deep holes called "banana holes." This may at first sound extremely unreasonable, since no known cephalopods (squids or octopuses) are found in fresh water. There is, however, evidence that some of these lakes and holes contain brackish water and may in fact connect to blue holes in the sea.

Bruce Wright's hypothesis that the Andros Lusca are giant squids cannot be dismissed.

However, it seems probable to me that the evidence presented, consisting not only of native rumors but also including so-called hard evidence—that is, tissue samples on which recent analyses with modern techniques have been carried out—establishes beyond reasonable doubt that very large octopuses exist somewhere in the Atlantic off the Florida coast. Whether these creatures explain the Andros Lusca tradition cannot be determined until deep-diving exploration is carried out in the area.

IV

Prehistoric Reptiles

in Africa?

On my bookshelf rests a work entitled *Old Fourlegs*. It was written by J. L. B. Smith, a chemist whose first love was ichthyology—fish and the study of fish. His ichthyological aspirations were rewarded in a once-in-several-lifetimes manner by his codiscovery of the coelacanth. The coelacanth, that marvelously ancient fish, is world-famous as a living example of the ancestral line of vertebrates from which all higher land animals arose. These fish, formerly known only from the fossil record and thought to have been extinct for sixty to seventy million years, need no further introduction.

But the story of their discovery by Smith and Dr. Marjorie Courtenay-Latimer, and its aftermath, are not so well known. As chronicled in *Old Fourlegs* it has been at one and the same time a haven and an inspiration to me. The trials and tribulations encountered by Smith, Courtenay-Latimer, and company had much in common with our own problems in our researches at Loch Ness, although we have not as yet reached a similarly happy conclusion.

One day while rereading portions of the Smith account, I was struck by a reference on page 189, which I must have read many times before. But that day, for some inscrutable reason, the words leaped out of the page at me. Smith had written that he had received a letter from the descendants of a missionary who had lived near Mount Kilimanjaro. This report from Germany gave a good deal of information about flying dragons they believed still to live in those parts. The family had repeatedly heard of them from the natives, one of whom had actually seen such a creature in flight close by at night. Smith added, "I did not and do not dispute at least the possibility that some such creature may still exist."

Although J. L. B. Smith is no longer with us, I immediately fired off a request to Margaret, his widow, asking her if she could find the correspondence referred to. In due course her reply arrived. She wrote me how disappointed she was that the letters from the German missionaries could not be found. She thought that the correspondence probably had occurred prior to the formation of the Department of Ichthyology at Rhodes University, when things were disorganized and letters could easily have been lost. A further check in the "Crackpot" file also was negative. Mrs. Smith suggested that she knew Marjorie Courtenay-Latimer had made at least one investigation of flying dragons many years ago. Perhaps she might know something helpful or might even have the missing correspondence.

I wrote directly to Dr. Courtenay-Latimer, who had by now retired to Tzitzikama, a remote area of South Africa. The information she provided was extremely interesting, although she knew nothing about the J. L. B. Smith correspondence with missionaries. She had indeed investigated what was considered a flying snake near Keetmanshoop in Namibia (formerly South-West Africa), but never established what the creature was, although she was convinced there was something out of the ordinary.

A summary of the reports regarding this creature follows: Farms in this area are often quite large, as much as 160 kilometers (100 miles) by 160 kilometers (100 miles), or 25,000 square kilometers (10,000 square miles). The main livelihood is derived from kana (a flowering plant) and colossal flocks of sheep. The natives on one particular farm in Keetmanshoop eventually left for the reason that the owner would not take seriously the allegation that there was a very large snake in the mountains where the sheep grazed and were shepherded. Having just lost all his help, the farmer sent his son of sixteen to tend the flocks of animals. When the boy did not return that evening, a party went into the mountains to search for him. They found him unconscious and brought him home. According to the attending doctor the boy was unable to speak for three days because of shock after he recovered consciousness. When questioned the boy related that he had been sitting under a shade tree quietly carving animals from pieces of soft wood when he heard a great roaring noise—like a strong current of wind. His immediate thought was that a "wind devil" was responsible, since such air disturbances are common in this mountainous area. Looking up, he observed what appeared to be a huge snake hurling itself down from a mountain ridge. As the creature approached the sound was terrific, combined now with that of sheep scattering in all directions out of the creature's path. The creature landed, raising a cloud of dust and a smell he described like burned brass. At that point he apparently lost consciousness from shock and fright. The incident was investigated by police and farmers some of whom actually observed the creature disappear into a crevice in the mountain. Sticks of dynamite were fused and hurled into the crevice. After the detonations a low moaning sound was heard for a short while and then silence.

Dr. Courtenay-Latimer arrived shortly thereafter, finding marks and trails made by the creature. She noted that the usual birds, rats, mice, and other small animals normally found in such areas were absent. She found no other trace of the creature.

In spite of Dr. Courtenay-Latimer's investigation and study of photographs of the marks and tracks of the creature, no explanation as to the nature of the creature is convincing. Could the creature have been an injured python that had therefore engaged in abnormal behavior and movement, as suggested by Dr. Courtenay-Latimer? According to her, literally anything is possible in this remote part of South-West Africa.

In my judgment, the injured-snake hypothesis fails to account for the considerable air disturbance reported, which suggests at least an anatomical air foil if not full-fledged wings. A snake, even a very large one, hurtling or falling over a ledge or mountain precipice hardly would disturb the air as described. In fact, it is hard to attribute such a disturbance even to a large gliding creature, suggesting instead that some kind of wing action must have been involved. However, if this were the case, it is strange that the boy made no reference to wings.

There are no known living truly flying reptiles, snakes, or snakelike lizards. There is a small species of lizard, *Draco volans*, found in the East Indies. These "flying lizards" have elongated ribs that support paired expansible membranes that enable them to make jumping glides from branch to branch. The gliding mechanism of these animals does not permit flight as in birds and bats or even extinct pterodactyls. There are also "flying geckos" (Kuhl's gecko, *Ptychozoon homalocephalus*) found in southeastern Asia that have lateral skin folds along the trunk of the body about half as wide as the animals themselves. An additional border of skin along the head and thighs continuing on the toes and tail completes the gliding surface. When legs and tail are extended rigidly, the folds of skin are stretched, acting as a parachute when the animal falls or jumps.

21. The Flying Dragon, *Draco volans*.

Lizards and geckos are not uncommon in South Africa, yet the comparison in the report was never to these animals, always to snakes. There is a so-called flying snake (*Chrysoplea ornata*) about 1.5 meters (5 feet) in length found in Borneo, which has a longitudinal ridge along each side of the belly. These Indo-Pacific arboreal snakes are able to drop from treetops over great heights, 15 to 20 meters (50 to 65 feet), and land successfully without injury. While this is neither flight nor gliding, it may be evolution in that direction, although at this stage the lateral ridge of scales is more useful for climbing than for gliding. Could a large variety of such lizards or snakes exist in South-West Africa and be responsible for the episode described? Or could some species of pterodactyl with elongated body and tail still survive, as claimed by the German missionaries?

There are other reports from Africa that are taken by some as referring to some species of pterodactyl. A friend, Jerry Clark, called my attention to an article in the journal *INFO* by Jan-Ove Sundberg, a Swedish journalist. Ostensibly the article deals with Irish lake monsters, particularly in Sraheens Lough. However, reference is made to strange flying reptiles reported in Kenya and Namibia.

Sundberg reported information provided by Mr. Carl Pleijel of the Swedish Museum of Natural History. Pleijel had been told that an English expedition in Kenya had observed a huge birdlike creature resembling the reconstructions of extinct "*Pterodactylus.*" The source was reluctant to make such a sensational claim publicly, and Pleijel stated he knew nothing about the members of the expedition.

The alleged sighting took place in March or April 1974. Sundberg obtained further information from a Swedish Museum official, who did not want to be named, that a similar creature was observed in Namibia, also in a swampy area, by an American expedition in late 1975. Allegedly a film was obtained in the latter case.

I wrote to Sundberg asking whether he could provide more concrete data privately. Sundberg was very co-operative but was unable to persuade his sources to "go public." Further

22. Pterodactyl in a typical batlike pose.

information regarding the sighting in Namibia would of course be most important relative to Dr. Courtenay-Latimer's report from the same region.

"Kongamato," a "flying dragon," makes an appearance in the book *On the Track of Unknown Animals* by Bernard Heuvelmans. Heuvelmans' data are based on Frank H. Melland's book *In Witch-bound Africa*, a serious study of the ethnography of the Bokaonde and their neighbors inhabiting the Kasempa district of northern Rhodesia (now Zimbabwe-Rhodesia). In Melland's study of the Kaonde he came upon a charm against the danger of river crossings: " *Muchi wa kongamato.*' In certain rivers at the fords or ferries there is a danger of being attacked by the kongamato ('? overwhelmer of boats'), which lives downstream of the ford, and which has the power of stopping the waters from flowing away, thus causing a sudden rise in the water level and overwhelming the passenger. To circumvent this, part of the root of the mulendi tree is ground by the traveler and mixed with water, the paste being put into a bark cup. Part of the root is cut into strips and tied in a bundle, which is carried when in the canoe or when crossing the dangerous ford on foot. When the kongamato comes the bundle is dipped in the medicine and the water is sprinkled therewith, which keeps off the kongamato and his flood."

Melland investigated the charm further and obtained a description of this creature. First he asked the natives, "What is the kongamato?" Answer, "A bird." "What kind of bird?" Answer, "Oh well, it isn't a bird really; it is more like a lizard with wings like a bat." The wingspread allegedly is from one meter to two meters (four to seven feet), with a general red color. It has no feathers but only skin and teeth in its beak. Melland showed the natives pictures of pterodactyls and other animals, and each native unerringly identified the pterodactyl as the kongamato.

Where exactly is this creature supposed to exist? According to Kanyinga, a native headman from the Jiundu country, the kongamato lives in the Jiunda swamp (see map). Although, this is only one of the possible areas, it seems to be the most likely, as Melland said he had never seen such a morass, 128 square kilometers (50 square miles) of swamp and dense vegetation: big trees and tangled undergrowth with matted creepers and exotic ferns.

The question in this business is the identification of the creature as a pterosaur. Heuvelmans records a couple of later references and even a possible explanation put forth by

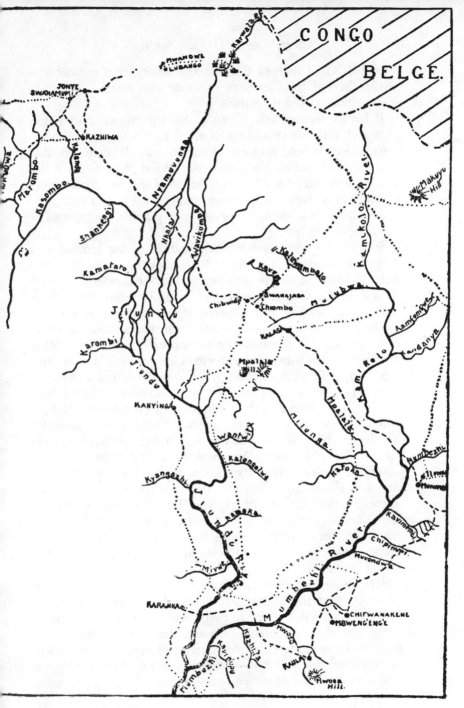

CONGO

BELGE.

23.

Professor C. Wiman of Uppsala University, that natives who earlier helped the Germans excavate pterosaurian bones in East Africa started the rumor.

It hardly seems likely, though, as Heuvelmans points out, that such a rumor should travel 1,600 kilometers (1,000 miles) unchanged, leaving no trace along the way. It seems possible that an unidentified creature exists. What then could it be? Heuvelmans suggests a large unidentified species of bat. None of the known bats have a wingspread as great as 2 meters (7 feet), although a Malayan species may reach a wingspread of 1.7 meters (5½ feet).

Support for the possible identification of kongamato as a large bat comes from zoologist Ivan Sanderson and his experience while leading the 1932 Percy Sladen Expedition to West Africa, in the Cameroons in the Assumbo Mountains. Sanderson was wading and hopping stone to stone in a steep-banked river when a large black thing the size of an eagle dived at him. He observed the head momentarily, presenting an open mouth with pointed teeth. Later at dusk the creature returned, with teeth chattering and wings making a swishing noise. The beast made straight for Sanderson's companion, Gerald, who ducked as the animal sailed off into the dusk.

Sanderson was told by the natives that this was "olitiau." Sanderson himself believes this was a bat, perhaps a really large variety of *Hypsignathus monstrosus* or hammerhead bat, which for some unknown reason does fly low over water, dipping. Heuvelmans objects that this species is hardly an aggressive type likely to attack man. The attack on Sanderson, however, occurred just after he had shot a large fruit bat, which fell into the river where he was wading. Clearly such an act could have triggered unusual behavior by another bat in the vicinity.

A point against this identification is the fact that Sanderson observed that the attacking creature had pointed teeth set apart approximately equal to their own width. This feature fits better with the carnivorous pterosaurs than with the specialized teeth of fruit-eating bats or the reduced dentition of insectivorous bats. Of the fish-eating bats none approach a size comparable to the observed creature.

Of course, Melland's kongamato may be something completely distinct from Sanderson's olitiau. It is very curious that the natives should ascribe to kongamato the ability to overwhelm boats. The natives definitely attributed amphibiousness to the kongamato, according to Melland, which struck him as mythical. But again, could the natives be right? Many authorities believe that some pterosaurs were also able to dive and swim efficiently. Such behavior could account for the native description entirely, in contrast to the bat idea, since there are no real swimming bats (although if a bat falls into water it is able to move on the surface by fluttering its wings, thus reaching the shore).

In contrast to some who state, "Today there is no possibility whatsoever of finding a flying reptile or any of its progeny in some lost corner of the world; all such reports can be nothing but hoaxes," I suggest we keep an open mind.

One who shares my viewpoint is James H. Powell, Jr. Powell is carrying on the search in the field for unidentified animals, including flying reptiles. He is a graduate of Columbia University, and has a Master's degree from Texas Technological University in Lubbock, Texas, and has studied herpetology at the University of Colorado. He began to do field work on the status and distribution of Morelet's crocodile (*Crocodylus moreleti*) in Yucatan and in Belize. He fell in love with crocodile field work and continued his studies in America, Africa, and the South Pacific islands. His extensive field work and his work as a member of the Crocodile Specialist Group of the International Union for Conservation of Nature and Natural Resources, coupled with his great interest in unidentified animals, especially reptiles, qualifies him as a cryptozoologist par excellence. This latter interest was kindled coincidentally by Heuvelmans' *On the Track of Unknown Animals*.

During his latest expedition to the Cameroons, Powell tried to check on Sanderson's olitiau, but none of the natives recognized the term. However, other cryptozoological inquiries were more successful and were of great interest to me.

Telephone discussions with Powell threatened to disrupt my financial stability, so it was agreed that he would come to

24. James Powell, scientific explorer
and crocodile expert.

Chicago so that information could be exchanged more effectively. He was particularly interested in the "flying snake" data
obtained from Courtenay-Latimer, while I in turn was most
anxious to explore any leads regarding strange African reptiles.
We were both interested in possible future co-operative investigations.

When Powell arrived he brought with him a copy of a newly
published book by Bernard Heuvelmans (in French only, as
of this writing) dealing exclusively with the possibility of the
survival of primitive reptiles in Africa. I examined this material
avidly, especially since it contained much new information.
Several evenings spent covering the cryptozoological topics
from the Indian Ocean to earth's poles were as delightful as
instructive.

A visit to the Field Museum to introduce Powell to some of
my professional friends there was arranged. Future expeditions

were discussed over lunch, including the possible participation of one or more museum specialists in some of our projects. Interest and excitement ran high as we discussed the botanical, zoological, and geological implications of our schemes!

It was agreed that Powell would make further preliminary investigations in several promising areas as time and financial support permitted. Eventually on the basis of these explorations a final choice for a full-blown expedition will be made.

Some of Powell's findings were most exciting. His investigations in Gabon, a former French West African colony, intrigued me greatly. Powell obtained much of his information through the good offices of the personnel at the Albert Schweitzer Hospital at Lambaréné, Gabon, while studying crocodiles. Quoting now directly from his note:

Albert Schweitzer believed in the sacredness of all life, not just human life. Therefore, when the staff of the Hôpital Albert Schweitzer at Lambaréné [Gabon] learned of the conservation nature of my work, they allowed me to use the hospital as a base. While there I became friends with a Swiss dentist, who had married a Fang girl from a village a short distance up the Ogooué from the hospital. Accompanied by him, I visited his wife's village, and there became acquainted with the village witch doctor. My dentist friend told me this witch doctor—a man of around seventy—was extremely intelligent, and so I found him to be. Using the dentist as interpreter, I questioned him as follows:

First, I showed him pictures of African animals found in the Gabonese jungles—leopard, gorilla, elephant, hippo, crocodile, etc.—and asked him to identify each one, which he did unerringly. I then showed him a picture of a bear, which does not occur in Gabon. This he could not identify. "That animal not live around here," he said. I then showed him a picture of a *Diplodocus* [a brontosaurus-ike dinosaur] from a children's book on dinosaurs and asked him if he could recognize it. "*N'yamala*," he answered, quite matter-of-factly.

I think *n'yamala* is the closest phonetic rendition I can give of the Bantu sounds. I asked my informant to repeat several times, slowly, and then I repeated it back to him so that he could check my pronunciation. Compare with the *amali* of Trader Horn ["The *Jago-Nini* they say is still in the swamps and

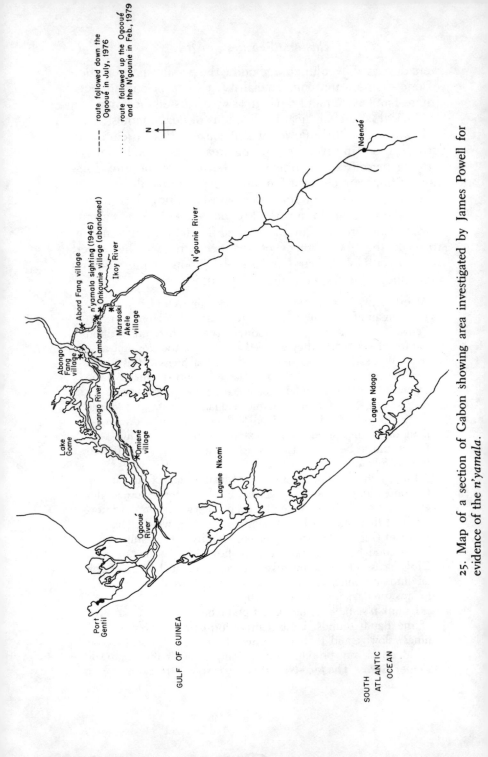

25. Map of a section of Gabon showing area investigated by James Powell for evidence of the *n'yamala*.

The labels on the map include:

Port Gentil

GULF OF GUINEA

SOUTH ATLANTIC OCEAN

Ogooué River

Lake Gome

Ouango River

Abongo Fang village

Omiené village

Lagune Nkomi

Lagune Ndogo

Lambaréné

Marsoski Akele village

Abord Fang village

n'yamala sighting (1946)

Onkounie village (abandoned)

Ikoy River

N'gounie River

Ndendé

N

- - - - route followed down the Ogooué in July, 1976

· · · · · · route followed up the Ogooué and the N'gounie in Feb., 1979 rivers. . . . Same as the *amali* I've always taken it to be. I've seen the *amali*'s footprint. About the size of a good frying pan in circumference and three claws instead o' five. . . . What but some great creature like the *amali* could account for the broken ivories we used to come across in the so-called elephant cemeteries? . . . That *amali*. I told you I've seen a drawing of him in those Bushman caves."] Amali; n'yamala; it seems likely that Trader Horn and I are trying to render into phonetic English the same African word.

The reader may not be familiar with "Trader Horn" and references to a strange unknown animal, the *amali* according to Horn. In 1927 a book appeared both in England and in America authored more or less by Alfred Aloysius Horn. I say more or less because it was a narrative of a boy trader's adventures in the 1870s in Africa, based in part on Horn's notes, who was in his seventies in 1927, but also on his almost weekly conversations with South African novelist Ethelreda Lewis, who put the whole thing together in a publishable form. These adventures, which are anecdotal, appeared under the title *The Ivory Coast in the Earlies* and, in the United States, as *Trader Horn*. Horn is a pseudonym, his real name being Smith, although Alfred Aloysius were Horn's real first and middle names. Some of the material contained in the book was considered quite racy and perhaps even scandalous at the time, which accounts for withholding Horn's real name, although his place of birth thirteen miles outside of Glasgow, Scotland, and other details of his early life are given.

Clearly these are reminiscences of an old man, so that circumspection must be exercised regarding his statements. Nevertheless, the remarkable references to the *amali* and their correspondence to Powell's findings one hundred years later are worth noting.

Powell continued:

I next asked my informant for more details on the *n'yamala*. He said it was a rare animal that was found only in remote lakes deep in the jungle. Only the very greatest hunters have ever seen the *n'yamala*. He himself had never seen one.

He then spontaneously added a detail that I found very

interesting: He said that the *n'yamala* lived on "jungle chocolate." My Swiss interpreter explained that "jungle chocolate" was the local term for a plant which grows near the banks of rivers and lakes and bears large, nut-like fruits said to be favored by this mysterious animal. One thinks immediately of Freiherr von Stein zu Lausnitz's description of the *mokéle-mbêmbe:* "It is said to climb the shore even at daytime in search of food; its diet is said to be entirely vegetable. . . . The preferred plant was shown to me; it is a kind of liana with large, white blossoms, with a milky sap and apple-like fruit."

Powell is quoting from an unpublished manuscript—a report by Captain Freiherr von Stein zu Lausnitz, who made a general survey of the Cameroons when they were still a German colony in 1913. Willy Ley published a translation of the description of the *mokéle-mbêmbe* from this report. "The animal is said to be of a brownish-gray color with a smooth skin, its size approximately that of an elephant; at least that of a hippopotamus. It is said to have a long and very flexible neck and only one tooth but a very long one; some say it is a horn. A few spoke about a long, muscular tail like that of an alligator. Canoes coming near it are said to be doomed; the animal is said to attack the vessels at once and to kill the crews but without eating the bodies. The creature is said to live in the caves that have been washed out by the river in the clay of its shores at sharp bends."

According to Heuvelmans, von Stein's report was confirmed in 1938 by Dr. Leo von Boxberger, who had been a German official during the German African colonial period. Von Boxberger wrote, "My own contribution to the subject is unfortunately very small. At the mouth of the Mbam in Sanaga in central Cameroons and on the Ntem in southern Cameroons, I collected a variety of data from the natives about the mysterious water-beast, but, alas, all my notes and also the local description of the animal were lost in Spanish Guinea when the Pangwe attacked the caravan carrying my few belongings. All that I can report is the name *mbokäle-muembe* given to the animal in southern Cameroons. . . ."

The belief in a gigantic water animal, described as a reptile with a long thin neck, exists among the natives throughout the southern Cameroons wherever they form part of the Congo basin and also to the west of this area, doubtless wherever the great rivers are broad and deep and are flanked by virgin forest.

Powell continued his interrogation, inquiring whether the *n'yamala* had a horn.

The witch doctor said no. This, of course, was not what I wanted to hear, so I pressed him more closely, asking if he was absolutely sure it didn't have some sort of a horn, or at least something on its head that might look like a horn. But he refused to change his story, and insisted that no, it didn't have any horn of any sort. While this marks a discrepancy from other accounts, it at least proves that my informant was not saying things just to please me, for I am sure he could tell that I wanted him to say the creature had a horn.

There was no money involved in any of this. The four of us— the witch doctor, a patient for whom he was prescribing fetish at the time of our visit, the Swiss dentist, and myself—were simply sitting in the village juju hut conversing as friends. The witch doctor's patient gave essentially the same account as did the witch doctor, though since we were all together this could not be considered as independent evidence.

A picture of a plesiosaur was also identified as *n'yamala*. Pictures of other dinosaurs (*Tyrannosaurus*, *Stegosaurus*, and *Triceratops*) produced the same negative result as the picture of the bear: These animals did not live around there, and were unknown to my informants. A picture of a pterodactyl was identified as a bat.

The following day I obtained a dugout and boatmen from the hospital and moved about 80 miles downstream to a small Omiené village in order to study *Crocodylus cataphractus* on the lower Ogooué. While based at this village I tried my picture test on a number of the Omiené. The results were consistently identical with those obtained at the Fang village. Pictures of a leopard, gorilla, hippo, elephant, and crocodile were all correctly identified. The bear was unknown. Pictures of a *Diplodocus* and a plesiosaur were both identified as *n'yamala*. *Tyrannosaurus*, *Stegosaurus*, and *Triceratops* were unknown. The pterodactyl was called a bat.

I hope I am not corrupting the natives too badly with my pictures of prehistoric animals!

When questioned about the habits of the *n'yamala*, my Omiené informants said that it lived far off in remote jungle lakes. None of them claimed to have ever personally seen it. I failed to ask about the horn.

So much for my Gabonese data. You can make of them what you will. For me, these leads, though inconclusive, were tantalizing. However, as my grant from the Explorers Club was for studying crocodile populations, I did not have the chance to follow any of them up. According to the official statistics I got from the American Embassy in Libreville, 80 per cent of Gabon is still relatively unexplored. I found the lower Ogooué between Lambaréné and Port Gentil incredibly wild and unspoiled—much to my pleasant surprise. Human population was very sparse, wildlife abundant. With its labyrinth of channels, papyrus swamps, and large lakes, this area would be an ideal last refuge for a relict population of large, aquatic reptiles. However, if the *n'yamala* is incompatible with hippos, then I wouldn't look for it in the main channel of the lower Ogooué; for hippos were so numerous in places as to constitute a hazard to canoe navigation.

Powell was aware that further data, possibly bearing on the *n'yamala* or *mokéle-mbêmbe*, had been obtained by Ivan Sanderson and Gerald Russell, an American naturalist during the Percy Sladen Expedition, already referred to in connection with the olitiau. Powell contacted Sanderson in 1970 for further information. Sanderson and Russell, while they were on the Mainyu River near the Mamfe Pool in West Cameroon, approached a place where caves with mouths were located in the cliffsides of the river. They heard a noisy commotion as of fighting beasts issuing from one or more of these caves. Suddenly they saw the top of something much larger than a hippo rise out of the water, again immediately submerging.

Above the Mamfe Pool on the upper Cross River, Sanderson told Heuvelmans, he had seen "vast hippolike tracks" although there were no hippos because this creature, the *mbulu-em'bembe* (Sanderson's spelling), drove them away.

In Sanderson's letter to Powell referring to Sanderson's observations and whether it might not have been a large

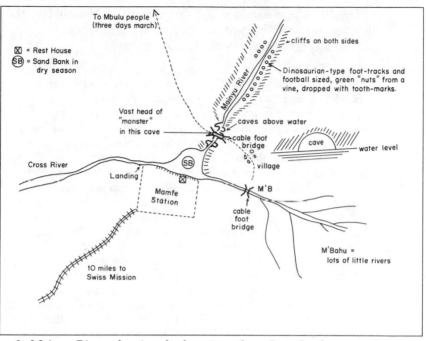

26. Mainyu River, showing the location where Ivan Sanderson and Gerald Russell observed their "monster."

crocodile, he wrote, "The thing we encountered and the tracks we found on the Mainyu River could not possibly have had any connection with any crocodilian. The effing thing's head was bigger than a whole hippo, and the tracks were sauropod." Sauropods, being those dinosaurs that became plant eaters, reached gigantic proportions and may have been at least semi-aquatic. To this group belong the well-known giants *Brontosaurus*, *Diplodocus*, and *Brachiosaurus*. Now not even Sanderson, whose zoological daring was second to none, was suggesting that one of these giants was present in the Mainyu River cave. Rather he was thinking of smaller varieties similar in form but a mere five to six meters (eighteen to twenty feet) in length. These would still dwarf a hippo, but would fit the descriptions and observations as to size and shape.

Powell reports his investigation of the area:

From Gabon I went to Mamfe, in West Cameroon, as I wanted to investigate the place on the Mainyu River where Ivan Sanderson and Gerald Russell saw their "monster" in a cave in 1932. I wrote Ivan about this back in 1970. He replied quickly and included a map showing the exact place where he had seen the animal. [See Illustration 26 with additional features added by James Powell obtained during his investigation.]

July and August are the height of the rainy season in West Cameroon. This year the rains had been exceptionally heavy, and access to Mamfe itself was difficult. The Mainyu, which here flows through a narrow, cliff-walled gorge, was a white-water torrent, unnavigable to man or dinosaur. However, as you can see from the map, a cable foot bridge now crosses the gorge directly above the center cave where Ivan saw the monster, so the site was easily accessible by trail. Owing to the swollen state of the river the caves were almost submerged, only their topmost portions being visible above water. Under the circumstances there was little I could do except photograph the site, and make a cursory exploration of the surrounding countryside on foot [Illustration 27]. Not entirely to my surprise, I didn't run into any dinosaurs.

Back in Mamfe, I again tried interrogation. My three principal informants were: the Presbyterian missionary, a seminary-educated local African; the prefect of Mamfe, who is also a noted hunter; another hunter, recommended by the missionary and the prefect as being extremely knowledgeable about the local countryside.

Unlike in Gabon, my "flash-card test" here produced only negative results. My informants' unanimous response to pictures of a long-necked sauropod dinosaur and a plesiosaur was that they were totally unfamiliar with the animal, had never seen anything like it, and were quite sure it did not occur in the area.

I next questioned them about the names *mokéle-mbêmbe* and *mbulu-mbembe*. Here the missionary proved extremely helpful, as he was a student of African linguistics, and had made a special study of the local dialects. None of my informants could recognize either term as the name for any local animal. According to the missionary, *okele*—without the *m*—can mean "to

27. A view of a typical cave on the Mainyu River in the Cameroons, in one of which Ivan Sanderson and Gerald Russell reported seeing a "monster"—that is, an unidentified animal.

take a bath" in one dialect, "to cry or weep" in another. *Mbulu* is the name of a tribe or clan that lives approximately three days' journey by foot to the north-northwest, along the trail which crosses the Mainyu above the caves [see map].

I also asked about "olitiau," the large, batlike creature Ivan and Gerald Russell encountered. The word was unfamiliar to my informants. Of course, I may have been pronouncing the African word so incorrectly that they did not recognize it. My picture of a pterodactyl was identified as a bat.

Finally, I asked if there were any animal legends connected with the caves on the Mainyu. Yes, they said, hippos lived in the caves, using them as dens during the dry season. In the rainy season, they were said to "hibernate" back in the caves, with only the tips of their nostrils protruding above water to enable them to breathe.

Now, this sounds like odd behavior for a hippo. On further questioning, the missionary explained that the local word for the hippopotamus was *nsok-nyen*, which means, literally, "water elephant." One is reminded of the *nzefu-loi* of Zaïre. In other words, the missionary explained, the tradition was that the *nsok-nyen* used the caves for dens and hibernated in them during the great rains. While *nsok-nyen* normally refers to the hippopotamus, it would probably also be applied to any large aquatic animal reminiscent of an elephant.

It may therefore be possible that a large, unknown aquatic animal does exist in the Cross River system. However, I do not think it has anything to do with long-necked dinosaurs—which doesn't make it any less interesting. The response to my *Diplodocus* and plesiosaur pictures was completely negative; and this stretch of the Mainyu River is much too near Mamfe, and the foot traffic over the cable bridge directly above the caves much too heavy, for a large, unknown animal not to give rise to a local tradition.

Clearly Powell came away with the impression that no unidentified semi-aquatic reptiles were to be found in the Cross River system, but our discussions revealed that Gabon might be more promising. Again many phone calls, lengthy and costly conversations. The question was whether to follow up the flying-snake business in South-West Africa, the *n'yamala* in Gabon, or have a further look in the Cameroons?

A long-distance phone call to Dr. Marjorie Courtenay-Latimer in South Africa eliminated the South-West African flying-snake matter, at least for the time being. Yes, she said, although it would be difficult on short notice, she could lead us to the area where the "flying snake" had been killed. However, she questioned the wisdom of investing time and money in the venture, since she felt the trail was far too cold. There had not been one solitary report from the region since the original episode. She had watched for further episodes but none had come to her attention.

The fact that the trail was indeed cold weighed heavily with us, much more than the dangerous political situation in South-West Africa (Namibia), with its border to the north shared with Angola. The choice was clearly between Gabon, a possible relict reptile, and something else in the Cameroons, perhaps unknown but no sauropod.

Powell agreed that Gabon and the *n'yamala* would be it. On January 31, 1979, he entered Gabon. Most of February 1 was spent preparing to enter the bush. On February 2 Powell reached Lambaréné, near the confluence of the Ogooué and the N'Gounié rivers. The Albert Schweitzer Hospital again served as a base of operations.

Michel Obiang, the witch doctor of the Fang people of the village of Obongo, who had provided most of the *n'yamala* information previously, was alive and well. During his earlier contact, Powell had come away with the distinct impression that Obiang had never himself actually observed a *n'yamala*, but that only the greatest hunters had seen it. Obiang now stated that he had seen a *n'yamala* when he was twenty-six years old, which would be around 1946, since he gave his age as fifty-nine. He described a spot about halfway up the N'Gounié River to the point where the Ikoy branches from the N'Gounié. There was a small cove off the main river where the water was deeper, and a small lake was located adjacent to the river. Obiang related how he had camped many days in the vicinity, building a hut for his greater comfort. He added that he saw a *n'yamala* come ashore during the early-morning hours and that normally the *n'yamala* remained in the water during the day but left the water at night, between midnight and about 5 A.M., to feed on jungle chocolate.

Of course, Powell inquired immediately whether it might be possible to visit this area. Obiang agreed to obtain a canoeist to take him to the exact location, but suggested it would be highly unlikely that one would be fortunate enough to observe a *n'yamala* in a single day, since patience and many days of surveillance were required. With the aid of the canoeist, Daniel, and Alec, a carpenter from the Albert Schweitzer Hospital, the location was reached in short order. Powell found everything exactly as described, a magnificent dense African rain forest with a small lake or pool perhaps 30 meters (100 feet) across near the main course of the N'Gounié. The

28. Michel Obiang (right) and Alec, an American carpenter, who accompanied Powell to the former *n'yamala* encounter site described by Obiang, standing in front of a huge kapok tree on the grounds of the Albert Schweitzer Hospital.

29. Downstream views from canoe and the shore at the *n'yamala* encounter site. According to Michel Obiang, the *n'yamala* surfaced in the small cove shown here, about midway between the camera and the small headland on the right bank of the river, and clambered ashore.

place was thick with flies and black ants, which made an extended stay a most unpleasant prospect.

Powell decided to make a depth sounding at the point where Obiang had observed the *n'yamala*. With the aid of a beer bottle and some line the depth was established at 5½ meters (18 feet). The sounding could not, however, be made until Obiang and Daniel had been put ashore, as they appeared to be extremely frightened that the sounding might rouse a *n'yamala*. Powell suggests that since Obiang appeared genuinely frightened, he did indeed believe that there were *n'yamalas* in the area. However, no *n'yamala* was seen during the short period of observation.

The description provided on this occasion was a creature with a long neck and tail about 10 meters (33 feet) from tip of snout to tip of tail, as strong as one of the caterpillar tractors being used in construction at the hospital at Lambaréné, weighing at least as much as an elephant. Two curious features attributed to the *n'yamala* were "fillets" or threadlike filaments at the back of the head and neck, and a pair of pouches in the vicinity of the shoulders or front legs. These pouches, it was alleged, served as storage places for the creature's food— "jungle chocolate," nuts, or fruits.

Powell was anxious to obtain independent corroboration of *n'yamala* as well as hard evidence, such as a bone or a piece of skin. On the way up the N'Gounié he had noticed a bleached antelope skull in an abandoned village, formerly occupied by the Onkounie, a branch of the Garoua people. He questioned Obiang as to whether a *n'yamala* skull might perhaps be preserved as a fetish, which is a common practice among the peoples in the area. Obiang replied, "Oh no, no, the *n'yamala* is the king of the waters. It never dies. No one ever kills a *n'yamala!*"

Powell and his group now proceeded farther up the N'Gounié about 30 kilometers (20 miles), midway between the point at which Obiang had sighted his *n'yamala* and the place where the Ikoy joins the N'Gounié. Here the village of "Marsoski" of the Akele people is located (the spelling of this name is of no significance since it appears on no map, but is as close a rendition of the sound as possible). The people were familiar with the term *n'yamala*, but their knowledge of it seemed much more vague. Opinions ranged from invisible animal; not flesh and blood; more like a genie; to the belief that a *n'yamala* lived in a pool near the Protestant mission at Ndendé near the Gabon-Congo border. None of the natives identified any of the pictures of dinosaurs, including the *Diplodocus*, as a *n'yamala*, and none claimed ever to have seen one.

Since the trail seemed to fade upstream, Powell again turned downstream to a point midway between the confluence of the N'Gounié and the Ogooué. There the Fang village of Abord produced more positive results. Three individuals, each independently, picked out the *Diplodocus* as being the *n'yamala* and gave descriptions similar to that provided by Michel Obiang.

Obiang suggested that if Powell wanted to see a *n'yamala* it might be better to travel down the Ogooué toward the coast to a wide part of the river where, on an island, a hippopotamus had been killed by a *n'yamala*. The native consensus is that the *n'yamala* is incompatible with hippos, in contrast to the generally benign interaction of hippos and crocodiles. However, lack of sufficient time and money prevented Powell from pursuing this avenue during this preliminary investigation.

If the *n'yamala* exists the identification of its food is of prime importance, since the association of an animal with its major source of sustenance is always very close. Powell contacted Paul W. Richards, the authority on African rain forests, describing the so-called jungle chocolate or wild mango as described by natives and by Ivan Sanderson. Richards tentatively identified the plant as one of the *Apocynaceae*, possibly a species of *Landolphia*. I might add that Heuvelmans came to the same conclusion independently.

Consideration of these aspects of the *n'yamala* tradition, regardless of whether it still exists, has led me to a possible solution to a controversy about the giant herbivorous dinosaurs that has up to now not been resolved. Two schools of thought have developed concerning these great sauropod reptiles. One,

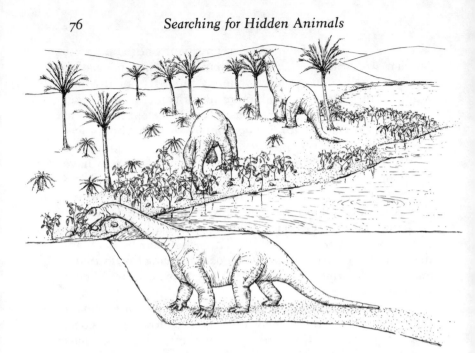

30. Sauropod dinosaurs shown in a variety of possible feeding modes. Restorations based on reconstructions of *Camarasaurus lentus* by C. H. Gilmore and *Camarasaurus supremus* by H. F. Osborn, C. C. Mook, and W. K. Gregory. A large adult is shown in the foreground shore-feeding while the bulk of the body is supported by water. Two smaller immature specimens with relatively shorter and thicker necks are feeding on the shore. An almost complete skeleton of *Camarasaurus lentus* indicated a height at the shoulder of 1.5 meters (5 feet), with an overall length of about 5.5 meters (18 feet). The hind feet had five digits with claws on three, while the front feet had only one claw. This specimen was an immature individual as evidenced by the conspicuous and unfused skull sutures. Some species reached overall lengths of up to 15 meters (50 feet).

the more traditional view, holds that the animals were primarily aquatic, that great bulk was supported by the water, and that the long neck allowed the body to be submerged in relatively deep water while the head was at the surface breathing. The fact that the nostrils were located high on the skull, rather than at the front, was cited as supporting evidence. Quite a few tracks of these animals have been preserved in mud, some of which clearly establish that the animals pulled themselves along by touching bottom only with the front legs. There is no track of the tail being dragged so that the tail must have been buoyant. Occasionally the light impression of a rear foot is seen when a change of direction was made by kicking down to the bottom with a hind leg. Other tracks, however, establish that the animals could come out on land, at least for a short while.

The problem with this view is that experiments have shown that animals, including man, cannot breathe when the rib cage is submerged very deeply. The water pressure prevents this, to say nothing of the staggering blood pressure required to counterbalance the hydrostatic pressure. As a consequence of these objections, an entirely different view has emerged, holding that the animals were primarily land animals, browsing on treetop foliage like giraffes.

Again great difficulties are encountered in explaining how the great bulk could be supported continuously on land, since the largest of these animals weighed more than a dozen elephants. On the other side of the coin, if the animals were semi-aquatic and fed on soft water plants, why did they develop the extraordinary long necks, since it has been demonstrated that it could not have been a breathing adaptation? Animals that feed on water plants generally have short necks. Another snag in this idea is that the teeth show much more wear than one would expect if soft water plants were being consumed. One suggestion accounting for this wear is to assume that the animals ate shellfish, rather than plants, tooth wear resulting from contact with the hard shells. No shells, which would probably be preserved, have been found in association with sauropod skeletons.

Now the investigation of the *n'yamala* suggests a hypothesis that would explain all these apparently conflicting data. The picture would be as follows: The animals were primarily aquatic although at least short excursions on land were possible, especially for the smaller forms. The great bulk of the body was supported by the water, and the massive legs were needed for limited activity on land. The long necks were developed not for breathing while the body was deeply submerged, but to reach suitable plants growing on the lake shores and riverbanks, while the body remained in the water comfortably supported. The "jungle chocolate," probably a species of *Landolphia*, grows along riverbanks and lakes and produces nutlike fruits that were or are part of the diet of these animals. The tough, hard shells of these fruits would account for the observed tooth wear and would not be expected to survive as fossils, as shells would. Thus the key element to an understanding of the sauropod lifestyle is that they were shore and riverbank browsers, rather than land treetop browsers or semi-aquatic consumers of water plants.

In view of these considerations, a positive identification of the *n'yamala* food plant, based on specimens, should be made, and an extensive survey of the Ogooué River and its tributaries is called for.

V

A Himalayan Mystery

An area of the Himalayas is of interest to us because of the "monster" called Buru. We will begin with a narrative written in the 1940s by a Mr. Charles Stonor:

> The vast jumble of mountain ranges which form the northeast frontier of India total more than twenty-five thousand square miles. The home of a million or more tribespeople of Mongolian stock, they are as fascinating and as little explored as any region in Asia. Starting with the Foothills, clad in tropical rain forest, infested with blood-sucking leeches, and almost uninhabited, range after range piles up, through each and every zone of climate, to the grand climax of the perpetual snows covering the gigantic backbone of the Great Himalayan Range.
>
> To enjoy the rare privilege of penetrating into these mountains is a rich and, there is no other word for it, magical experience. At one moment you are enjoying the generous hospitality of a Planters Club in the civilized and well-groomed world of the Tea Gardens in the Plains of the Brahmaputra valley. A short march and you start to climb, scrambling and stumbling up and down narrow footpaths. Huge trees, festooned here and there with exotic orchids, meet in a canopy overhead. Or you are boulder-hopping along the bed of a river in the last stages of its journey from the Snows. Pied Kingfishers dart up and down, and now and again a Giant Heron—one of the world's rarest birds—flaps majestically by.

Every so often you fall in with a party of Dafla tribespeople on their way to trade in the Plains, swashbuckling, happy-go-lucky warriors wearing cane helmets, often carrying short Tibetan swords, each with a bow and a quiver of arrows slung across his back. After two or three days you come out of the heavy forest and into the country of the Daflas: to be entertained to a mug of millet beer in the smoky gloom of their bamboo long-houses, the walls adorned with row upon row of trophies of the chase.

Leaving their country with a pang of regret—the Daflas are enjoyable people to mix with—you are soon up to five thousand feet, and in an almost temperate climate. The path winds through a small forest of magnificent Pine trees, then suddenly, abruptly, in complete contrast to all that has gone before, you come out of the forest to a great swampy plateau.

Locked away in the heart of the mountains the plateau totals some twenty square miles; completely irregular in its outline it includes countless bays and inlets, surrounded by bracken-clad spurs, thickets of barberry and deciduous trees and creepers, giving, in autumn, the golden and russet beauty of an English landscape; followed in the spring by great sheets of mauve primulas, and with the more distant crests of the encircling mountains crowned by forests of pine and rhododendrons.

Fully in keeping with the enchantment of its setting the plateau is the sole home of a very remarkable people—the Apa Tani tribe. As different as chalk from cheese to their harum-scarum Dafla neighbours, the Apa Tanis are twenty-thousand strong and live close-packed in seven great villages of bamboo houses dotted around the fringes of their swamp.

The Apa Tanis are in the so-called Neolithic stage of culture, on the same level as the tribal peoples of Borneo, the Philippines and the Naga Hills of Assam, with the same close-knit tribal organization, and worshipping the spirits of the forest, the chase, the crops, and so on. Stop among them for even the shortest of visits, and you very soon realize you are dealing with an exceptionally clever people, as shrewd and as hard-headed as they are intelligent. To take but one side of their lives, like most of the teeming population of these mountains the Apa Tanis are first and foremost self-supporting farmers. And, purely from their own resources and an inborn flair, they have built up and developed a system of husbandry that can stand comparison with any agricultural community in our own civilization.

Most remarkable of all is their intense isolation from the outside world. Small parties wend their way down to trade in the Plains of Assam during the winter months. Otherwise most of them literally never go more than a day's journey from the valley. In effect the Apa Tanis are a race of self-contained islanders, producing their own food, keeping their own livestock, growing, weaving, and dyeing their own cotton, cultivating their own groves of bamboo for house-building. Through sheer ability they have built up over the Ages a miniature civilisation: a civilization complete in all respects but one—knowledge of the Written Word.

I have had the great good fortune to be among the first handful of visitors to the valley from the outside world; accompanying the late Philip Mills, a senior official of the Indian Government and an anthropologist of international repute. Before we went a strange rumour had filtered back that the Apa Tani valley was once the home of "Monsters": and we lost no

31. The lost valley allegedly the habitat of the "Buru," or monsters. The valley is very irregular in outline, with innumerable bays and inlets.

time in delving into this. Yes, our hosts assured us, it was perfectly true. And this is the story they told us.

Long ago, just how long ago no man knows, the forefathers of the Apa Tanis had their home in the mountains away to the east of the valley. For some reason they left it and migrated westwards. During their wanderings they came on the valley. They found it quite uninhabited, and what is now the plateau was a great swampy lake with water "much deeper than the height of a man." The exact site where they first pitched camp is still pointed out; and they found the valley so well suited for their rice cultivation that they decided to settle there and make it their permanent home.

The lake was the home of great aquatic beasts the like of which they had never seen before, and to which they gave the name *Buru*. The Buru was a heavily-built, cumbersome animal, fifteen feet or so in length with a long and thick neck, and a broad head tapering to a prominent snout. There were three hard plates on the head, one on top, and one on each side. The tongue was long and forked, after the fashion of a snake. There were teeth "flat like those of a man": and according to some accounts there was a pair of small tushes in each jaw. The body had a girth such as "a man could just put his arms around," and measured some eighteen inches across the back. A row of blunt spines ran down the back and along each side. There were four stumpy limbs, with feet "like those of a burrowing mole." The Buru had a thick and powerful tail, three or four feet long, and on each side were broad and deeply-fringed lobes. The skin was fish-like and the colour mottled blue/black above and whitish below.

THE HABITS OF THE BURU:

There were many of them, and first and foremost they were aquatic, keeping to the deeper water, so that they were not very often seen. In the summer months they sometimes crawled out onto the banks to bask in the sun. In winter they disappeared into the mud on the bottom and were never seen. Now and again they appeared above the surface of the water, when they gave a coarse, bellowing call.

They were believed to have been vegetarian, and were always nosing about in the mud, weaving their way through the swamp with their long necks, when the hard plates on the head were brought into play. They did not lay eggs, and the young were born alive in the water.

The Buru "did everything with its tail," and a tradition tells of a man who speared a young one he surprised asleep on a mud-bank, whereupon he was attacked by the mother, who caught him round the legs with her tail and pulled him into the water where he was drowned.

HOW THE BURU BECAME EXTINCT:

They were not looked on as dangerous to Man, and for long the Apa Tanis were content to live and let live. But as time went on the population increased, and more and more of the swamp was needed for rice cultivation. So it was decided to start in and drain the lake by broadening a narrow gap at the south end, where a meandering stream leaves the valley.

From then onward the Burus were in the way and had to be got rid of. As the water drained off by slow degrees they were trapped in the deeper pools, and finally destroyed by hurling rocks onto them, and burying them under wood and stones. The poor beasts used to wave their heads and necks from side to side in their death struggles—a graphic touch—and the blood flowed up and coloured the water red.

With future excavations in mind I asked if it was known where they were killed. Most certainly it was. Accompanied by Elders of the tribe I trudged through the sodden rice plots to be shown four sites. Although my guides could pin-point them exactly, the first two had nothing to distinguish them from the rest of the swamp. The third site was some distance out from the bank and marked by a pool some yards across; quite clearly it must have been the remnant of a deep pool in the primeval lake. I was also told it was the only patch in the valley it has never been possible to drain enough for cultivation. The fourth site—also some way from the bank—is marked by a sizeable oblong of rushes in sharp contrast to the rice plots around it. Why, I asked, has it not been absorbed into the cultivation? Because in days gone by there was a big mound here, built up when the Burus were destroyed and buried. By slow degrees it has sunk into the mud, leaving this last vestige.

It was most striking that not only did the Apa Tanis know the precise location of each burial site, but they were just as positive over the historical order in which the pools were filled in, in the

32. A traditional site where Burus were killed, still marked by a pool in the rice fields.

long-drawn-out process of extermination, which they believe to have taken generations. By general consensus this last site, marked by the rushes, was the last refuge.

Had any bones ever been found? Seven generations ago a man, by name Takhe Saha (I spoke with his descendants), found a skull, which was like a pig's but with a longer snout. Soon afterwards his son died and he threw it away thinking it had brought him bad luck.

WHAT WAS THE BURU?

Soon after recording the Buru tradition I consulted an eminent biologist. He turned it down flat. "The trouble is the whole story is too good to be true." And at first glance the pieces of the jigsaw do seem to dovetail into one another rather too well; the appearance, the habits, the extinction, all add up to a distinctly plausible story.

But let us be fair and look at the other side of the medal; let us above all judge the whole story within the framework of its setting and remember that the Apa Tanis, intense in their isolation, are completely unaware that the Buru was unique to their valley. For all they know or care there are or were colonies here, there and everywhere. Philip Mills and I were the first outsiders ever to question them on the subject, and while we were struck by their completely matter-of-fact attitude, they on their side seemed equally perplexed as to why anyone should be so interested in what was to them a matter of everyday knowledge.

So far so good. But, is it possible that a tribal people with no knowledge of the written word could hand down the whole saga, intact and unembroidered, purely by word of mouth? Emphatically, Yes! To turn to another part of the world. Before the coming of the White Man the Maori tribes of New Zealand had a vast store of traditional knowledge, handed down over many generations, the truth of which nobody doubts. I have talked with the grandson of a Maori chief who could tell me the name of the boat, the name of each member of the crew, and where it was beached when his ancestors first reached New Zealand way back in the fourteenth century. The Maoris also had a great store of traditional memory of the Moas, the huge flightless birds their forbears exterminated in the past. I wonder if their tradition would have been believed had they not been proved up to the hilt by discovery of bones!

Without writing, without mathematics, tribal people such as the Apa Tanis must have some form of yardstick for simple measurements so as to cope with the realities of every-day life. In common with many peoples on their level of culture they have adopted the very practical method of direct comparison with parts of the human body. It was both fascinating and convincing to see the Buru so described, tersely and to the accompaniment of much pantomime.

The neck was the length of a man's arm, the limbs of a forearm, the tail of an arm, plus the width across the body, and to the elbow of the other arm. And so on. The lobes along the sides of the tail were copied by arranging leaves along a stick, and the bellowing call was imitated. Surely it is a fair guess that the name Buru was coined from the call.

The blend of measurement, pantomime and imitation—re-

33. Drawing of the Buru by the late nature artist Neve Parker based on verbal descriptions.

ducing the whole story to its simplest terms—was absorbing to watch and could so easily have been handed down over the generations without any pointless embroidery.

What was the Buru? I for one find it impossible to doubt the truth of the story. The appearance and the habits strongly suggest a giant member of the Lizard family. Fossils have proved that huge aquatic Lizards once existed, so that the Buru might have been a lone survivor. Or, and perhaps more likely, it could have developed from a more modern type, sealed off in the primeval lake, free from natural enemies and free to evolve in its own cumbersome way until the arrival of Man. Of such was the story of the most grotesque of all birds, the Dodo. And, are there not giant lizards—the Komodo Dragon—still surviving in the isolation of the Indonesian Islands?

One last word. The bed of the Apa Tani plateau is many feet deep in acid mud. A good preserver of bones and not difficult to excavate.

The story seemed plausible as Stonor maintained, but I certainly was not going to start and stop with Mr. Stonor and his story. Who was Stonor and what was he talking about? I began with his reference to Philip Mills, who I found was J. P. Mills, M.A., C.S.I., C.I.E., one of the greatest authorities on the tribes of the Assam frontier, and certainly no fly-by-night crackpot, so if Stonor had visited the Apa Tani with Mills as claimed, Stonor's story became that much more acceptable. Stonor's statement about a strange rumor that had filtered back from the Apa Tanis' valley of "monsters" also needed checking. What rumor, coming from or repeated by whom? Fortunately the reference to Mills led me to the answer and to the first discovery of the Apa Tani and their valley. My search led to an article published in the *Illustrated* London *News*, November 8, 1947, written by Christopher von Fürer-Haimendorf, Ph.D., professor of anthropology at Osmania University, Hyderabad, India. The article was entitled "The Valley of the Unknown." The summary at the beginning of the article stated that in 1944–45 Professor C. von Fürer-Haimendorf had carried his investigations of native tribes between Assam and Burma into a district in the North of the Balipara Frontier Tract and there discovered the Valley of the Apa Tanis. Here then was the original discovery of the mysterious valley, but what about the alleged "monsters"? I scanned the article several times, finding only one reference, which was apparently the source of the monster rumor.

In the context of describing the valley, von Fürer-Haimendorf wrote, "The bottom of the valley—according to local tradition once a marshy swamp inhabited by lizardlike monsters . . ."

Further checking revealed that shortly after the publication of this article, Charles R. Stonor and J. P. Mills twice visited the area, and that in 1948 C. R. Stones, accompanied by Ralph Izzard, correspondent for the London *Daily Mail*, and Frank Hodgkinson, an expert cameraman and veteran of many

strange expeditions, led a sortie to investigate the matter of
the Buru further. Charles R. S. Stones, B.S.C., was in 1948
the agricultural officer, North-East Frontier, Tribal Area,
Shillong, Assam, and as an agricultural zoologist was much
interested in strange animals. An account of this expedition
and its results was published by Izzard in 1951 in a book
entitled *The Hunt for the Buru*. The book makes interesting
reading and we of course learn why the expedition was a
failure as far as the "Buru" was concerned. It also contains an
authoritative chapter written by J. P. Mills describing everything that is at present known of the Buru.

The seeds of failure were already contained in the fact that
Stonor had received further information about an area near
the Valley of the Apa Tanis known as Rilo, where the creatures
were reported as still being alive, whereas the Apa Tanis said
they had killed the last specimen many years before. Izzard's
and Stonor's expedition set out to find the live beast and, as
is so well told in Izzard's book, their search for a living Buru
at Rilo was unsuccessful. This failure may have been, according to them, because proper climatic conditions at Rilo during
the expedition's stay never did materialize. According to the
natives, warm weather coupled with a conversion of the swamp
with its pools into a lake were absolutely essential. Stonor and
Izzard, however, appear to have concluded that there simply
were no living Burus and that their efforts should have been
directed at excavating remains, rather than playing the long
shot.

This latter assessment is probably the correct one in view
of the somewhat unreliable impression the Rilo tribesman
projected, in contrast to the Apa Tani. There the matter stands
to this day, C. R. Stonor having died by this time.

What can we conclude from all of this?

Regardless of whether or not live Burus still exist, it seems
probable that they once did, and very recently indeed. It is
also likely from the descriptions that the animal was a reptile
(much more unlikely a large amphibian). I will proceed with
a detailed analysis of the characteristics of this animal and
what it might be or was after I have described another living
species that I believe is most relevant to this question.

From the account of J. P. Mills (in Izzard's book) and my information from Stonor we can, I believe, accept the following: First, that this "valley of the unknown" exists approximately 1,600 meters (5,000 feet) above sea level, situated in the outer Himalayas of the North-East Frontier of India, at latitude 27° 35" N, and longitude 93° 50' E. According to Mills the whole area of the valley, which is surrounded by mountain ranges of 2,000 to 3,000 meters (6,500 to 10,000 feet) in height, is 32 square kilometers (12½ square miles) or rather more, the central area consisting of irrigated rice fields. The cultivated area represents approximately 50 square kilometers (20 square miles). It is irregular in shape, with many large and small inlets of flat land running in between low, projecting, and bracken-covered spurs, on which the seven large villages of the tribe are located. The valley is, in effect, an elevated plateau surrounded by a rim of mountains, and lies between two river valleys: that of the Kamla to the north, and that of the Panior, (or Panir) to the south, both of which are some 600 meters (2000 feet) below it. There is no area comparable to it in this region of the Himalayas, and it is reminiscent on a minute scale of the great valley of Nepal. Temperatures may reach freezing in winter, with regular snowfalls. In summer temperatures rarely rise much above 20°C (70°F), although rainfall then is usually very heavy.

Mills goes on to observe that the center of the plateau is quite clearly a drained lake or swamp, the whole of which is now irrigated rice fields, with the exception of a small area at the south end, which is a waterlogged, shallow swamp. The plateau is roughly bisected longitudinally by the Kal River, a small stream rising in the northeast section of the surrounding hills, and leaving the plateau at its southern end to join the Panior River some miles to the south. In the plateau itself the Kal River is a stream of moderate speed, running between low banks that are largely artificial, and winding through the cultivated paddy swamp.

It leaves the valley by an extremely narrow gap, and thereafter becomes a mountain torrent that rushes down a deep valley. The south end of the valley is closed except for the narrow outlet of the Kal River. Neither the Apa Tani

Plateau nor the surrounding country has ever been surveyed, but from superficial observation of artificial drains and ditches, and of the swamp itself, the bed of the valley appears to consist of a thick layer of silt superimposed on gravel.

The descriptions obtained by Mills through interpreters independently from several villages agree in most details with Stonor's version. Mills points out that neither interpreters nor informants had any inkling of the possible scientific interest in their tradition, and there can be no question of their having embroidered their accounts to suit preconceived notions.

Mills returned in 1946 and obtained a second account from Tamar of Hang, an old and much-respected Apa Tani priest, some seventy years of age. Mills had not questioned him in 1945, so was able to get an additional completely independent report. Mills reports the questions and answers verbatim in Izzard's book, including exact descriptions of the four traditional sites where the Burus were killed and buried, later confirmed by Stonor and company.

The accounts collected in 1945 and 1946 were quite similar, although there were some discrepancies. The main point of physical difference is that earlier versions described limbs, while Tamar said there were none, although Mills believes Tamar was trying to explain that there were no limbs as he understood the term. He referred to paired flanges of the thickness of a man's arm, which were used in burrowing, and were in pairs according to Mills, very reminiscent of the accounts given by other men of short limbs. The priest used a snake for descriptive comparison, but made it clear that the animal was not a snake. Mills notes that comparisons were never made to crocodiles.

One other piece of information recorded by Mills, of importance to future investigations, should be noted. The Apa Tani told him that they never dug or excavated any of the Buru burial sites, but that seven generations back, a man named Takhe Saha of Hang village by chance found a Buru skull in a corner of the central flat called Chagho, as already reported by Stonor. Whether or not the skull was of a Buru, we of course cannot determine. This single episode of the chance discovery of a bone suggests that the burial sites have indeed probably been left intact waiting for future investigators.

Let us now turn to another area of Asia, specifically some tiny islands of Java located in the Lesser Sunda chain. Again the original primary information is represented by tales and rumors from natives in the area. In 1910 Mr. J. K. H. van Steyn van Hensbrock, first lieutenant of infantry and civil administrator on the island of Flores, heard from natives that giant lizards were to be found near a place called Laboean Badjo and that similar animals were to be found on the nearby island of Komodo. The natives called these creatures *boeaaja darat* (land crocodile).

Lieutenant van Steyn van Hensbrock resolved to check on these rumors as soon as the opportunity afforded itself, possibly if he should be assigned duty on Komodo Island, upon which the rumors appeared to be centered. He actually did draw duty on Komodo shortly, and there found a Mr. Kock and Mr. Aldegon, part of a pearling fleet working in the vicinity, both being in addition keen hunters. They told him that indeed giant lizards reaching lengths of 6 to 7 meters (19½ to 23 feet) were present and that they had shot several specimens of that size. They stated that the animals were withdrawing to the mountainous areas in retreat from increasing intrusion by man. They believed that the animals lived exclusively on land, digging lairs under stones and rocks, into which they retired at night. During the day they stalked deer and pigs, having excellent eyesight but extremely poor hearing. The legs and necks were long and the animals walked with torso well above the ground and could move with great rapidity. Van Steyn van Hensbrock obtained one specimen during his stay measuring 2.2 meters (7 feet, 2 inches).

This information together with a photograph and the skin was sent to P. A. Ouwens of the Zoological Museum at Buitenzorg, Java, who promptly published the information in the *Bulletin du Jardin Botanique de Buitenzorg* (1912), naming the animal *Varanus komodoensis*. The existence of the giant lizard now proved, further specimens were wanted. Ouwens sent a native collector to Van Steyn van Hensbrock on

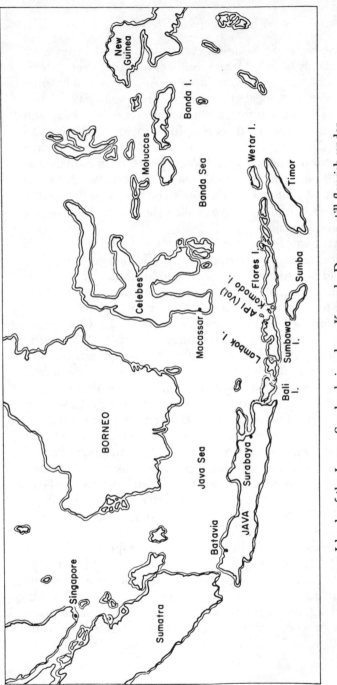

34. Islands of the Lesser Sunda chain where Komodo Dragons still flourish under Indonesian governmental protection.

35. Museum group of the Komodo Dragon, *Varanus komodoensis*, consisting of specimens collected by the Burden expedition.

Komodo. The collecting expedition was quite successful, obtaining two live juveniles about 1 meter (3 feet, 3 inches) each and two adults 2.9 and 2.35 meters (11 feet, 4 inches, and 9 feet, 4 inches) long. For the lieutenant the search was over. He was transferred to Timor, so the collection of further specimens had to proceed without him. He did provide one further interesting bit of information, however, that one of his men, a Sergeant Beker had shot a 4 m (13 ft) specimen.

As usual, man had begun to exterminate this rare and marvelous form of animal life by hunting and killing specimens, always singling out the largest, most spectacular examples for destruction. The Burden Expedition of 1926 collected further specimens, including twelve obtained for the American Museum of Natural History and two live individuals for the Bronx Zoo. W. Douglas Burden described his expedition in a book entitled *Dragon Lizards of Komodo*. Not only did he collect specimens, but also he reported much of interest resulting from observation of these creatures in the wild. Important to us are his observations of the aquatic behavior of these animals, which had been reported by the natives to be strictly terrestrial.

Burden describes how one evening five lizards were released on the beach as a test, to determine swimming ability and whether or not the animals would take to the sea of their own free will—an important question to Burden and others, bearing on whether these giants could have migrated via island hopping from Australia, where fossil remains of close relatives are abundant. "Of five lizards let loose, one large and one small one immediately fled to the sea, without the slightest hesitation. Two others headed for the jungle, while a fifth ran down the beach for 150 yards, went up into the grass, and then deliberately walked down to the water's edge, and proceeded to swim far out into the bay. The largest one which had taken to the water immediately submerged for a full two minutes, and then reappeared 100 yards away, swam down the beach for half a mile, and ambled slowly off into the jungle."

Clearly the natives were wrong in stating the lizards were strictly terrestrial.

The demand for these giant dragons was now great and native poachers began to decimate the population. Fortunately the Dutch Government intervened to protect these animals, which exist to this day, being also protected by the present Indonesian authorities. The range of the lizards was found to be restricted to only four islands, Komodo and Flores as mentioned, and also Rinja and Padar. Padar is a small pile of volcanic rock hardly capable of supporting large animal life. The Komodo dragon survives there by digging out sea turtle eggs.

Anyone observing these great reptiles alive cannot help being impressed. I recall my own wonder while observing a 3-meter (10-foot) specimen in the San Diego Zoo, head raised above 50-centimeter (2-foot)-high grass, forked tongue lancing in and out. Consider what a 7-meter (23-foot)-long specimen would look like under these conditions, if one believes the early reports of lengths up to 6 or 7 meters (19½ to 23 feet) . Today most authorities doubt that even the largest males exceed 3 meters (10 feet), certainly no more than 4 meters (13 feet). However, large sizes are certainly possible, since fossil remains of a closely related species from Australia (*Varanus priscus*) with a similar configuration may have reached lengths up to 9 meters (30 feet). More conservative estimates based on comparisons of skeletal material of komodoensis with the Australian fossils would range from 4½ to 7 meters (15 to 23 feet).

The genus *Varanus* is very old indeed, already a group differentiated from other lizards 60 million years ago. The closest living relative is *Varanus varius* [much smaller, 2 meters (6½ feet)] of Australia, living in the same regions where related fossils are most abundant.

All varanid lizards, also known as monitors or goannas, are carnivorous and most are terrestrial, although *Varanus salvator* is aquatic (known as the water monitor). Even many desert species swim quite well, while others stay in or near water. When swimming they fold limbs against the body, propelling themselves by undulating body and rudderlike tail from side to side. Some monitors even sleep in the water, keeping the head above the surface. All are diurnal, reaching maximum activity when the sun has warmed the environment. Aside from serving as a swimming organ in some species, the tail may be prehensile and can be a formidable weapon, delivering powerful blows. However, the most effective weapons are the teeth and daggerlike claws.

Prey are detected by sight and by the olfactory sense of the long, forked tongue, which is snakelike. Snakes in fact are presumably the varanids' closest relatives, contrary to what one might suppose.

The foregoing descriptions of the appearance and habits make these types of animals serious contenders for close relatives of the "Buru," which may live, at least until recently, in the lost valley of the Apa Tani.

Let us pursue this point further and see just how well a species of *Varanus*, perhaps as yet unknown, might fit the Buru data.

1. As to size, Burus have been reported to be 3½ to 4 meters (11 to 13 feet) in length, completely consistent with the size of the larger monitors.

2. The head is 50 centimeters (2 feet) long, elongated snout, flattened at tip. Eyes behind the snout. Again completely consistent, especially the eye location agreeing with the extension of the mouth beyond the eyes.

3. Teeth are described as "flat like those of a man," except for a pair in the upper and lower jaws, which were large and pointed. Not consistent with the strictly carnivorous habits (including carrion and eggs) of the monitors, but in agreement with the belief of the natives that Burus were vegetarians.

4. The neck elongated, slightly less than 1 meter (3 feet) in length, capable of being stretched out or drawn in. Quite compatible with monitors, particularly *Varanus komodoensis*, which has a neck more elongated than is usual for most lizards.

5. General body description: Tail 1½ meters (5 feet) long with fringed lobes forming a row along either side beginning at the anus, is in good agreement with characteristics of some lizards and even some snakes. The fringed lobes may represent lateral scutes or dermal armor as found in some lizards and crocodiles, although the latter is ruled out rather conclusively by other features.

6. Forked tongue clearly puts the Buru in the reptilian class, lizards or snakes, and rules out crocodiles, alligators, gavials, etc.

7. Legs were 50 centimeters (2 feet) long, equipped with claws, which looked like the "forefeet of a burrowing mole." This feature is very much like the majority of monitor lizards, even the aquatic ones such as *Varanus salvator*, and again rules out the crocodiles and alligators with partially webbed digits.

We must note, however, the major contradiction introduced by the account of Tamar of Hang, who stated that the animal had no legs. There are of course lizards that have only rudimentary limbs or even none at all, especially certain burrowing types. Mills thought Tamar was trying to say that the animal had no limbs as he understood the term. Tamar's references to lateral paired flanges used for burrowing are according to Mills very reminiscent of the accounts by other men of short limbs.

8. There is general agreement that the Buru's tail is prehensile. It is reported to do "everything with its tail" and one account has a man being grasped by the tail. Again this feature is most compatible in that a variety of lizards do have prehensile tails, including certain species of monitors.

9. The skin was described as similar to a snake or a scaleless fish, which again is in agreement with the lizard hypothesis. Three lines of short, blunt spines were reported along the back and sides, certainly a not uncommon reptilian characteristic.

The color of dark blue blotched with white with a white underside can also be matched in the reptilian world, including lizards.

10. All reports agree that the Buru was almost entirely aquatic and was seldom seen because it lived in water deeper than the height of a man and put its head out of the water, reminiscent of the behavior of certain aquatic monitors. It is also said to bellow hoarsely. Tamar stated that the animal occasionally came out of the water in warm weather and lay curled up on the bank. He also confirmed the bellowing sound, which is more like a crocodile than the hiss of the "Komodo dragon."

11. When questioned as to how the Buru bred, most natives said they did not know. Tamar, however, stated definitely that the young were born alive and no eggs were laid. This would not fit the monitors, since they all lay their leathery-shelled eggs, but in other reptiles, including some lizards and snakes, the young are born alive, the egg being retained in the body cavity till hatching. This characteristic in many instances appears to be an adaptation to an aquatic environment, which would be most consistent with the lifestyle of the Buru.

12. Dormancy during the dryer, colder winter season is completely compatible with reptiles, including certain lizards. That the animals should become torpid and inactive seasonally as conditions become unfavorable is a very widespread characteristic of cold-blooded animals such as reptiles, which are in varying degrees at the mercy of the environmental temperature and conditions.

Taken all together, the reports suggest that a large unidentified species of aquatic lizard lived or lives in the swampy lake regions of the outer Himalayas of Assam.

The animals probably are now extinct in the Apa Tani Valley, but precise locations of remains are known and should not be too difficult to excavate. Recovery of subfossil bone and tissue would provide a definitive answer as to the nature of these unusual creatures.

VI

"Alice in Wonderland" Birds

The Indian Ocean is an interesting place, especially the islands, volcanic and otherwise, that rise above the ocean surface. Of all places in the world, they have in the past and in some cases may still harbor some of the strangest birds on or off record. The largest of these islands, the Malagasy Republic (formerly Madagascar), lying just off the eastern coast of Africa, is the repository for a variety of unique animals and plants.

We will concern ourselves with only one of these creatures, a giant bird (*Aepyornis maximus*), flightless to be sure, but standing 3 meters (10 feet) tall with legs massive enough to bring to mind an elephant and believed by some to be the basis for the *Arabian Nights* roc. Undoubtedly Madagascar was known to the Arabs in pre-Columbian times, and during the time of the Crusades, southeastern Asian sailors—Malays and others—began to make contact with the area. It is even possible that knowledge of these birds was possessed by the ancients, for Herodotus wrote that during discourses with Egyptian priests he was told that beyond the Nile lived great birds capable of carrying off a man. Marco Polo also reported

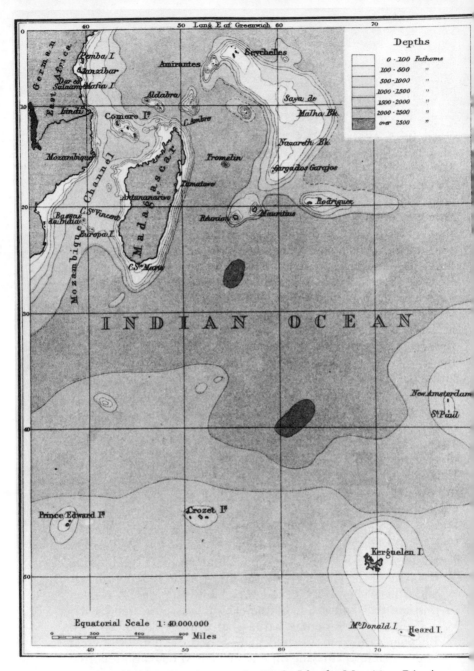

36. Mascarene Islands, showing the Dodo Islands, Mauritius, Réunion, Rodrigues, and Nazareth Bank.

37. *Aepyornis maximus*, the giant flightless bird of Madagascar.

the existence of large birds from islands south of Madagascar.
Could these reports have been inspired by such Madagascan
giants as *Aepyornis maximus?*

Bernard Heuvelmans believes that the first written reference
to *Aepyornis* was recorded by Admiral Étienne de Flacourt in
Histoire de la Grande Isle de Madagascar in 1658. The references reads as follows: "Vouroupatra, a large bird which haunts
the Ampatres and lays eggs like the ostrich's; so that the people
of these places may not take it, it seeks the most lonely places."
Heuvelmans adds in a footnote that the term "vouroupatra"
was either misunderstood or misspelled by de Flacourt, the

Malagasy word for bird being *voron*, so he thinks the word should be "voronpatra."

In any case, subsequent travelers on the island discovered giant eggs that suggested giant birds (I say "suggested" because the relation between egg size and bird size is by no means precise, some large birds laying rather small eggs, and vice versa, there are absolute limits, of course: Clearly a hummingbird could not lay an ostrich-sized egg). In spite of these eggs the large ostrichlike birds of Madagascar did not officially become recognized until 1850, 200 years after de Flacourt's writings.

The scientific report establishing the existence of these creatures was published by Isidore Geoffroy-Saint-Hilaire based on the evidence of three eggs. The eggs of *Aepyornis maximus*, as named by Geoffroy-Saint-Hilaire, were sent to him by Monsieur de Malavois, a colonist of the island of Réunion, east of Madagascar. The eggs had been obtained from natives in Madagascar by Captain M. Abadie. Since then more than fifty eggs have been obtained, the largest of which measured over 38 centimeters (15 inches) in length. Skeletal remains, most incomplete, also are in hand, but compared to the abundant moa remains, to be discussed later, the quantity of *Aepyornis* material is minuscule. Dr. Walter Rothschild, a great student of extinct birds, lists in his now rare book *Extinct Birds* three genera containing twelve species. The listing of so many species, however, when based on so little material, can hardly be accepted. More realistically there probably were three species, represented by the genera listed. L. Monnier, a taxonomic lumper, reduced the multiplicity of species to three in 1908, creating one new species in the process, *Aepyornis graciles*. Size variations and sexual differences between males and females and juveniles probably account for most of the variations on which the multiple species were based. However, there was at least one smaller species, smaller than an ostrich, represented by remains labeled *A. hildebrandti*.

The questions of interest to us are, of course: When did these birds become extinct? Or, in fact, are they extinct? Heuvelmans is convinced that there is no hope of finding a living specimen, because the swampy forest areas that he believes were their habitats have dwindled as a result of reduced rainfall due to deforestation by man. This view may turn out to be correct, but caution is in order when pronouncing bird species out of existence. Time and time again, a bird species thought to be extinct has turned up. The reasons why the species declined or even became extinct are most important in making a judgment as to whether a small population may still persist.

The bones are not always found where the birds actually lived, but often in places where rains and running water have carried them. So far most *Aepyornis* remains are found in the South and Southwest buried in the sand dunes of the seacoast. Most investigators agree that the birds lived in the forests, especially in the open glens and clearings. Again there is agreement that deforestation played a major role in the demise of *Aepyornis*. If the view that the birds lived in forest clearings rather than swampy areas is correct, this is the habitat to be examined.

Bones showing crocodile tooth marks have been obtained, proving that birds were present in lake and swampy regions. However, it seems reasonable to relate this to a compression of the overall *Aepyornis* feeding range by drought due to deforestation as already mentioned. The swampy areas would be the last affected, and so the birds may have been forced into the inhospitable crocodile-infested swamps, subsequently succumbing to crocodile depredation. Of course, under extreme survival crisis adaptation may be very rapid and any remote unexplored areas should be examined.

According to natives the *Aepyornis* was alive at least up to 1867, and some maintain to this day that the smaller variety still lives in certain remote forests. It is true that great mountain lakes have dried up and swampy forest areas are much smaller. Yet some remain and no one can say what might be found there. This opinion is shared by at least one correspondent of mine attached to the American Embassy at Tananarive. At the very least additional subfossil skeletal material might be collected that would be very welcome in any museum.

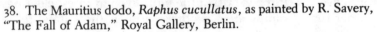

38. The Mauritius dodo, *Raphus cucullatus*, as painted by R. Savery, "The Fall of Adam," Royal Gallery, Berlin.

Let us turn our attention now to other flightless birds, thought to be extinct, for which the odds for a surviving species are perhaps slightly better. Most everyone has heard about dodos, especially if they were exposed to Lewis Carroll's "Alice in Wonderland" as a child. Many people are unaware that the dodo was a real bird and existed on at least three islands in the Indian Ocean—Mauritius, Réunion, and Rodrigues—in recent historical times, and that at least two live specimens found their way to Europe in the seventeenth century. Since dodos had evolved into a flightless condition they were effectively isolated genetically by their island habitats and so a different species was found on each island. The Mauritius variety is the one best known and is the basis for illustrations found in "Alice in Wonderland."

Like Madagascar, the three islands, known collectively as the Mascarene islands, after their Portuguese discoverer, Pedro Mascarenhas, are found in the Indian Ocean. They also were probably known to the Arabs, as established by maps dating from the thirteenth century. The largest of the three, Mauritius, lies about five hundred miles east of the African coast at 38° E longitude and about 20° S latitude, with an area of 1800 square kilometers (seven hundred square miles). The Portuguese did not colonize the island, although domestic animals such as hogs and goats were released there, with dire consequences for some of the indigenous animal life. The Dutch arrived with eight ships in September 1598 under the command of Admiral Jacob Cornelius van Neck. Van Neck published a detailed journal of these voyages, which includes the first description of the Mauritius dodo as follows: "Blue parrots are very numerous there as well as other birds; among which are a kind, conspicuous for their size, larger than our swans with huge heads only half covered with skin as if clothed with a hood. These birds lack wings, in the place of which three or four blackish feathers protrude. The tail consists of a few soft incurved feathers, which are ash-colored. These we used to call Walghvogels ("nauseating birds") for the reason that the more and the longer they were cooked the less soft and more insipid eating they became. Nevertheless their belly and breast were of a pleasant flavor and easily masticated."

Not only did van Neck describe the creature, but also he brought back a living specimen to Holland in 1599. This specimen appears to have survived in captivity for years, and was painted at least fourteen times (Illustration 42).

Four years later, in 1603, another Dutch fleet arrived at Mauritius. The account of the voyage and visit in the form of a journal kept by Reyer Cornelisz, a captain under the command of Admiral van Heemskerk, was not published until 1646. The dodo is mentioned, but no new data were recorded. Dr. Masauji Hachisuka, one of the great students of the dodo and other extinct birds, documents twenty references up to 1681 to the dodo. These statements represent practically all of the knowledge we have about the life habits of the bird as observed by these early explorers.

The birds appear to have been fearless of human beings, which certainly contributed to their extinction, as dodos (despite van Neck's criticism) were killed for food. They are described as serene or majestic, bold in their walk. The birds were unable to fly or swim even when forced into water, although they were reported to be fast runners.

Other live specimens were brought to Europe, and possibly to Japan, between 1600 and 1666. Dr. Hachisuka summarizes the number of live dodos exported from Mauritius as follows: Holland, 4 females, 5 males; England, 2; Italy, 1; India, 2; and Japan, 1. There is some uncertainty attached to this list, since there may well have been more that have gone unrecorded. Remains of these specimens are practically nonexistent. The only parts that have survived are the head and right foot of one of the English specimens and the left foot of the other specimen. As for the former, in 1683 this stuffed specimen existed intact, listed in Tradescant's *Collection of Rarities Preserved at South Lambeth*, published in 1656. A dodo from the island of Mauritius is found in the list of "whole birds." The specimen became part of the Ashmolean Collection at Oxford, England, but probably because of its poor condition was ordered burned in 1755, only the head and right foot escaping. The *Catalogue of Many Natural Rarities*, 1665, lists a leg of a dodo. This left foot, different in size from the right foot of the other specimen, is preserved in the British Museum.

As time passed doubts began to arise as to whether there ever really was such a creature as the dodo. This may seem strange to the reader, but memory is short, and finding little or no concrete evidence soon becomes blank, collectively or individually.* Now, however, as a result of searches and excavations on Mauritius, skeletal material, including complete skeletons, is found in the collections of museums of many countries.

What happened to the dodo on Mauritius? The last report of a live dodo there is contained in a British Museum manuscript concerning a visit in 1681. Pigs had been introduced into the islands and by the early 1700s large numbers

---

* This observation should be kept in mind when judging native tradition relative to possible extinct animals. It is certainly remarkable how well "uncivilized" cultures, without writing, are able (at least in some cases) to preserve information for several hundred years.

of hogs were present, to say nothing of monkeys, also reported to be present in great numbers. The pigs created destruction and probably were the main cause of the demise of the dodo, although man's killing of these flightless and vulnerable birds certainly was a contributing factor. By 1693 no dodos were to be found on Mauritius.

Our description of the bird rests upon written records, paintings, skeletons, and subfossil skeletal remains. There is some inconsistency in this evidence, especially in the case of written descriptions and pictures.

The plumage ranged from light blue-gray to much darker blue-blacks and brown. The great zoologist A. C. Oudemans, who also studied dodos, believed the lighter individuals were males, the darker females. There certainly were sexual differences, including variations in tail feathers and eye color. The appearance of young dodos in the flesh can only be deduced from pictures that leave much to be desired as to accuracy, although the general color of juveniles resembled the adult females, with somewhat more yellow.

The bill of these birds was peculiar and deserves some comment. This bill as commonly portrayed is perhaps the most distinctive feature and indeed lends an "Alice in Wonderland" aura to the bird. However, this configuration is only one of several, which varied according to sex, season, stage of development, and even from individual to individual. It has been suggested that some of this variation resulted from an annual molt, which included the bill in addition to the feathers. Other features such as horny outgrowths and ridges appear to have been developed only during the breeding season. The bill color ranged from yellowish-brown to reddish-brown to darker brown around eye and nostril.

The fact that the birds molted also may have contributed to color variations and accounts for the disparity seen in pictures, some of which depict a large, fat, round form of body, while others show a lean bird. The lean form probably was characteristic of the nonbreeding season, October to March, while the fat form was typical during the dry, cool season from March to September, which also was the time of breeding. The change from a fat to a lean condition had a profound effect on the appearance, changing the apparent position of the wings and the tail.

The feet of these strange birds also were unusual in that they were four-toed, whereas the ostrich has three toes, suggesting that they were not related. The males had small feathers covering the ankle, whereas the females had no feathers on the legs or feet.

Dodos, being birds, must have laid eggs. According to one early account the dodo laid a single egg—"they lay one egg, which is white, the size of a half-penny roll"—probably the size of the largest goose eggs. This single egg is somewhat atypical, as most *Columbidae* (pigeons), the group to which the dodos belong, lay two eggs, although there are a few species that do in fact lay only one egg.

Since dodos had only rudimentary wings, nests were made on the ground, adding to their over-all vulnerability to predators, including man.

There is only one reference to the food of the dodo, and this reference, although anonymous, is probably correct in stating that dodos fed on raw fruit.

Hachisuka has pointed out that the tooth-billed pigeon of Samoa, with a beak similar in structure to the dodo's, eats fruits and berries. Since flight was impossible, the dodos were restricted to fallen fruits, or at best low-growing berries.

This then is a general description of the strange birds known as dodos. Study of skeletal remains clearly establishes that they are related to pigeons, although forming a distinct family from pigeons proper. There was only one species of dodo on the island of Mauritius and it is certain that there are none left there alive today. It probably evolved from a flying form that settled on the island and adapted to survival on the island, which did not require flight. On other islands in the area, other species of dodos, probably derived from a common (flying) ancestor, were found.

On the island of Réunion, some 200 kilometers (130 miles) southwest of Mauritius, there were two distinct species of dodos, although the existence of one of these as a separate

39. The white dodo of Réunion, *Victoriornis imperialis Hachisuka*.

species, the white dodo, has been disputed. According to Hachisuka, who named the bird *Victoriornis imperialis* in 1937, except for its white color it was in general very similar to the common dodo of Mauritius. Be that as it may, of interest to us is that the Réunion dodo, probably because the island is larger, was most certainly still alive in 1746, although by 1801 a survey of the island revealed no dodos.

The existence on Réunion of a closely related species known as a solitaire also has been put forth. Hachisuka conducted extensive research, which he believes confirms it. Early authorities, Strickland and Rothschild, had originally postulated the existence of such a variety. Hachisuka does not question the existence of the Réunion white dodo, but writes, "After a careful examination of Lestrange's description of a living

40. The solitaire of Réunion, *Ornithaptero solitaria* (de Sélys-Long-champs), male (right), female (left).

dodo which he saw in London, and a comparison of it with the accounts of Carré and Du Bois, which latter accounts Strickland and Rothschild conjectured to refer to a hitherto unnamed species of didine bird, I am convinced that I have found in four published pictures further confirmation that such a species did really exist in the island of Réunion. I am prepared to show, therefore, that the bird described by Lestrange was of a species closely allied to the solitaire of Rodrigues and misidentified by all previous writers as a white dodo." He further draws the conclusion, based on pictorial evidence, that at least four specimens of the Réunion solitaire, so called because they always go alone, were at one time or another imported into Europe, between 1561 and 1657. He then goes on to make his case, carefully sorting out historical references, dates, and pictures, which we need not go into here.

A serious problem with the hypothesis that such a bird existed is that no remains of the alleged creature are in hand. However, the absence of subfossil material is purely negative and by no means disproves the hypothesis. I submit that on the strength of evidence put forth by Hachisuka and others an extensive search for Réunion solitaire remains should be made in areas other than those known to have been occupied by the Réunion white dodo. It seems likely that two such closely related species would hardly be competing in the same ecological niche.*

There can be little doubt that no living specimens exist today, since what little historical evidence exists suggests that this variety became extinct at least seventy years before the white dodo, probably around 1669.

There is another small island, with an area of about 110 square kilometers (43 square miles), 640 kilometers (400 miles) east of Mauritius, known as Rodrigues, officially discovered by the Portuguese navigator Diego Fernandes Pereira in 1507. Almost a hundred years elapsed before even transient inhabitants arrived, probably contributing to the survival at least for a time of local animals and plants. Eight French Protestants led by François Leguat settled on the island in 1691. They remained only two years, but were followed by other French colonists.

Leguat described his surroundings including the animals and plants that he observed and, of interest to us, a dodo or solitaire. At one point Leguat's very existence, to say nothing of his accuracy or veracity, has been questioned. However, subsequent scholarship has established that not only did Leguat live on Rodrigues for two years, but also that he was undoubtedly an intelligent, well-educated, and trustworthy observer. His written account published in 1708 contains no less than twenty-eight drawings of solitaries, all quite consistent

---

* We must keep in mind, however, that bones are not always found in the original habitat of the animal in question. For example, a river that is fed both by upland and lowland watersheds might carry the remains of an upland species along with remains of a lowland species to a common site such as a silted delta, where both types of remains might be deposited together.

with each other, but depicting certain osteological peculiarities that led students to question their accuracy.

Another written description of the Rodrigues solitaire, although anonymous, was discovered in the French archives in Paris in 1825, and is worth reproducing here.

The solitaire is a large bird, which weighs about forty or fifty pounds. They have a very big head, with a sot of frontlet, as if of black velvet. Their feathers are neither feathers nor fur; they are of a light gray colour, with a little black on their backs. Strutting proudly about, either alone or in pairs, they preen their plumage or fur with their beaks and keep themselves very clean. They have their toes furnished with very hard scales, and run with quickness, mostly among the rocks, where a man, however agile, can hardly catch them. They have a very short beak, of about an inch in length, which is sharp. They nevertheless do not attempt to hurt anyone, except when they find someone before them, and when hardly pressed try to bite him. They have a small stump of a wing which has a sort of bullet at its extremity, and serves as a defense. They do not fly at all, having no feathers to their wings but they flap them and make a great noise with their wings when angry and the noise is something like thunder in the distance. They only lay, as I am led to suppose, but once in the year, and only one egg. Not that I have seen their eggs, for I have not been able to discover where they lay. But I have never seen but one little one alone with them, and if any one tried to approach it, they would bite him severely. These birds live on seeds and leaves of trees, which they pick up on the ground. They have a gizzard larger than a fist, and what is surprising is that there is found in it a stone of the size of a hen's egg, of oval shape, a little flattened, although this animal cannot swallow anything larger than a small cherry-stone. I have eaten them; they are tolerably well tasted.

Subsequently a great deal of fossil and subfossil remains were discovered in various caves. Detailed study of this skeletal material established that Leguat's observations were indeed correct, and today the nature of the osteology of the Rodrigues solitaire is as well known and well established as that of any other bird, living or extinct.

Having established the reliability of Leguat's reports in

41. The solitaires of Rodrigues, *Pezophaps solitarius* (Gmelin). Nest with egg, male (right), female (left).

general, we will consider another unknown bird described by Leguat, whose existence rests on his report alone. In the view of most ornithologists, it is a never-never bird, which never existed or at most was really a flamingo, rather than an unknown species. This bird was supposed to have existed on all three of the Mascarene islands—Mauritius, Rodrigues, and Réunion. It has been named, in spite of its nebulous existence, *Leguatia gigantea*, the giant water hen.

Leguat's description was as follows: "One may see many kinds of certain birds which are called Giants because they lift their head for about the height of six feet. They are mounted extremely high and have a very long neck and the body is not larger than that of a goose. They are altogether white except for a small red patch under the wings. They have a beak like that of a goose, but a little sharper. The toes of the feet are separated and very long. They occur in marshy places. The dogs often attack them because they do not have time to lift themselves from the ground. We saw one in Rodrigues, such

42. The giant water hen, *Leguatia gigantea* (Schlegel) (left), and the flightless giant gallinule, *Cyanornis caerulescens* (de Sélys-Long-champs) (right).

a bird, and we took it by hand for it was very fat. It was the only specimen which we saw here, which made me believe that it was probably driven hither by a storm whose force it could not resist. The flesh is very good."

This bird has been classified by some as an ostrichlike bird or even just a flamingo. Hachisuka disposes of these identifications by careful comparison and establishes that the bird was a species of water hen. He also provides a satisfactory answer to the question: How is it that Leguat is the only writer who has observed this gigantic water hen of Mauritius, while the voyagers who visited the island before him speak of several other most remarkable birds they met with, but do not mention this one? The answer, Hachisuka believes, is that the voyagers only reported what they saw in areas they frequented, which generally were close to the places where their ships were anchored and did not include the marshy areas of the interior, which was the habitat of the giant water hen. Leguat and his colonists, on the other hand, lived on Rodrigues for two years and undoubtedly made many excursions to the interior and remoter parts of the islands during their sojourn there.

No remains are in hand to corroborate Leguat, and there can be no question that the birds are now extinct on the three Mascarene islands. But fossil material may of course exist, waiting to be discovered.

If there are no longer any dodos or giant water hens on the three Mascarene islands, must we conclude that it is absolutely impossible that there could be present-day survivors? Not as long as unexplored and uninhabited islands exist in the Indian Ocean in the general vicinity of the areas where these birds once existed. For a clue as to the best place to begin a search, we note François Cauche's report of an expedition he led to Mauritius in 1638, published in 1651.

In Cauche's account he calls dodos *oiseaux de Nazaret*. In 1948 Willy Ley, our romantic zoologist, proposed that the idea that dodos existed on an unknown island of Nazareth was all a mistake. Ley's explanation begins with the correct French translation of the Dutch word for dodo, *walghvogel*, as *oiseaux de nausée* (again, nauseating birds). Cauche, Ley said, serving the birds on Mauritius, probably concluded that the birds may be stupid, comical, or strange, but certainly not nauseating, and instead designated them with the place name Nazareth, which in French sounds similar to *nausée*. This, according to Ley, led to subsequent books recording the dodo of Nazareth Island.

Ley pointed out that there was no Nazareth Island. Even though marked on some maps, it really represented one of the Mascarene islands but was given an incorrect position. Earlier, A. C. Oudemans, a zoologist of stature and a student of dodos, found that Ilha de Nazare appears on older Portuguese maps, but is now known as Île Tromelin, and implies that a search of this island might reveal something interesting, either subfossil material or live dodos. Tromelin is somewhat to the north of the Mascarenes.

In 1962 Willy Ley published a revised version of his earlier works that includes references to dodos. He repeats his earlier view as to Cauche's probable mistake, but now refers to Oudemans and the island of Tromelin. Further, he acknowledges that Nazareth also appears on modern charts, but refers to a bank rather than an island, distinct from Tromelin. He writes, "Nobody knows much about Île Tromelin. The latest edition of the Admiralty Charts states that its position may be five miles off on the map." He further states that as long as there is an uninvestigated lead left the book should not be closed.

This state of affairs intrigued me mightily. I proceeded to obtain the latest available nautical chart of the area from the U. S. Naval Oceanographic Office. This chart, entitled "Plans in the Indian Ocean H. O. 3864, No. 61551," proved to be exceedingly interesting. In the lower right-hand corner was a large insert labeled Île Tromelin located 15° 53′ S latitude and 54° 31′ E longitude based on a Madagascan survey in 1959. The map shows the presence of a meteorological station, presumably automatic, and a small airstrip. Inquiries to the French Government, who supposedly own the island, have drawn a blank, as has a search of the World Weather Organization's listing of weather stations for that area. What all this

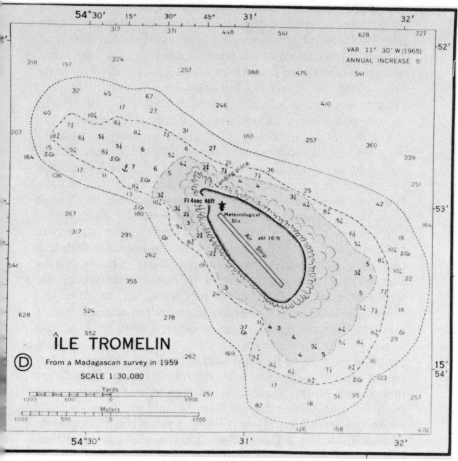

ÎLE TROMELIN

From a Madagascan survey in 1959

SCALE 1:30,080

43.

means I do not know except that a careful search of Ile Tromelin is in order.

The chart showing Île Tromelin is really a map of the Cargados Carajos Shoals based on a British survey of 1846. These shoals include a variety of small islands, most of them untouched or unnoticed by man. Albatross Island, for example, is reported to lie 1 kilometer (0.6 mile) northward of its marked position in 1962. The area is extremely hazardous for landings by small boats, since no vessel can approach safely from the seaward side because of reefs and shoals. The map states that the eastern coasts were sketched in 1825 from small boats that penetrated from the western side, noting only when trees could be observed, but that never actually landed. Perhaps a dozen small unexplored islands exist that might indeed yield some plant and animal surprises if investigated.

The burning question is: How stable an environment do these islands, at most 2½ to 5 square kilometers (one or two square miles) in area, provide for living creatures? Certainly one would not expect large populations of large animals. However, the Komodo dragon already discussed, the largest living lizard, lives on very small islands indeed.

We began our search in this chapter with the giant *Aepyornis* of Madagascar and will conclude with another large flightless bird, even taller than *Aepyornis* although not as heavy. To do that we will shift our attention to two islands far to the southeast, known collectively as New Zealand.

New Zealand is an interesting place, self-contained, which may still harbor very strange creatures. One such is the primitive lizardlike tuatara, a living fossil with an unusual structure on its head that is a kind of third eye, quite common among reptiles millions of years ago in the Triassic Period, but nonexistent to any degree in most other living reptiles. We could list many other strange New Zealand creatures, but our interest here is moas. There still lives today a small living form of moa known as a kiwi. There is some question as to how kiwis should be classified, but that they are a small type of moa, or are at least an offshoot of a common ancestor, is supported by the fact that a similar form known only from a skin taken from a native chief's ceremonial dress is in hand, even though no living specimen has ever been obtained. There is a good chance that this unknown bird, probably as big as a large turkey, may still lurk somewhere in the remote areas of the islands. Perhaps if a living specimen is obtained it will turn out to be a variety of moa known as *Megalapteryx* (meaning big Kiwi).

44. *Dinornis maximus*, the tallest of the New Zealand moas.

What exactly were these moas? T. Lindsay Buick, one of the greatest students of the moa, writes as follows: "The native term moa is one that has been popularly applied to the gigantic struthious [ostrichlike] bird—the largest in the world—known to science as *Dinornis*, once an inhabitant of New Zealand, but now confidently assumed to be extinct." *Dinornis* is related to ostriches, rheas, emus, cassowaries, and of course kiwis, as already mentioned. Although taller than *Aepyornis*, the eggs were somewhat smaller, about 20 centimeters by 15 centimeters (8 inches by 6 inches) for some species.

Moas existed in recent historical times but have been in the world for millions of years, as established by fossil bones in addition to the subfossil remains, which are in hand and attest to their recent demise.

No one knows exactly how and when knowledge of the moa reached European consciousness. In fact, there are mysteries surrounding a number of aspects of the moas' sojourn on this earth that have not been cleared up to this day, but regarding which we will suggest at least the more plausible solutions.

A curious fact is that the white man was in contact with the native population of New Zealand, the Maoris, for some time before we hear or read anything about maos. It is indeed surprising that these giant birds, the largest in the world, some species standing 3.7 to 4.3 meters (12 to 14 feet) high, surrounded with romantic notions and legends, were not immediately precipitated on the first explorers of New Zealand. No mention of or references to moas can be found in early reports of New Zealand visits. These include Tasman, 1642; Captain James Cook, 1769; Admiral d'Entrecasteaux, 1807; John Liddiard Nickolas, a missionary, 1814; M. Lesson, a naturalist, 1824; and John Rutherford, who lived with some Maoris between 1816 and 1826.

We first hear about moas from J. S. Polack in 1838 in his book *New Zealand*. Polack was a trader who originally visited New Zealand in 1831, and during his initial stay till 1837 he not only saw and handled moa bones but also learned much about the Maori legends and traditions regarding these birds. Some of these stories were marvels indeed. The birds were

45. *Euryapteryx elephantopus*, the bulkiest of the New Zealand moas.

monstrous animals living high on the mountains, fed on air, and guarded by two giant tuataras, who kept incessant watch while the great moas slept. If one approached the moas' abode one would be immediately killed by trampling. This man-destroying bird was reported to reign on the great mountain known as Whokapunoke.

The reference to the lizard guards is interesting. Tuataras, the small reptiles with a third eye, are of course found in New Zealand as already mentioned, but none are larger than 65 centimeters (2 feet). Actually, New Zealand is devoid of large quadrupeds of all types, although there are other native traditions that refer to at least one large lizard and possibly an unknown mammal called *waitoreke* by the natives. One wonders whether large monitor lizards, such as the Komodo dragon, may have at one time inhabited New Zealand.

Captain Cook, who made inquiries about the natural history of the country, was told by a chief, Tawaihura, that there were giant snakes and lizards in the country. The lizards were alleged to be 2½ meters (8 feet) long and as thick as a man's body. They attacked and devoured men, lived in burrows, and could be killed by building fires in the burrow openings. The size and shape of these lizards certainly are reminiscent of *Varanus komodoensis* discussed in Chapter V.

Why was Captain Cook given such natural history details about these reptiles, but nothing about moas? The answer became apparent over the years as the earlier distribution and persistence of moas in New Zealand were established. Whether or not you heard about moas depended on where and to which tribes you talked. New Zealand consists of two islands, called North and South, both of which had moas widely distributed. However, North Island gradually lost its moa population before South Island. So, if you talked to native tribes who were late arrivals on North Island, they knew little or nothing about moas. In contrast, others in different localities claimed to have hunted the birds for food in their youth.

The moas did finally find their way into Western science via a thighbone fragment obtained by Dr. John Rule from a friend, John Williams Harris. Harris was an educated trader

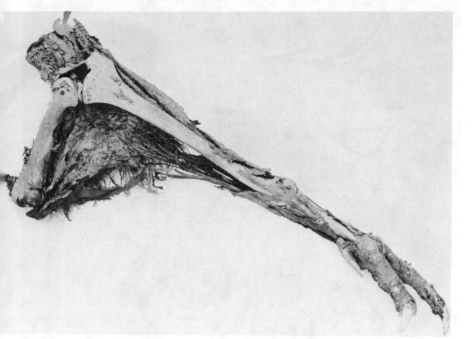

46. Recent moa remains (dried leg of *Megalapteryx*).

who married a New Zealand native. In 1838 Dr. Rule brought the bone fragment to the attention of Professor Richard Owen, the greatest comparative anatomist of the day.

Owen at first regarded the fragment as nothing more than an ox bone, but at the insistence of Dr. Rule that the fragment was part of the leg bone of a giant bird, he studied the fragment more carefully. It is a tribute to his genius that he concluded, objectively, contrary to many zoological preconceptions of the day, that:

"Any opinion as to the specific form of this bird can only be conjectural, but so far as my skill in interpreting an osseous fragment may be credited, I am willing to risk the reputation for it on the statement that there has existed, if there does not now exist in New Zealand, a struthious bird nearly, if not

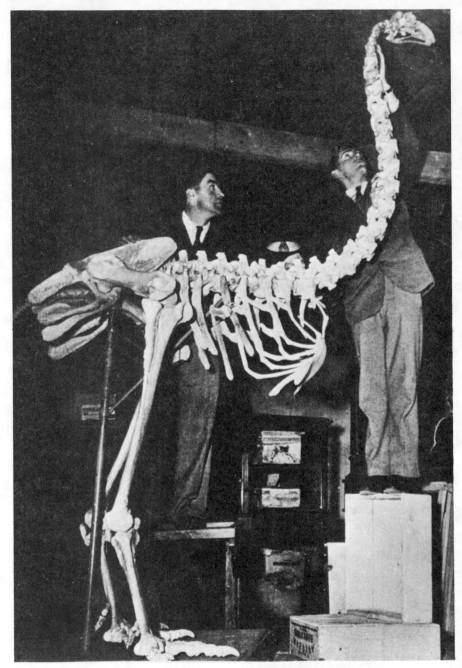

47. Assembled skeleton of *Dinornis maximus*.

quite, equal in size to the ostrich, belonging to a heavier and more sluggish species."

His colleagues laughed, for they believed he had gone too far on the strength of a single fragment of bone. Owen stood firm. In the years to follow Owen was thoroughly vindicated and New Zealand was subjected to what might be termed a "bone rush." Bones were collected from thousands of individuals, finally comprising five genera of large birds with perhaps two dozen species. A picture gradually emerged that New Zealand had been occupied by a variety of successive and in some cases contemporaneous species of moas with the distinct possibility that some might still be alive, or at least have become extinct very recently.

At first there was even controversy over whether or not the birds had ever been contemporary with the Maoris at all. This point was eventually laid to rest when stone ovens, as used by Maoris, were discovered containing great numbers of charred bones, corroborating the Maoris' statements that the moas were hunted for food. Large numbers of subfossil bones were also found in caves. Some clearly had been deposited there by man, but in other cases it became clear that moas had entered caves for shelter. As would be expected, many bones were found in dunes and river deltas, where they had been carried from the mountains by rivers.

At this point a remarkable discovery was made, that the bones from hundreds, even thousands of moas were found in close array in various swamps. Amazingly, in some arrays all the leg bones were found in a vertical position, just as they would be if the birds were standing there alive. What could be the explanation? To this day no one knows. Ingenuity and explanations multipled. Once the swamps were lagoons; perhaps the cold drove the birds into the water, assuming of course that the lagoons contained thermal springs. Alas, geological analysis of the areas proved that the lakes and springs were not thermal. Could the Maoris have driven huge flocks of moas into the lakes to better be able to kill their quarry? If that were the case, why had they left all the carcasses, which supposedly were the objectives as food sources? There are other theories, but all fail in one way or another.

The most probable explanation of the leg-bone finds is that fire was the agent responsible for occasionally forcing large flocks into the lakes. Formerly, before the advent of man, both North Island and South Island were heavily forested, and forest fires must have decimated the landscape at times. Active volcanoes were present, and natural agents such as lightning certainly played a role. In some instances the frightened birds, congregating in the lakes to escape the flames, were probably asphyxiated by smoke and gas from the burning forest, leaving tremendous numbers of dead birds.

Other unanswered questions were: When did the Moas become extinct? Or indeed, are they extinct? Again controversy reigned supreme. To be sure, there were Maoris who claimed to have participated in moa hunts in their youth. Some of these natives were certainly deemed reliable, and on this and other evidence it appeared that a few live moas were present at least on South Island in a district known as Otago as late as 1830. Many of the bones discovered appeared so fresh as to have been part of live birds only yesterday. Some even had flesh and feathers still adhering. Others were clearly old, even true fossils.

In 1828 a most convincing piece of evidence was discovered in the form of the complete moa remains of *Megalapteryx didinus* at Queenstown. Examination of the carcass revealed even such fragile organs as the tongue and eye to be intact. The carcass could not be more than fifty years old. All along there were natives from the interior who insisted that the bird was still alive there. They were able to describe a moa hunt in such detail that only a hardened skeptic could fail to be impressed.

This discovery still did not settle the matter. Special conditions that preserved tissue could always be claimed by those who believed moas had become extinct a long time ago. The years passed until the extremely important objective carbon-14 dating technique was discovered in the late 1940s by Professor Willard Libby, the teacher at the University of Chicago from whom I learned physical chemistry.

A drowned moa, genus *Dinornis*, with a full crop of food still intact, was obtained, and a C^{14} date was determined on the plants contained in the stomach. The technique destroys the sample—so better to sacrifice a few plants from the stomach than part of the precious specimen. The results were very important because the *Dinornis* was the type that was believed to have become extinct well before the Maoris arrived in New Zealand. The proponents of that view were not happy, because the result indicated that the bird died about A.D.1300, just about the time the major migration of Maoris arrived. For most that settled the matter: *Dinornis* was contemporary with man in New Zealand.

To this day there are claims that a contemporary moa has been observed. On this question T. Lindsay Buick, a keen student of the moa, wrote as follows:

"It is reasonably certain that no European whose word is above suspicion ever saw a living moa. In 1823 a man named George Pauley told Meurant, the southern interpreter, that he had seen a moa near a lake in the interior of Otago. He described it as a monster six meters (twenty feet) high, an exaggeration not surprising, since their acquaintance was very brief. No sooner had the man and the bird sighted each other than, as Pauley says, 'I ran from it, and it ran from me,' so that, by mutual consent, the crisis was soon over, and our information is tantalisingly brief and amazingly inaccurate."

Buick reports another episode: "In 1850 Lieutenant A. Impey, of the Bengal Engineers, conducted an overland expedition, via Marlborough, in the hope of finding a route to Canterbury, but did not succeed in getting through. When some of the party returned to Wellington they reported that they had seen two large birds like emus, on one of the hillsides, but, in his official report, Lieutenant Impey made no reference to the matter, which would hardly have been the case had the incident actually occurred on the journey."

I might comment on this latter assessment by Buick, which in my experience is not a valid conclusion. More often than not, controversial matters, either from fear of ridicule or other repercussions, are left out of official reports, and Lieutenant Impey should not be doubted on that account.

In 1878 the following newspaper story appeared in the Otago *Witness*:

"A gentleman recently returned from Maiau [North Canterbury] and in whose integrity and intelligence we have the fullest confidence, informs us that there appears to be very little doubt that at last the moa has actually been seen in the flesh. The story is current, and generally believed in the Waiau district, and our informant states that he took the trouble to see the runholder on whose station the bird had been seen, who states there can be no doubt but that a very large bird—much larger than any emu—exists in the back portion of his run on the west side of the Waiau, and adjoining the large bush which stretches to the West Coast. This gentleman has repeatedly seen its tracks and footmarks, and on a recent occasion his shepherd—an intelligent man— started the bird itself out of a patch of manuka scrub, with his sheep-dog. The bird ran from the dog till it reached the brow of a terrace above him, some thirty or forty yards off, when it turned on the dog, which immediately ran into the shepherd's heel. The moa stood for fully ten minutes on the brow of the terrace, bending its long neck up and down exactly as the black swan does when disturbed: It is described as being very much higher than any emu ever seen in Australia, and standing very much more erect on its legs. The color is described as a sort of silver grey with greenish streaks through it."

This account rings an authentic note, but still it is only an anecdote, not a fresh drumstick. With that I will leave the reader to judge any future reports of live moas.

VII

Living Trilobites?

Back in time some incredible six hundred million years ago, when life was in the first flush of its dawning, there were trilobites: marine arthropods with exoskeletons that, according to the fossil record, suddenly appeared in the Lower Cambrian, forming groups so structurally distinct that intergroup relationships remain obscure. We can infer, even without direct fossil evidence, that in the prior epoch, the Pre-Cambrian, trilobites must have been the most advanced and ubiquitous species.

Animals do not arise spontaneously fully formed out of the slime of primeval deeps. Perhaps trilobites, in their evolutionary childhood, had no exoskeleton, no hard parts that could be fossilized, but only soft tissue easily eaten by predators or destroyed by the natural vicissitudes of marine conditions. To date the mystery of their origin has not been revealed in the fossil record. However, by studying their morphology (form and structure), we can establish that their ancestors must have been the segmented worms.

From the Cambrian on, aeon after aeon these animals thrived and flourished, leaving an abundantly prolific record of their heyday, spanning an incomprehensible three hundred fifty million years of existence, compared to man, who has

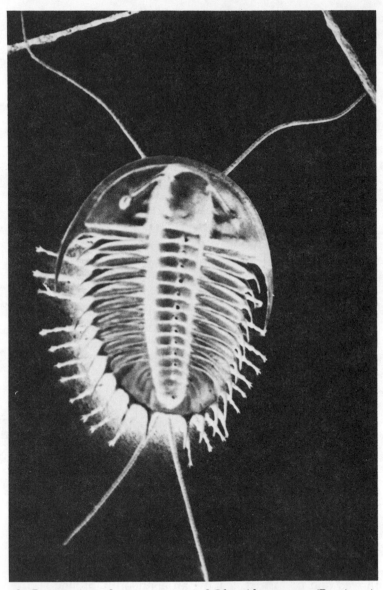

48. Botton view of reconstruction of *Olenoides serratus* (Raminger), a Middle Cambrian trilobite.

existed as man, or man-ape, for only four million years. Trilobites from earliest times were well adapted to numerous environments in the Paleozoic seas, for they changed very little during this era. Gradually, as we approach the end of the Permian Period (two hundred million years ago), their numbers dwindle and no fossil remains are found. Other life forms have arisen and now hold the ascendancy.

What exactly were trilobites and why are they regarded as so zoologically interesting? As the first group of highly organized creatures, they possessed, as shown by researcher Riccardo Levi-Setti and others, remarkably sophisticated compound eyes, with which to view the depths of ancient seas. Levi-Setti, a physicist at the University of Chicago, interpreted lens structures discovered by E. N. K. Clarkson, paleontologist at the University of Edinburgh, showing that these incredible animals had developed a unique feature among life forms: Their eye lenses were shaped to correct for optical aberrations with design elements discovered by Descartes and Huygens, two members of the human species, five hundred million years later—life forms, incidentally, who were completely ignorant of trilobites and their marvelous optical achievements.

Further, these creatures had the same ancestors as all arthropods, those animals with skeletons outside rather than inside their bodies. Arthropods surpass all other animal types in number, variety, and diversity of distribution. These include such well-known groups as insects, spiders, and crabs. Clearly the trilobites, creatures that exhibited such an early and successful diversity of life forms, are of great zoological interest.

Now, the question: What were these creatures? Knowledge of these animals dates from 1698, when Lhwyd published the first scientific report in England. Lhwyd's term for these strange fossils was "trinuclei." In 1745 Karl von Linné (better known to us as Carolus Linnaeus, the Swedish scientist who established the binomial naming and classification of animals), described a number of varieties, designating them *Entomolithus paradoxus*. *Paradoxus* reflects the uncertainty as to how these creatures should be classified. Linnaeus himself was not

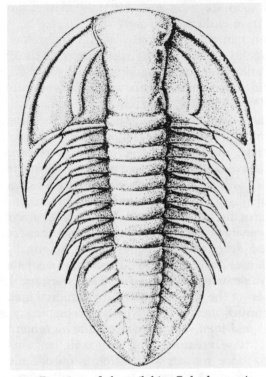

49. Drawing of the trilobite *Polypleuraspis*, showing the three body divisions from left to right, and also the three major body divisions, head or cephalon, body or thorax, and tail or pygidium.

far off the mark, believing them to be insects. Subsequently other names were proposed, but the term *Trilobitae*, proposed by Walch in 1771, stuck. The term, later changed to *Trilobita*, referred to the distinct side-to-side body division into three parts, literally "three-lobed" (Illustration 49).

Until 1870 only the exoskeleton was known and no one was sure what these creatures might be. Early on, in contrast to the brilliant insight of Linnaeus, many zoologists regarded them as the shells of unusual clams. One French zoologist, Latreille, stated that as far as he was concerned they *were* clams until someone found legs. The existence of legs had been suspected, but since the fossil remains showed only the top side, such inferences were vague and not widely accepted.

Some remains were strangely curled up, much like "wood lice,"* which proved to be the key to the mystery. In 1876 an American scientist, C. D. Walcott, approached the problem with a hacksaw, opening over 3,000 curled-up trilobites. On some 270 of these he found legs! In 1870 another scientist, Billings, published a description of the legs of a species known as *isotelius*, which flourished in the North American Ordovician Period. Walcott's original observation of legs was confirmed between 1895 and 1920, when beautifully preserved specimens showing all the legs (more properly appendages, since not all turned out to be legs) were discovered.

Preservation of these animals occurs in two ways: either by the direct deposit of minerals in the exoskeleton, gradually replacing the original material, or by external and internal molds. In some cases the original material of the hard parts is actually preserved, not being replaced by minerals. Some of the best preserved specimens showing all the soft parts have been found in black shale and very fine-panned limestone. In the latter case the limestone can be dissolved away by acids, leaving the most delicate structures intact.

Most of the remains range in size from 3 to 10 centimeters (1 inch to 4 inches), although the giant of the group, *Urolichas riberoi*, was 70 centimeters (28 inches) long. Now a very curious thing was noted about the size range of these fossils. Whole series of size gradations, one blending into another, were seen. The smallest were less than 1 millimeter (1/25 inch) in length and were little more than tiny shields. As they increased in size they showed more and more of the features of the larger fossils.

The conclusion was inescapable! These series represented

---

* Seen by anyone who has ever lifted a stone or piece of wood, which has lain undisturbed on the earth. These isopods, more of which later, are arthropods at least distantly related to trilobites.

developmental stages or a successive series of larval (juvenile) forms, each cast being the molted outer shell as the animal outgrew its own skeleton.

Three main phases were identifiable. The smallest and first stage was called protaspis, the intermediate stage meraspid, and finally the holaspid phase. The trilobite of course existed in a preprotaspis state as an egg, but remains of this phase, *sans* exoskeleton, have not been preserved, or at least have not been found.

The adult form is generally elliptical, divided not only from side to side, but also from front to back. The front portion, as you might expect, is called the cephalon (head, or head shield); the main body is called the thorax, terminating with the third part, the tail or pygidium. In some species the segments of the pygidium can hardly be distinguished from the thoracic segments, the whole forming a continuous sequence. The marvelous eyes already referred to appear early as eyelobes in the first larval stages. The main part of the body (thorax) consists of articulated segments, the last of which articulates with the tail or tail shield. The pygidium (tail shield) is formed by fusion of the rearmost segments. In those species without a distinguishable pygidium this fusion is incomplete or absent.

The appendages include the front pair, which are antennae, followed by pairs of legs decreasing gradually in size, one pair per segment. In a few species the rearmost appendage also appears to be antennaelike. The appendages are called biramous, meaning they consist of two parts (Illustration 50). They appear to have served a triple function—walking, swimming, and breathing.

The principal part was the walking leg or telopodite and a second gill-bearing branch or pre-epipodite. These are basically like a half feather consisting of a shaft bearing a fringe of bladderlike filaments.

How were these strange appendages used? The telepodite clearly was a walking leg, used for crawling over the sea bottom, on floating objects, and possibly on various types of marine growths such as seaweed. Trails, technically called *Cruziana*, are abundantly preserved in periods when trilobites

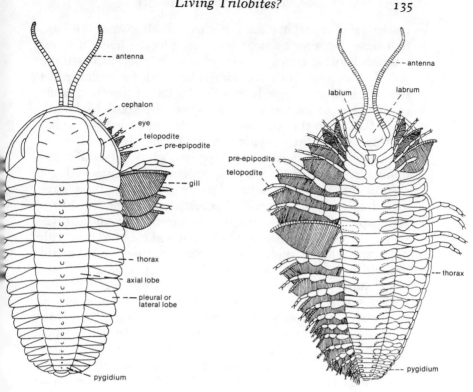

50. Sketch of the Ordovician trilobite *Triarthrus eatoni*, including soft parts. Left, top view; right, bottom view.

flourished and are conspicuously absent in periods later than the Permian when trilobites had by and large disappeared. This association led to the identification of Cruziana as trilobite trails. Further study has confirmed this observation (Illustration 57).

As more remains in which appendages were preserved were studied, it became clear that some of them were used for digging in bottom ooze. Most Cruziana trails end in a subcircular indentation, which suggests that the animals responsible for these trails buried themselves in soft sediment.

Telepodites may also have been used for swimming, but the

consensus of expert opinion is against this idea, since it is hard to believe that animals as primitive as trilobites had a nervous system advanced enough to co-ordinate the movements of the same appendage both for swimming and for walking. In swimming all legs move forward or backward together, while in walking some legs move forward while others push backward. Does this mean that the animals could not swim? Not at all, for this is where the pre-epipodites or featherlike organs come in. Their general paddlelike shape strongly suggests a swimming adaptation with an oarlike function. The attached frill or filament clearly was a breathing organ but also may have served as part of the paddle, operating more or less like a venetian blind, being feathered during the forward stroke, very little resistance encountered, followed by a 90° turn with maximum surface applied to the water during the backward propulsive stroke. This idea is doubly attractive because water would have to be circulated around the frills to provide the oxygen supply. This could be done by "fanning" but would be even more effectively accomplished by swimming movements.

Sensory organs other than the eyes and antennae are not well understood. The eyes, however, are so remarkable that we shall discuss them in more detail. Our understanding of trilobite eyes is due in large part to Clarkson's extensive study of different types of trilobite eyes and their structure and to K. M. Towe, the scientist who showed that calcite crystals (calcium carbonate in hexagonal form) must have been present in the eyes of the living animals. For the particular kinds of trilobite eyes, called "schizochroal," Clarkson and Levi-Setti provided an analysis pointing to optimization of the eye optics. The excellence of the compound eye, first seen in trilobites, is established by the fact that most arthropods today still follow closely the trilobite design. One curious fact is that not all trilobites had eyes, although most did. In some species the eyes were so large that a large portion of the head was taken up by these organs. The presence of such organs should provide us with clues as to the life habits of these animals.

The compound eyes of trilobites were of two types. One type consisted of many small lenses closely packed and covered

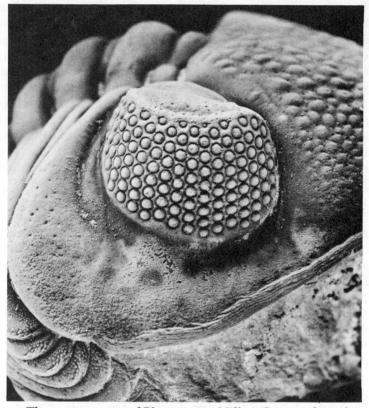

51. The aggregate eye of *Phacops rana Milleri* (Stewart) from the Devonian Silica shale of Sylvania, Ohio (×15).

by a thin membrane or cornea. A second type consisted of fewer but larger lenses with a cornea covering each lens (Illustration 51). The number of lenses in the first type ranged from one hundred to fifteen thousand; in the second type, two to four hundred. It is in the latter type that Clarkson and Levi-Setti discovered the remarkable evolutionary optimization of the optical function.

In 1973 Levi-Setti was having coffee with Dr. E. N. K. Clarkson at the Oslo International Conference on Trilobites.

Dr. Clarkson, as noted, had made a detailed study of the trilobite eye, revealing many heretofore unknown structures. Levi-Setti came back to Chicago with some napkin sketches of doublet lenses split by a curious wavy surface. He was convinced that trilobites had tried to correct their optics. The surprise came when he discovered how they had done this. While he was browsing through the works of Christian Huygens, the father of wave optics, published in 1690, he noticed a description, with an outline of a particular kind of lens, known technically as *aspherical aplanatic*. Remarkably the outline resembled the wavy shape in Clarkson's sketches of the trilobite eye lens.

Huygens referred to earlier results by Descartes in his work *La Géométrie* of 1637. Levi-Setti to his delight and surprise found another construction, somewhat different, but designed by Descartes for the same purpose. This matched a second version of the trilobite lens. Levi-Setti writes, "Armed with the conviction that trilobites had solved a very elegant physical problem and apparently knew about Fermat's principle, Abbe's sine law, Snell's laws of refraction, and the optics of birefringent crystals, I set about to inform Dr. Clarkson of the meaning of his trilobites' lense shapes"—marvelous indeed for a lowly forerunner of insects five hundred million years ago, when the eyes in all other animals were primitive and inefficient, in some cases little more than light-sensitive spots, only able to distinguish between light and darkness. One other characteristic of trilobites deserves comment. Most if not all were able to roll themselves up so that only the hard shields would be exposed. This defensive and protective maneuver was similar to what armadillos and hedgehogs do today. When trilobites enrolled a variety of spines assumed positions protruding rather than lying flat so as to deter a predator from its purpose. This was possible because the segments of trilobites were hinged with anatomical stops and interlocking features. Trilobites appear to have been not only good optical physicists but also mechanical engineers.

Since we cannot travel back in time to observe living trilobites, anything we say about their mode of life must necessarily include guesses based on the structure and environment in which these animals must have lived. All were aquatic and were able to crawl along the sea floor. In some cases the trails lead to the animal itself, in its burrow in the mud. For some the burrow was no doubt a temporary refuge from predators; for others it became a way of life.

Some trilobites were shy, small-particle feeders, while others with jaws of sorts may have hunted prey. Some of the more streamlined species were active swimmers, perhaps swimming upside-down like the horseshoe crab. Levi-Setti comments that the swimmers had the larger eyes commanding an imposing view of the ocean bottom. Those forms with eyes protruding like turrets must have been able to lie buried in the ocean bottom, able to see all without themselves being seen.

Now could such animals still be alive today? We must be careful to separate possible from probable. If we ask, "Is it possible?" the answer must be "Yes"; assessing the probability, however, is another matter. Relevant to this question is the fact that a trilobite relative, in the sense that it shared a common trilobitelike ancestor, is among us, alive and well. This descendant is *Limulus polyphemus*, the horseshoe crab, another living fossil in its own right, having also survived from the Cambrian, 550 million years ago. There have been differences of opinion as to what this animal is. First, it is not a crab; it is perhaps best described by the late zoologist Willy Ley as part "crab," part "spider," with a good deal of "scorpion" thrown in, plus a fair-sized remainder uniquely *Limulus*. Actually the animal belongs to the *chelicerata* subphylum, which includes spiders.

Our interest resides in the fact that the horseshoe crab is an offspring of the same breed that gave rise to the trilobites. We know this from at least two lines of evidence. The most important is that the early larval form of the horseshoe crab is very similar to trilobites and recapitulates the trilobite head and tail. Second, certain fossil members of both groups are so similar that one is hard pressed to decide which is which (compare Illustration 52 with Illustration 53).

Today only five species of horseshoe crabs remain: *Limulus*

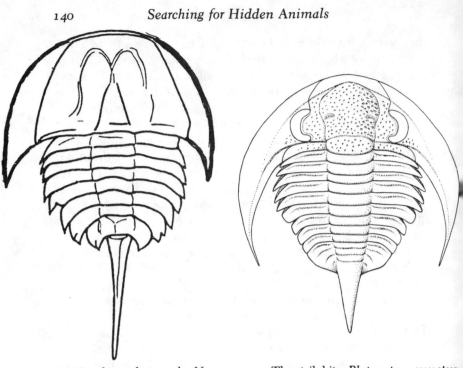

52. A primitive horseshoe crab, *Neo-belinuropsis rossicus* (Tschernyshew), from the Upper Devonian (×5).

53. The trilobite *Platyantyx arcuatus* (Billings), showing reconstructed exoskeleton (×2.3).

polyphemus (Atlantic horseshoe crab) and four Asian species belonging to two genera, *Trachypleus* and *Carcinoscopinus*, found along the coasts of Japan through the East Indies and Philippine islands. The largest of these animals reach lengths of 60 centimeters (2 feet) and are brown in color. The large head shield has undoubtedly served its protective function well, helping this animal to flourish for over 500 million years. This shield (or carapace) is shaped like a horseshoe—thus its common name, horseshoe crab. Mostly the animals crawl and dig in shallow coastal waters searching for organisms such as mollusks, worms, algae, and almost anything that can be scavenged. The food is picked up by the *chelicerae*, a pair of antennae or feelers that bear claws and could also be considered

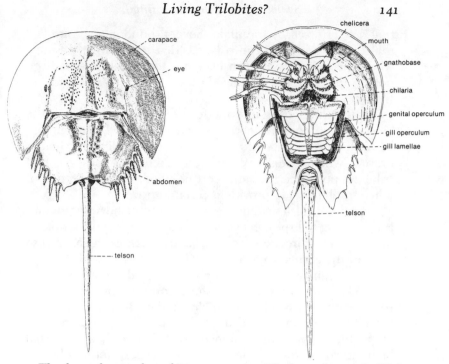

54. The horseshoe crab or king crab, *Xiphosura polyphemus*, top view.

55. The horseshoe crab, *Xiphosura polyphemus*, showing appendages on one side (bottom view).

legs. Bona fide crabs have two pair of these; so at least in this respect *Limulus* cannot be considered a crab. The mouth of the horseshoe crab is located just behind these clasping antennae surrounded by five pair of legs, the upper portion of eight of these helping in grinding or shredding food material. The legs are also used for walking, burrowing, and as paddlers when this strange creature swims, in an upside-down position. The first pair of these most versatile legs aid the male in mating, since the tips are modified into hooks that are used to hold onto the female. During the mating period in spring the female crawls ashore, with three or four smaller males clinging to her, each trying to push the other out of the way. At the high-tide mark the female digs a hole and deposits eggs that are fertilized by the male. Several hundred eggs are laid that hatch in a month into larvae that grow larger, molting when the external skeleton becomes too small. As has been noted, the first larval stage bears a close resemblance to trilobites.

Another interesting internal feature of these animals is the blood, which does not carry oxygen via the red hemoglobin. Instead, oxygen is bound by a blue copper pigment, hemocyanin, which is dissolved in body fluid. It is possible that trilobites possessed the same sort of blood. Only dissection of a live trilobite could provide a certain answer.

A final conspicuous anatomical feature of horseshoe crabs is the strong tail spike called a telson. This tail spike is able to move in any direction, serving as a steering organ. It also enables the animal to turn over when lying on its back.

These animals are still very abundant and not about to die out. This fact suggests that some form of true Cambrian trilobite might possibly still be alive today. To the extent that trilobites were shallow coastal dwellers like the horseshoe crabs, they apparently no longer exist. The only hope would be that some forms adapted to a deeper, more obscure environment and there have found refuge. Members of one of the greatest and most successful scientific expeditions, the voyage of H.M.S. *Challenger,* December 21, 1872, to May 26, 1876, seriously believed that living trilobites might be dredged up from the ocean bottom. Thousands of new species were in fact discovered; the report and results from this voyage fill fifty volumes, but no trilobites! In hindsight the article on trilobites in the eleventh edition of the Encyclopaedia Britannica (1911) states that the *faint* hope of dredging living trilobites from the sea floor was not realized.

According to Willy Ley, a few years prior to the *Challenger* voyage someone announced a real live trilobite raised from a depth of 1,200 fathoms or 2,200 meters (7,200 feet). The news was believed unhesitatingly—but then it turned out to be only something resembling a trilobite and from a lesser depth.

Although Ley gives no further information, the reference is probably to the discovery of *Serolis trilobitoides* by James

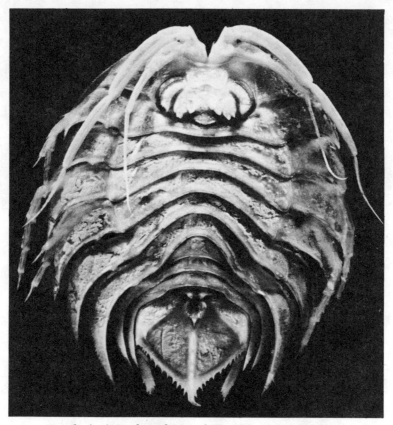

56. A giant abyssal isopod (*Serolis trilobitoides*).

Eights in 1830. These animals, first mistaken for trilobites, are certain primitive crustaceans related to crabs known as isopods, which include wood lice already noted (Illustration 56). The giants of these forms may be 50 centimeters (18 inches) in length.

In 1830 James Eights, naturalist and corresponding member of the Albany Institute, New York, found himself on the shores of Patagonia. He was there in the capacity of scientist to the exploring expedition of 1830. In those days a scientist (naturalist) was a scientific jack-of-all-trades, responsible for collecting meteorological, geological, botanical, and zoological data, and anything else that might even remotely fall in the broad class of natural philosophy or science.

During a calm period the seamen accompanying the expedition amused themselves by catching some of the fine bottom fish to improve the expedition's diet. Eights examined the stomach contents of some of the then undescribed species, particularly *Phycis*, caught by the seamen. To his surprise he found a strange olivaceous green creature, about 3 centimeters (little more than 1 inch) in length. The animal was clearly some sort of crustacean, but he was amazed at the remarkable resemblance to *Paradoxus boltoni*, a trilobite believed to be extinct for millions of years. He writes, "I was convinced that this animal came nearer to the long-lost family of trilobites than anything hitherto discovered."

After collecting a variety of specimens the expedition moved on to Cape Horn and to the New South Shetland Islands. These clusters of rocks rising precipitously from the southern seas, up to 1,900 meters (6,000 feet), covered with heavy masses of snow, divided everywhere by straits and indented by deep bays or coves almost continuously swept by fierce gales, impressed Eights greatly. Unexplored and inhospitable, they would yield further zoological surprises.

Here Eights found more of the strange crustaceans, presumably from the great depths of the surrounding ocean. This undoubtedly explains Willy Ley's statement that first reports placed the habitat of these animals in the ocean depths, rather than the more moderate depths subsequently established. Eights himself discovered further specimens along the coasts of Cape Horn. In general, cold Antarctic waters and the eastern coast of South America, including a few other deep-water occurrences, represent the present range. Eights named these animals, some specimens as large as 7 centimeters (3 inches), *Brongniartia trilobitoides*—*Brongniartia* in honor of Professor Alexander Brongniart, who first attempted a systematic arrangement of trilobites, and *trilobitoides* in recognition of their resemblance to trilobites. Today, because of zoological factors unknown to Eights, the generic designation *Brongniartia* has been replaced by *Serolis*.

These creatures, except for the fact that they have two pair of antennae as compared to one pair in the case of trilobites, are so structurally similar that they may well have functional analogies. This was evident to me when I compared the hypothetical suggestions of trilobite locomotion and behavior while watching a motion-picture film of living specimens of *Serolis*, provided by Levi-Setti.

While not relevant to this discussion, it is of interest that Eights noted four species of seals, one of which was unknown to him. He identified the sea elephant, sea leopard, and fur seal. The term sea leopard, a popular designation for the Weddell seal, should not be confused with the leopard seal *Hydrurga leptonyx* discussed in Chapter II. It may in fact be that Eights' unknown seal was just this species. Consider his description: "There is also a fourth species, which I have no recollection of ever seeing the slightest notice of. It is probably not common, as I saw but one; it was standing on the extremities of its forefeet (flippers), the head and chest perfectly erect, abdomen curved and resting on the ground, the tail was also in an upright position." He then speculates that this animal may be responsible for the "mermaid" myth. He continues, "When I approached within one hundred feet, it threw itself flat and made rapidly for the sea: It appeared about twelve or fifteen feet in length, and distinctly more slender in proportion than any of the other species, so much so that the motion of the body when moving seemed perfectly *undulating*. Some of the seamen had seen them frequently on a former voyage, and mentioned that they were known among sealers by the name of *sea serpent*, from the circumstance."

More recently, in 1967, I was invited by Ralph Buchsbaum, professor of zoology at the University of Pittsburgh, to give a seminar on our researches at Loch Ness. During the social hour after the presentation one of his colleagues told me about experimental photography of the sea bottom that was in progress. He stated that photographs of fresh tracks identical to the *Cruciana*, the fossilized trilobite tracks, had been obtained. He expressed the hope that traps could be lowered to catch whatever was making these highly suggestive tracks. As far as I know the nature of these tracks was never determined

57. A cruziana, or fossil trilobite trail, from Bell Island, Newfoundland. Trail width, about 3 centimeters (1.25 inches).

and nothing was ever trapped, because of a subsequent loss of funding for the project. The business of identifying sea-bottom trails and tracks is a tricky one and to infer living trilobites from a track is even more tricky. A marvelous collection of sea-bottom tracks and trails is presented in a book entitled *The Face of the Deep* by B. C. Heezen and C. D. Hollister. Only a tiny fraction of aquatic animal tracks have been identified, so that fertile ground for new discoveries is indeed abundant.

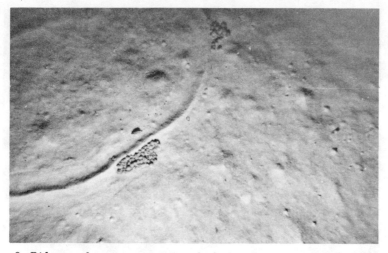

58. Ridge marks representing a trail of a large animal with associated ovoid pellets. Depth, 3,162 meters (2 miles), eastern scarp, Manihiki Plateau, equatorial Pacific. Field of view, about 1.5 meters (5 feet) by 1.75 meters (6 feet).

Heezen and Hollister describe one dramatic photograph (Illustration 58) that they say gives the distinct impression that the ridge marks the trail of some large animal that may perhaps have been 20 or 30 centimeters (8 or 12 inches) wide. Associated with these broad ridges and furrows are piles of round or ovoid pellets approximately the size of golf balls. The animal that made these tracks and balls is still unknown, and according to Heezen and Hollister may be some still-undiscovered sea monster, perhaps some gigantic crab, since some fiddler crabs work sediment into small round balls.

Large "tread tracks" looking like giant tire tracks are shown in Illustration 59. These mysterious deep-sea trails begin and end abruptly, compounding the mystery. In one case the trail ends in a deep cylindrical hole. Again the animals responsible for these tracks are unknown, although one might speculate that they were made by large mud-eating starfish.

A great many extremely interesting underwater photographs of tracks and trails, in some cases including unidentified

59. Large "tread trail" tracks, meandering with prominent lateral impressions, depth 4,410 meters (2.7 miles), continental margin of southern Chile.

creatures, have been published. During the period 1959–65 the sea bottom of the Indian Ocean was intensely studied under the auspices of the International Indian Ocean Expedition. Some of the results have been published by the USSR in the Geological-Geophysical Atlas of the Indian Ocean. Included are pages of superb underwater photographs of the seabed. Many strange tracks, fecal material, and burrows are to be seen. One clearly shows a strange, unidentified, wormlike animal at a depth of 5,197 meters (about 3 miles) (Illustration 60).

Trails and tracks are not the only evidence of sea life known and unknown that can be read on the seabed. Excrement and fecal material of marine creatures are often seen and photographed and in some cases may lead us to still unidentified creatures. In most cases the fecal form and consistency give some clue as to the type of creature that produced it. Meat eaters tend to produce a loose consistency, vegetable eaters a more firm material, and deposit eaters a very compact and

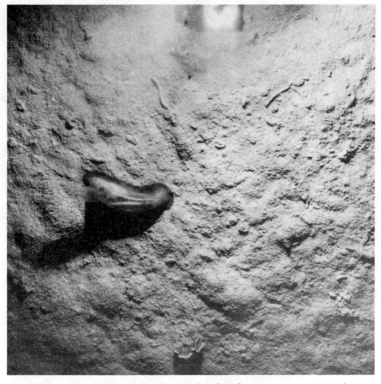

60. Strange wormlike animal at a depth of 5,197 meters (3 miles) in the Indian Ocean. Diameter of compass shown at edge of photograph is about 7.5 centimeters (3 inches).

stable form of excrement. Heezen and Hollister point out that marine fecal material has not been studied very much because of the difficulty in sampling. Fecal materials picked up in deep-sea dredges are undoubtedly destroyed when raised to the surface, and remains that may reach the surface are washed away when the collected animals are sieved from the sediment. Underwater photography of the ocean floor, however, appears to be a promising tool for future cryptozoological expeditions.

While not impossible, it is most improbable that living

trilobites still exist. New fossil species, however, will certainly be discovered. Today there are a variety of collecting areas. One of the most spectacular is located in Manuels, Newfoundland. In the gorge of the Manuels River are found shalebeds representing the Middle Cambrian, containing fossils of giant trilobites, known as *Paradoxides*, some of the large specimens reaching lengths of 25 centimeters (10 inches). Perhaps 90 per cent or more of the fossils contained in this site remain to be discovered.

VIII

Maybe Animals of South America

South America! A vast unexplored continent, laced with mighty rivers and impenetrable jungles, teeming with lost cities and civilizations, immeasurable wealth in gold and jewels, strange peoples, miraculous plants and springs of water that cure disease and restore youth, and, last but not least, fabulous unknown animals!

Such was the picture painted by the early Spanish conquistadors, returning from their explorations of this new, magical land. Obviously reality must fall far short of such promise. The acquisition of riches was the overriding concern of these conquerors, rather than thirst for new knowledge, although in some cases, especially among the Catholic priests who accompanied the expeditions, a more learned motivation was evident. Even when this was the case, information rarely became available to the rest of the world, since Spain jealously guarded newfound secrets, burying them in her governmental archives.

The true openers of South America were the later explorer naturalists, who collected, measured, and reported the results of their work to the entire world. Undoubtedly even these early naturalist explorers, less credulous than conquistadors, were influenced by the profusion of fabulous tales. Clearly no land could possibly contain all of these marvels, but allowing for the disparity between fact and fiction, South America has been disappointing from a cryptozoological viewpoint. Of course, some quite marvelous animals have been discovered, but nothing like the tremendous wealth of large animals found in Africa. We may well ask, given a continent as large as South America, containing over 7½ million square kilometers (3 million square miles) of jungle in Brazil alone, where are the large quadrupeds comparable to Asian and African elephants, rhinoceroses, hippopotami, giraffes, and the like? Where are the large primates comparable to gorillas and chimpanzees?

The reason for the lack of large advanced mammals in South America is now more or less clear. With only occasional exceptions, South America is a land harboring very primitive mammals known as *Edentates* (toothless),* which arose from even more primitive mammalian forms (the protoinsectivores) at the beginning of the Tertiary Period of the Cenozoic era, some one hundred million years ago.

At one time South America was joined to Africa, and then separated, as now established by continental drift. There has been much controversy over the "simpleminded" observation that the continents, if pushed together, fit rather well, especially if one takes into account the shorelines as they existed in the geological past. Originally the proponents of this idea were laughed at as "childish," whereas today the reality of the separation of a single ancient land mass in the Southern Hemisphere is well established. There is far too much geological evidence to cite here, so I will mention only the two most important types of data. One is a study of the remanent magnetism of rocks. Remanent magnetism is the magnetism frozen into a rock at the time the rock was formed. The paleomagnetic data that have been gathered at a great expense of human effort are best explained by the theory of continental drift (Illustration 62). The second extremely compelling evi-

---

*A misnomer, as only a few species are literally without teeth. The teeth are generally numerous but very small.

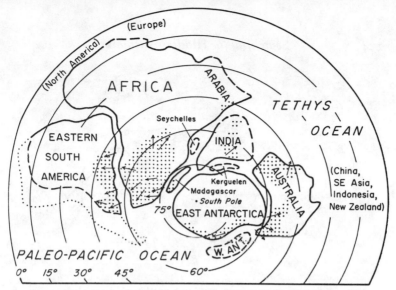

61. Reconstruction of the ancient continent of the Southern Hemisphere. The stippling and arrows show the glaciers and their movement. Dashed and dotted lines indicate changes in the shapes of the continents.

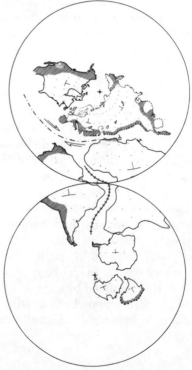

62. Reconstruction of the positions of continents in the geologic past from paleomagnetic data. A single geologic period (Jurassic) is shown.

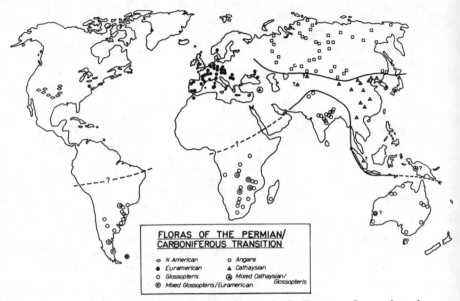

63. Distribution of latest Carboniferous/Early Permian floras plotted on the present continent positions.

dence is the discovery of the distribution of fossil plants, especially a genus known as *Glossopteris* (Illustrations 63 and 64), which indicates that a humid, temperate climate existed over the range indicated, including Antarctica. Again, these data make the most sense if these areas were once a single land mass. Clearly if this idea is to explain in large part the kinds of animals in South America, especially the edentates, the separation must have occurred prior to the time when the higher mammals had evolved; or prior to or during the protoinsectivorous stage of mammalian evolution.

Again, it is gratifying for this hypothesis to report that the best geological evidence establishes that considerable separation had occurred by the end of the Jurassic and the beginning of the Cretaceous Period, which precedes the Tertiary. Thus a single hypothesis elegantly explains a mass of data that at

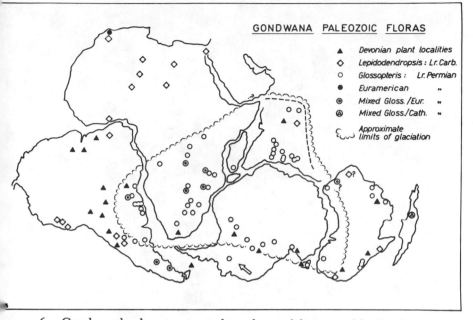

64. Gondwanaland, reconstructed on the model proposed by Smith and Hallam (1970), with the South Pole based on the Permian continent positions suggested by Smith, Briden, and Drewry. The distribution of fossil plants (Illustration 63) would be explained by this model.

one time required the most ingenious, but unlikely, hypotheses of land-bridge formation and destruction coupled with additional unlikely concatenations of events.

In this way, the South American life forms were separated from the mainstream of evolution in Africa, where the large African quadrupeds evolved to the present stage. This explains why South America is zoologically a land of edentates; but why do we not find other large forms comparable to but differing from African species, which evolved in their own right in South America? The answer to this question is that indeed this did occur, and the cryptozoological aspects of the question will be addressed in the pages that follow.

65. The electric eel, *Electrophorus electricus*.

Aside from edentates there were some rather marvelous animals discovered by early naturalist explorers. Georg Marc-graf (1611–44), one of the earliest explorers, described the electric eel *Gymnotus carapo*. A fish that produced an electric current was certainly a marvel, but since the nature of electricity was not understood at the time, little was made of this prodigy. The natural history of another species, *Electrophorus electricus*, measuring up to 3 meters (9 feet) in length, was published by Richter in 1929. However, not until 1805, when Alexander von Humboldt studied and experimented with this giant of the electric eel group, did the Western world begin to appreciate these strange creatures. Humboldt, perhaps the greatest of the South American explorer-naturalists, had known about this creature and was most anxious to obtain specimens during his expedition through South America, 1799–1804. Humboldt's expedition was perhaps unique in that it was purely scientific in nature, with the specific purpose of collecting plants and animals and studying whatever natural phenomena might be encountered.

This was in contrast to the first and earlier scientific expedition led by the French explorer-scientist Charles-Marie de La Condamine. Zoology was purely ancillary to his main purpose of measuring the length of a degree of arc on the surface of the earth in the vicinity of the equator. The reason for making such a measurement was to determine whether Sir Isaac Newton's hypothesis that the earth was flattened at the poles was correct or whether the French Cassinians, who maintained that the earth was elongated in the direction of the poles, were right. The only experimental way to settle the matter was to compare the length of a degree of arc at the equator and near one of the poles. After much controversy the French Académie des Sciences commissioned two expeditions to carry out this work. One, under the command of M. Maupertuis, would go to Lapland; the other would go to Peru and would be led by the distinguished mathematician and geodesist, Charles-Marie de La Condamine. Thus the first truly scientific expedition to South America was mounted in 1735. The task was carried out as planned, proving that Newton was correct, which is quite a story in its own right; however, many new plants and animals, too numerous to list here, were also discovered.

Getting back to Humboldt and his electric eels. For quite a while Humboldt was unsuccessful in obtaining specimens, primarily because the reputation of these creatures was so bad that the mere mention of them to the Indians evoked terror close to panic.

His luck turned when he reached Calabozo, a small town in Venezuela, halfway between Caracas and the Orinoco River. Calabozo was nothing in itself, but it was located in a swampy region that abounded in the notorious electric eels. These fish were actually related to carp, although they certainly looked like eels. As was to be established later, they could

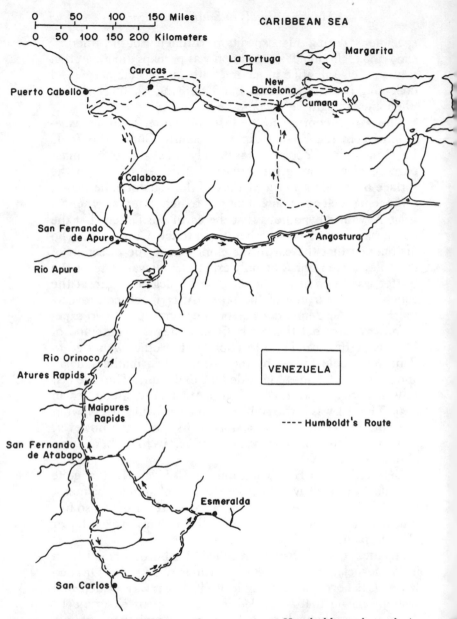

66. Map of Venezuela showing the route von Humboldt took exploring and specimen-collecting, 1799–1804.

deliver up to 650 volts at up to 2 amperes in air; somewhat less in water. The electric field allegedly could kill or stun large animals (horses) and might even stun or kill a man. At Humboldt's request the Indians agreed to provide him with some specimens.

First they rounded up two or three dozen horses and mules, which they herded into the pools infested with electric eels. Encircling the pool using spears and sticks, they forced the poor horses to remain in the pool. The eels, disturbed by the horses' and mules' trampling, rose to the surface delivering electric shocks in all directions. The horses and mules in utter terror, foaming at the mouth, were in great confusion, continuously trying to escape from the pools. Some were so severely shocked that they sank to their knees or fell down, and a few actually drowned.

Eventually the strength of the shocks decreased so that the situation calmed down to the point where the Indians harpooned some of the eels that approached the shoreline. Some were only slightly injured so that Humboldt actually had live specimens to experiment with. Eventually all were killed and dissected, forming a spectacular addition to the specimen collection.

The accomplishments of Humboldt and Aime Bonpland, his best friend and partner, an excellent botanist, received world acclaim. Among those later inspired by the exploits of these two was young Charles Darwin, who regarded Humboldt's "personal narrative" almost as magical. When the opportunity arose in 1831 for Darwin to accompany as a naturalist Captain Fitzroy, who would command a vessel on a two-year voyage to Tierra del Fuego, Darwin's delight was without bounds. Little did he realize that this voyage and his reading of Humboldt, whom he regarded as "the greatest scientific traveler who ever lived," would change his entire life and eventually lead to a theory of the origin of species.

We raised the question as to why there were no larger edentate quadrupeds in South America, since one might expect such evolutionary forms to develop even though the edentates were isolated from the mainstream of mammalian

67. *Megatherium americanum*, pampean of Argentina, the largest of known ground sloths.

evolution. When Darwin arrived in Patagonia a gaucho showed him a place that contained the bones of monsters "created by the devil." Here indeed were the missing giant quadrupeds, a giant sloth as big as an elephant, known as *Megatherium*, large toxodonts (described by some as a cross between a woodchuck and a rhinoceros), giant armadillos, one species (*Doedicurus*) with a tail much like a medieval spiked mace—lost-world animals by anyone's criteria. The effect on Darwin of collecting and handling these remains of ancient creatures, now supposedly extinct, cannot be overestimated. It led him to note the similarity of some fossils to existing animals, rather than regarding them simply as extinct animals, as had been done heretofore. Thus the germ of the idea of the evolution of life forms was born.

Long after Darwin had left South America, events and discoveries led to a startling question: Was it indeed a fact that

68. A pampean toxodont, *Toxodon burmeisteri*.

all of these great creatures had vanished from the face of the earth, or might a few still survive in the lost wildernesses of Patagonia?

To this day there is no pat answer to this question. The matter is complicated, facts almost inextricably mingled with false claims, exaggerations, misrepresentations, and wild speculation, to say nothing of instances of outright fraud. Bernard Heuvelmans in his book *On the Track of Unknown Animals* has gone a long way toward untangling this mess. I will summarize the data for the reader, sorting out the facts, adding and clarifying when possible.

As usual we begin with native legends. The two major sources are the Tehuelche pampas Indians of southern Patagonia and their neighbors, the Araucans. The stories refer to at least two different kinds of animals, and in some cases the two appear to be found together, although other explanations are possible.

69. *Nesodon imbricatus*, representing a different stage of development. The remains of the creature were discovered by Charles Darwin.

The Tehuelche (or Tzoneka, as they call themselves) describe animals as large as cattle, but with much shorter legs, armed with claws. Often the animals are represented as amphibious, digging burrows in the ground, sleeping by day, nocturnal in their habits. Much has been made about the alleged attribute of imperviousness to arrows and bullets, but it is not uncommon for aboriginals to ascribe invulnerability to creatures, regardless of fact.

Further details were recorded by Professor Florentino Ameghino, an Argentine paleontologist, who for better or for worse got involved in the whole matter at the turn of the century (1898).

In one of his published papers Ameghino related that a Tehuelche Indian named Hompen, while traveling from Senguer to Santa Cruz, had met an *iemisch* that had barred his way on the road. He claimed to have shot the creature dead

70. Pampean glyptodonts: *Doedicurus clavicaudatus* and *Glyptodon clavipes*.

with some dispatch. *Iemisch*, which translates to "tiger of the water," was the Indian name for this creature. The Indians maintained the animal was amphibious and walked as easily on dry land as it swam in the water. This characteristic is, as we shall see, most valuable in establishing a probable zoological identification. This information comes from the Tehuelche Indians via Carlos Ameghino, a brother of the paleontologist, who spent a great deal of time traveling in Patagonia collecting data. He further stated, "Today it [the *iemisch*] is confined to the center of Patagonia, in caves and lairs on the banks of Lakes Colhué, Fontana, and Buenos Aires, and the Rivers Senguer, Aysen, Huemules. But according to tradition it once spread north as far as the Rio Negro; and in the south, as old Indians recall, it used to live in all the lakes on the eastern slopes of the Andes, right down to the Straits of Magellan. Thus, around the middle of the century, an *iemisch*, which had come down from lakes in the Andes by the Rio Santa

Cruz, landed on the northern bank of this river near Pavon island. The terrified Indians fled into the interior, and as the only reminder of its inopportune arrival gave the deserted place the name it still bears today: Iemisch Aiken (that is, '*iemisch*'s harbour or port of call'). This animal is of nocturnal habits, and it is said to be so strong that it can seize horses with its claws and drag them to the bottom of the water. According to the description I have been given, it has a short head, big canine teeth, and no external ears; its feet are short and plantigrade, with three toes on the forefeet and four on the hind; these toes are joined by a membrane for swimming, and are also armed with formidable claws. Its tail is long, flat and prehensile. Its body is covered with short hair, coarse and stiff, of a uniform bay colour. Its size is said to be larger than a puma's, but its paws are shorter and its body thicker."

Professor Ameghino, unfortunately, proceeded to make the data conform to his hypothesis that the *iemisch* referred to the giant sloths, extinct or otherwise, which were present not only in the fossil record, but also in the form of quite fresh skin. Pieces of "fresh bone and skin" of these sloths had been popping up almost regularly and were causing a great deal of interest among zoologists and paleontologists. The pieces of hide, still with hair and small embedded bones, were unquestionably from supposedly extinct giant ground sloths, such as mylodon, megatherium, glossotherium, and other related forms. The only question was: "How fresh" was this material?

Subsequent investigation revealed that some of the skin that was still supple—with a coating of dried blood serum adhering to the edges, which had clearly been cut by man—had come from caves. Thorough excavation of one of these caves, known as Cueva Eberhardt, included an inner chamber, which revealed some most remarkable facts and artifacts.

Near the place where the first skin had been found, a second rolled-up skin came to light. The list of findings included a kitchen midden; human remains; heaps of dung (some as large as an elephant's); bones, including a sloth skull, showing the marks of man's attempt to club the animal; and fodder suitable as food for large herbivores. The application of modern

71. Ground sloth *Mylodon robustus*, pampean of Argentina.

scientific methods, including carbon-14 dating, established that the dung in the mylodon caves was some ten thousand years old, at which time the creatures were undoubtedly widely distributed.

The original conclusion was that the giant ground sloths were contemporaneous with man and were kept in a semi-domesticated state in the cave! (Heuvelmans claimed they were really not domesticated, but were driven into the caves periodically and kept entrapped for future food.) Alternately it may be that the sloths were "cave sloths" in analogy to cave bears, feeding on plant materials at night, but retiring to caves by day. In any case, the great quantity of dung clearly establishes that a succession of several animals had to have been involved, rather than a single isolated case.)

Rumors persist of such animals in the flesh, but to date none have come to hand. These sloth tales clearly do not fit the *iemisch* description; they refer to burrowing, in most cases

72. Giant armadillo (*Priodontes giganteus*).

harmless animals. These reports come not only from the
Tehuelche, but also from the Gennake and the Araucans. In
1875 an old Indian chief named Sinckel showed Dr. Francisco
Moreno, of the La Plata Museum, who was deeply involved
in the sloth business, a cave that was said to be the lair of one
of these unknown animals, which were called "ellengassen."

Ramon Lista, another authority, reported that the Tehuelche believe there are large four-footed animals in the
Santa Cruz territory. One story has it that a whole family of
Indians was once carried off by these creatures. Heuvelmans
cites more reports, all of which show that the Indians have
legends related to the sloths, differing from those referring to
the *iemisch*.

Heuvelmans documents in considerable detail the various
efforts and pieces of evidence and reports that lead to a clear
identification of the *iemisch* as an otter. The major contribution comes from the research of Dr. Robert Lehmann-
Nitsche, anthropologist of the Natural History Museum of La
Plata. His most fruitful approach was to trace the meaning of
the word *iemisch* in the Tehuelche and Araucan languages.
This word and related forms all referred to some sort of otter,

probably *Lutra felina* according to Dr. Lehmann-Nitsche. However, he finds it difficult to reconcile the reputed ferocious nature of the *iemisch* with this small and rather harmless creature, concluding that the explanation is that the *iemisch* has to some extent been confused with the jaguar.

Heuvelmans appears to accept this idea, although he does so perhaps reluctantly and raises the question of whether this could not be a species of giant otter, such as is found in Brazil.

In my opinion the Tehuelche *iemisch* is not a composite of the jaguar and the otter at all. First we note that *Pteronura brasiliensis*, the giant South American otter found in Venezuela, Guyana, Uraguay, Brazil, and the North of Argentina, reaches an unusual size. Six-meter (20-foot) lengths have been reported but never verified. Official zoology texts set the average size of these animals at a length of 1.4 meters (5 feet) weighing 24 kilograms (50 pounds). Except for size and the number of toes on the webbed feet, the description fits remarkably well with the Indian description of the *iemisch*. Peter Fleming, a reliable correspondent for the London *Times*, has reported some relevant data in his book *Brazilian Adventure*, published in 1934. Fleming accompanied an expedition into Brazil that had been organized to determine if possible the fate of Colonel Percy Fawcett (more of whom later). His narrative of this adventure is utterly delightful, but our concern at this time is page 157 only. The expedition is at the time described on the Araguaia River in central Brazil.

He writes, "We ourselves were animal fanciers for a time. The Araguaia—and for all I know the other great rivers of central Brazil—are inhabited by a kind of otter not found elsewhere. It is a huge beast and is said to measure as much as ten or twelve feet in length; though the biggest adult that I saw out of the water was not more than seven feet long."

A 3- or 4-meter (10- or 12-foot) specimen would certainly qualify for the "water tiger" of the Tehuelche.

Now my suggestion as to the nature of the *iemisch* is that it is a rare, large, ferocious species or subspecies of otter related to Pteronura, but not identical to it. Its range is restricted and may still be shrinking. Whether or not the

73. Giant otter, *Pteronura brasiliensis*.

Indians are right about the number of toes one does not know, since the known species of otters have five digits on each foot, although length of claws and extent of webbing vary from species to species.

It may be that certain anatomical peculiarities of the feet may result in a visual impression of three toes on the forefeet and four on the hind feet. In every other characteristic, including the proverbial elusiveness of some species of otter, the correspondence is too great to explain in any other way.

There is yet one further South American enigma that would be satisfactorily explained by a giant southern otter. I refer to reports of an alleged Patagonian plesiosaur. The whole matter has been reported in some detail by Peter Costello in his book *In Search of Lake Monsters*. We will concern ourselves only with the reports proper to see if a probable zoological identification can be made. The reader if interested will be able to obtain further details from Costello's book.

The first report of this large marine animal was received by Dr. Clementi Onelli, director of the Buenos Aires zoo, in 1897. While traveling in Patagonia a Chilean farmer reported unusual night noises, described as sounding like a heavy cart traversing a pebble beach, coming from White Lake. During moonlit nights, a large animal was observed swimming in the lake, with a long reptilelike neck protruding from the surface. If even a slight noise was made, the creature would submerge.

The next report listed by Costello also involves Dr. Onelli. Allegedly a Norwegian named Vaag, while exploring the Rio Tamanga, found huge animal remains and some tracks. Costello says Onelli thought the tracks might belong to a plesiosaur, which seems rather surprising, since we really don't know what plesiosaur tracks might look like, although one can, of course, speculate.

In 1913 Onelli received a similar report from an Englishman from the Santa Cruz area.

In 1910 a George Garrett provided the following information to the *Globe* of Toronto:

So far as I know, my son and I are the only white men who have ever caught sight of one of these antediluvian monsters. It was about the year 1910. Having pioneered a peninsula on that most beautiful lake, Najuel Huapi, I was appointed manager of a newly formed company.

At that time I speak of, the government engineer was surveying the property, and my son and I were navigating him and his staff of assistants around the wild, rugged coasts of the peninsula. We had put the engineer, his men and instruments ashore, and were sailing about for pleasure, with about half a gale of wind. We were beating windward up an inlet called "Pass Coytrué," which bounded the peninsula. This inlet was about five miles in length, a mile or so in width, and of an unfathomable depth. Just as we were near the rocky shore of the peninsula, before tacking, I happened to look astern towards the centre of the inlet, and, to my great surprise, I saw about a quarter of a mile to leeward, an object which appeared to be fifteen or twenty feet in diameter, and perhaps six feet above the water.

Having time only for a glimpse, as the boat was now racing within a few yards of the rocks, I told my son to keep his eyes on the curiosity while I tacked our somewhat cumbersome craft. This was accomplished with all speed, and in the twinkling of an eye we were tearing towards the spot—when the thing disappeared. Only a very few minutes could have elapsed ere we were tearing towards the spot where the object had been, but there was not the slightest trace of it in the clear waters of the lake. On mentioning my experience to my neighbors they said the Indians often spoke of immense water animals they had seen from time to time.

In 1922 Onelli received a letter from an American prospector named Martin Sheffield, who had observed large tracks while looking for gold in the Andean foothills of Chubut Province near a lake in the Esquel region of Patagonia. Bushes and undergrowth were described as crushed by deep marks that could only have been made by a large animal. The tracks, according to Sheffield, disappeared into the lake.

Sheffield is further quoted as stating that he observed an animal in the lake with a huge neck like a swan, making movements suggesting a body like a crocodile.

This last report was too much for Onelli, who proceeded to mount an expedition to find Sheffield's animal. The expedition reached the area and actually investigated several lakes. Investigation consisted mainly of observation and the detonation of depth charges. While in the field Onelli heard further reports and rumors of monsters in other lakes. In spite of all efforts nothing definitive resulted.

From the vantage point of 1980, and fourteen years of work at Loch Ness, Scotland, where the difficulties of tracking an aquatic animal were underscored, it is not difficult to understand Onelli's failure. We must remember that in 1922 sonar had not been invented, nor was underwater photography in a sophisticated state.

That there were or are fairly large semi-aquatic animals, having a configuration more or less like the popular conception of a plesiosaur, seems to me to be entirely likely. However, the animals are not primitive reptiles, but giant otters probably related to *Pteronura brasiliensis*. I should emphasize that I do not believe the Indians have confused or fused the traits and characteristics of jaguars with those of ordinary small otters, as has been suggested heretofore. It is my judgment that a separate species or subspecies of otter, much larger than ordinary otters, extremely surreptitious and rare, probably accounts for the *iemisch* and Patagonian plesiosaur reports.

The possible persistence of relict species in South America is not the only kind of exotic zoology attracting our attention. Evidence can also be adduced for other large, unidentified animals. Some of the most reliable evidence can be found in the notes and diaries of Lieutenant Colonel Percy H. Fawcett, perhaps the greatest South American explorer of all time. Colonel Fawcett spent nineteen years searching for a lost city, which he believed was inhabited by a highly civilized race of white people; in this he was a romantic and a dreamer, but when it came to reporting what he had observed and measured, he was unfailingly accurate.

Fawcett originally served in the Royal Artillery of the British Army, but had in addition to his military skills acquired the necessary training for boundary-survey work. The life of an artillery officer in home stations was not the cup of tea that interested Colonel Fawcett. In 1906 there were many boundary disputes among the various South American countries, particularly Bolivia and Brazil. Bolivia had requested the Royal Geographical Society to act as a referee, and to recommend an experienced army officer for the work. The president of the Royal Geographical Society was aware of Fawcett's talents and interest, and after discussing the matter with Fawcett, recommended him for the post. Thus began Fawcett's nineteen-year career of measuring and surveying the trackless jungles of South America. Actually, the activity amounted to exploration and permitted Fawcett to pursue his search for lost cities and peoples, till he disappeared in the Mato Grosso jungle in 1925, which is another story in itself.

Fawcett recorded most of what he experienced and observed during his years of exploration, which in many cases include references to animals, known and unknown. We will quote some of the more interesting passages. Many of these reports were made while Fawcett was on the River Acre, a tributary

74. Map of South America showing rivers that were explored by Colonel P. H. Fawcett.

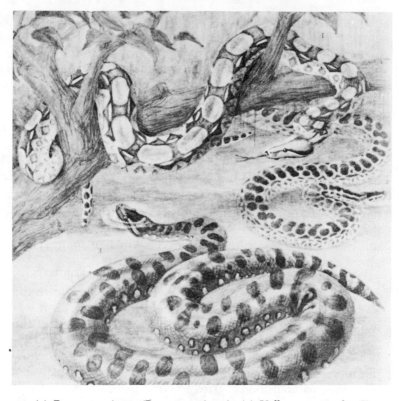

75. (1) Boa constrictor (*Boa constrictor*). (2) Yellow anaconda (*Eunectes notacus*). (3) Anaconda (*Eunectes murinus*).

of the River Purus, which in turn flowed into the Amazon.

Fawcett wrote: "In the Purus and Acre is found a large catfish called the Pururucu, whose tongue, tough as the sole of a shoe, and like it in form, is used as a rasp for grating food and polishing wood. Stingrays are common here because of the sandy riverbed; and I shot an eleven-foot crocodile, a rarity so far up river. The manager at Yorongas told me he killed an anaconda fifty-eight feet long in the Lower Amazon. I was inclined to look on this as an exaggeration at the time, but later, as I shall tell, we shot one even longer than that."

Later he reports the episode as follows: "We were drifting

easily along on the sluggish current not far below the confluence of the Rio Negro when almost under the bow of the
igarité there appeared a triangular head and several feet of
undulating body. It was a giant anaconda. I sprang for my
rifle as the creature began to make its way up the bank, and
hardly waiting to aim smashed a .44 soft-nosed bullet into its
spine, ten feet below the wicked head. At once there was a
flurry of foam, and several heavy thumps against the boat's
keel, shaking us as though we had run on a snag.

"With great difficulty I persuaded the Indian crew to turn
in shorewards. They were so frightened that the whites showed
all around their popping eyes, and in the moment of firing I
had heard their terrified voices begging me not to shoot lest
the monster destroy the boat and kill everyone on board, for
not only do these creatures attack boats when injured, but
also there is great danger from their mates.

"We stepped ashore and approached the reptile with
caution. It was out of action, but shivers ran up and down the
body like puffs of wind on a mountain tarn. As far as it was
possible to measure, a length of forty-five feet lay out of the
water, and seventeen feet in it, making a total length of sixty-
two feet. Its body was not thick for such a colossal length—
not more than twelve inches in diameter—but it had probably
been long without food. I tried to cut a piece of the skin, but
the beast was by no means dead and the sudden upheavals
rather scared us. A penetrating, foetid odour emanated from
the snake, probably its breath, which is believed to have a
stupefying effect, first attracting and later paralysing its prey.
Everything about this snake is repulsive.

"Such large specimens as this may not be common, but the
trails in the swamps reach a width of six feet and support the
statements of Indians and rubber pickers that the anaconda
sometimes reaches an incredible size, altogether dwarfing that
shot by me. The Brazilian Boundary Commission told me of
one exceeding *eighty* feet in length! In the Araguay and
Tocantins basins there is a black variety known as the Dormidera, or 'Sleeper,' from the loud snoring noise it makes. It
is reputed to reach a huge size, but I never saw one. These
reptiles live principally in the swamps, for unlike the rivers,

which often become mere ditches of mud in the dry season, the swamps always remain. To venture into the haunts of the anaconda is to flirt with death."

When the 19-meter (62-feet) snake was reported in England, Fawcett was promptly branded a liar. To the contrary, I believe he did indeed report the size of the snake truthfully. We should remember that Fawcett had plenty of experience in measuring and carried appropriate equipment for boundary-survey work, and I see no reason to doubt him or to assume he made a mistake.

Both Tim Dinsdale, of Loch Ness fame, and Bernard Heuvelmans, in their books, record a variety of anaconda reports, ranging to the colossal length of 60 meters (200 feet), which is a pretty tall order to swallow.

Officially zoologists allow that anacondas reach lengths of 9 to 10 meters (29 to 33 feet). A 10-meter (33-foot) specimen is actually preserved at the Institute of Butantan in Brazil. If we are extremely generous and permit an increase of 75 per cent in length for rare outsize specimens, we come up with about 18 meters (58 feet), or something close to Fawcett's 19-meter (62-foot) specimen. From Fawcett's description it is clear that this animal was the ordinary anaconda (*Eunectes murinus*) in spite of its size. The New York Zoological Society at one time offered $500 to anyone who could capture a 12-meter (39-foot) specimen, but to date none has been produced, which of course proves nothing.

Now we can be reasonably certain that if much larger specimens exist they are most probably a different species, since the size range required is too large to include all individuals. The consensus among those who take the giant-snake matter seriously is that this is the case. The natives themselves maintain this, and Fawcett alludes to the black variety known as "Dormidera." In South America, especially in the Amazon basin, the existence of a giant constrictor, probably an anaconda known as *sucuriju gigante*, is stoutly maintained. Whether this is fact or exaggeration we cannot decide in our laboratory, but only in the jungles of South America.

References to giant snakes were not all that Fawcett reported, which might be of interest to the cryptozoologist. During a mapping excursion up the Yaverya, a small tributary of the River Acre, he wrote the following: "It was a difficult stream to negotiate owing to the snags and fallen trees, and the work was made harder by the amount of shirking that went on whenever my back was turned. Protruding from the surface of a hardened clay deposit in the riverbank well upstream we found the skull and some bones of a petrified saurian. The skull was over five feet long, but too damaged by the action of water and pebbles to warrant its removal, though I did manage to collect a few black teeth which happened to be intact. Not far away was the skeleton of an even larger monster, plainly to be seen at the bottom of a deep, quiet pool, but there was no way of getting at it."

This area discovered by Fawcett, if relocated, would be an excellent one to excavate so that one could determine what type of beasts were represented. Fawcett refers to "petrified" remains and one cannot be sure whether he means "fossils" or for that matter whether he would be able to distinguish between encrusted recent "green" bones or true fossils. If the former should turn out to be the case, the find would be extremely intriguing!

There are still other references, not to possible fossil remains or recent extinct forms, but to currently existing behemoths. The statements are in general too vague to make any specific judgments, with perhaps one or two exceptions.

He wrote: "In the Paraguay River there is a fresh-water shark, huge but toothless, said to attack men and swallow them if it gets a chance. They talk here of another river monster—fish or beaver—which can in a single night tear out a huge section of riverbank." The shark reference may well represent a variety of bull shark, *Carcharhinus leucas*, which at least in one case, in Lake Nicaragua, has adapted and thrives in a completely fresh-water environment. Further, pregnant females prefer rivermouths where the water is at least partially fresh.

The other river monster—fish or beaver—undoubtedly refers to the giant river otter *Pteronura brasiliensis*, already alluded to.

76. Brazilian bush dog, *Icticyon venaticus*.

Fawcett continues: "The Indians report the tracks of some gigantic animal in the swamps bordering the river, but allege that is has never been seen. The shark exists beyond doubt; as for the other monsters—well, there are queer things yet to be disclosed in this continent of mystery, and if strange, unclassified insects, reptiles and small mammals can still exist there, mightn't there be a few giant monsters, remnants of an extinct species, still living out their lives in the security of the last unexplored swamp areas? In the Madidi, in Bolivia, enormous tracks have been found, and Indians there talk of a huge creature described at times half submerged in the swamps."

Later while writing about his work on the Peruvian-Bolivian boundary he again refers to strange beasts of the Madidi: "In the forests were various beasts still unfamiliar to zoologists, such as the mitla, which I have seen twice, a black doglike cat about the size of a foxhound.* There were snakes and insects

* Most probably the Brazilian bush dog, *Icticyon venaticus*.

yet unknown to scientists; and in the forests of the Madidi some mysterious and enormous beast has frequently been disturbed in the swamps—possibly a primeval monster like those reported in other parts of the continent. Certainly tracks have been found belonging to no known animal—huge tracks, far greater than could have been made by any species we know."

To this day we have no clue as to the possible nature of the Madidi monsters. The area associated with the River Madidi, a tributary of the River Beni of Bolivia, if carefully explored, might yield some interesting discoveries.

It is interesting to note that Bruce Chatwin, recently traveling in southern South America, still reported stories of strange creatures in his excellent travel book *In Patagonia*, published in 1977. The situation in the Mato Grosso, up to now the remotest area of the Brazilian jungle, is completely different.

In 1925 Fawcett believed he knew where the lost city of an advanced white people, referred to as "Z" by Fawcett, was located, and with his son mounted his last expedition. The last word came from Dead Horse Camp at 11° 43′ S latitude and 54° 35′ W longitude, close to the source of the River Manitsaua Missu, a tributary of the River Xingu. Neither he nor any member of his expedition was ever heard from again. In spite of Fawcett's admonition that if anything happened to him, no one was to come after him, numerous expeditions did make an attempt, without success, to determine his fate. Legends have sprung up and tall tales abound, but there seems little doubt that he and his party were killed by hostile Indians.

Today the Brazilian Government has constructed a great highway across Brazil through the very region, which in Fawcett's time was probably the most remote place on this earth. Research stations exist and farms are being shaped out of the jungle.

Alas, there is no lost civilization, although plenty of new plants and animals are being discovered. There still remain some remote unexplored areas in this vast area, so the final word is not yet in. Patagonia, especially the Argentinian

PATAGONIA

ARGENTINA

CHILE

ATLANTIC
OCEAN

•Santa
Cruz

Tierra del
Fuego

N

portion, still has remote areas, as does Bolivia. Whether any new large quadrupeds (four-legged animals) will be discovered remains to be seen. The reader should not be unduly discouraged by the fact that construction of a highway through the vast Mato Grosso (1¼ million square kilometers or 500,000 square miles) has revealed that Fawcett's romantic dream of a lost civilization does not exist where he thought it did. To either side, along tributaries of the Amazon and the Orinoco rivers, surprises, both zoological and archaeological, are still waiting for the intrepid explorer.

IX

The Strangest Animals
Without Backbones

Sea serpents! This is a subject that has intrigued both seafarers and landlubbers alike for hundreds of years, if not thousands. To this day no satisfactory explanation has been found for some of the reported observations, in spite of the heroic efforts of Bernard Heuvelmans to sort out the data in his encyclopedic book *In the Wake of the Sea-Serpents*. To be sure, a partial solution is in hand for certain types of observations. Certainly mistaken identities figure largely in the sea-serpent saga, as do such embarrassing errors as taking a large seaweed for a serpentlike animal.

The reader will recall observations of "Caddy" along the coast of British Columbia in an earlier chapter, and the idea that a primitive whale *Basilosaurus*, although rare, may still be cruising the western Canadian coast. We cannot rule out that such creatures may also be found in other areas of the earth's oceans. New species of whales are still being discovered, and there are one or two so rare that very little is known about them.

I now wish to bring to the reader's attention another group of animals, which I believe represent a piece in the picture of

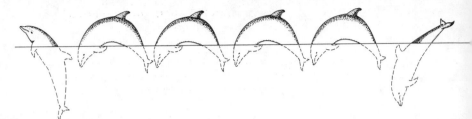

78. A group of stringing dolphins has been frequently suggested as being mistaken for a vertically flexing sea serpent as shown in caricature. Such errors of observation may occasionally be made, but dolphins rarely remain in such uniform lines very long. It is doubtful that observations of dolphins account for more than a very few sea-serpent reports.

the sea-serpent puzzle. The animals in question are practically unknown to anyone except the professional zoologist. Yet they are so remarkable and interesting that it seems strange that little if anything has been written about them in a popular vein.

We need to devote a few words in the form of a brief zoology lesson to describe exactly what these animals are and how they are related to the rest of the animal kingdom. There are three groups (orders) of these animals, known as *Doliolida*, *Pyrosomida*, and *Salpida*; however for simplicity we will refer to all of them in general as salps, which, strictly speaking, is incorrect.

The salps belong to a larger group (subphylum) known as tunicates, so named because the outer part of the body consists of a tough, semitransparent "tunic" composed of material much like cellulose as found in plants. In some cases many individual animals are embedded in a common tunic, thus forming a large colony. Many species are permanently attached to stationary objects; only the free-swimming types, which form large colonies, are of interest to us in the sea-serpent context.

These animals as a whole are of great interest to zoologists because they represent a kind of transition between animals without and with backbones. The adult tunicates have no

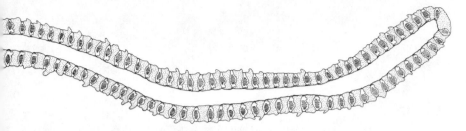

79. A long, cylindrical colony of *Pyrosoma spinosum*. Each individual animal is oriented in the same way, with the mouth at the outer surface of the tube. Water and food are taken in through the mouth and ejected into the common colony cavity, or cloaca, which provides jet propulsion by the combining of the jet action of each animal imbedded in the gelatinous envelope. The overall length has been observed to reach 10 meters (33 feet). The length of each individual ranges from 10 to 20 centimeters (4 to 8 inches).

backbone, not even the notochord, which is found in all the embryonic forms of animals with backbones. This notochord is a cartilagelike flexible bar that extends the length of the body, giving support to the rest of the body organs, muscles, and tissues. In adults this bar is replaced by the vertebral column or backbone. The larvae of the tunicates, however, are free-swimming animals that resemble tadpoles and that have well-developed notochords, indicating that they are descended from the ancestors of backboned animals.

Some representatives of these animals were known to Aristotle, but it was not until the early part of the nineteenth century that their true nature and relationships were recognized. There is a remarkable alternation of generations, in which one form with certain characteristics follows another form with somewhat different features. For example, budding forms alternate with sexual forms and solitary forms alternate with aggregate or colonial forms.

While details of body organization vary from species to species, all free-swimming forms move by jet propulsion. These types have a barrel-shaped body with two main openings at opposite ends of the body cavity so that water and food particles are taken into one opening, analogous to a mouth, passed through the body cavity or atrium, and ejected though

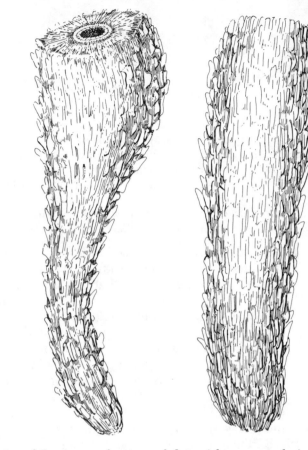

80. Views of colonies of *Pyrosoma atlanticum:* left to right; open-end view; view showing narrow and wide aspects; and a top view showing only a slight tapering over the entire length of the colony.

the atrial aperture, or cloaca. The body cavity is surrounded by muscle bands that can contract, driving water out of the atrial cavity, pushing the animal forward.

These animals as individuals range in size from 1 millimeter (¹⁄₂₅ inch) to 23 centimeters (9 inches) in the case of *Salpa maxima*—certainly not creatures that could be mistaken for giant sea serpents. However, the characteristic of certain species to form giant colonies of many individuals is what interests us and is relevant to the sea-serpent problem.

Of the tunicates the *Pyrosoma* are most spectacular because they form colonies that look like a thick-walled tube or cylinder closed at one end. As early as 1886 the scientists of the Talisman Expedition described a cylinder of *Pyrosoma spinosum* 2 meters (7 feet) in length. Later, in 1902, tubes of *Pyrosoma indicum* were found in the Indian Ocean averaging 2.5 meters (8 feet) long by 20 to 30 centimeters (8 to 12 inches) in diameter, the largest reaching astonishing lengths in excess of 4 meters (13 feet). At this writing tubes of *Pyrosoma spinosum* have been recorded with lengths even greater—no less than 10 meters (33 feet), certainly a respectable size for a real live sea serpent.

Such gigantic tubes floating at the surface might be mistaken, as are certain types of seaweed, for sea serpents, but should hardly explain observations where the creature was seen undulating along. Actually, these giant cylinders do just that! Each individual in the tube is embedded in the tube wall with the mouth pointing out and the cloacal opening into the central cavity of the tube, so that the jet of water from each individual joins with that of every other, resulting in a pro-pulsive jet of water squirting out of the open but constricted end of the tube, driving the entire tube or colony along. The natural flexibility of the longer tubes results in a remarkable serpentinelike undulatory movement.

In general the younger, smaller individuals are more or less transparent, but as they age and grow larger they develop bluish or yellowish colors. The *Pyrosoma* have been so named (*pyrosoma* means "fire body" in Greek) because they possess luminiscent organs, containing luminiscent bacteria that can be stimulated mechanically or otherwise to give off yellowish to bluish-green light. The exact mechanism of this phenom-enon is not understood.

While the general shape of the colonies is often a fairly uniform cylinder, one end may be flattened or enlarged, as shown in Illustration 80. When this occurs in a long cylinder, a tadpolelike configuration is apparent.

The reader may agree that such cylinders could explain some 10-meter (30-foot) or even 12-meter (40-foot) sea serpents, but hardly the 20-meter (65-foot)-to-30-meter (130-foot) varieties, setting aside the 60-meter (200-foot)-plus reports as exaggerations.

The answer may lie at least in part with the *Salpida* or true salps. As mentioned before, these animals show marked generation changes, consisting of two forms. One, called the oozooid, is a solitary animal, has no male or female sexual organs, but reproduces by a structure called a stolon by budding. These animals are called "nannies" or "nursemaids" because they have no sexual organs.

The other type of individual, which is produced by budding from the stolon, is known as the gonozooid and becomes a sexual animal as it matures. It is this latter type or gonozooid that is of great interest to us. The remarkable feature about the young zooids growing from the stolon is that they remain attached for a long time, thus producing gigantic chains that may exceed 25 meters (80 feet) in length!

These giant chains are rare, shorter lengths being much more common. If the giant unbroken chains are rare, observations of them at the surface are even rarer. Most seafarers, to say nothing of the casual sea voyager, would not be able to recognize the true nature of such creatures when observed.

The question that immediately comes to mind is whether or not these salp chains are capable of independent movement, as are the tubes of *Pyrosoma*. As far as the very long chains are concerned we should explain at once that no one really knows. Most zoological textbooks make no reference to the movement or nonmovement of chains per se. A few state that as chains break off the whole aggregate assumes a pelagic existence, "pelagic" meaning that they are not attached to the sea bottom but move about, swimming or drifting with currents.

The well-known and authoritative *A Textbook of Zoology* by Parker and Haswell describes how the salp chains are formed. "The chain of zooids formed on the stolon breaks off in lengths which swim about intact while reproductive organs develop in the individuals." This, however, hardly settles the matter, since a great deal regarding movement of salp chains, especially long ones, remains to be explained.

In searching the literature devoted to salps I found an article by Ellis L. Michael of the Scripps Institution for Biological Research of the University of California, carrying the formidable title "Differentials in Behavior of the Two Generations of *Salpa democratica* Relative to the Temperature of the Sea," published in 1918 by the University of California. Contained in this article is information that throws a lot of light on the possible sea-serpent-salp chain connection suggested here. The entire article is most interesting, as Michael is able to explain much about the behavior and relative numbers of short and long salp chains in warm and cold ocean water, to say nothing of the details of motion of these various forms. One section of his paper, dealing with the theory of motion and behavior of the salp chains, is of great interest. I will summarize the relevant points. Solitary forms are most abundant on the surface when the temperature of the water is high. Aggregate forms are most abundant on the surface when the temperature is low. In general he found that both types, solitary individuals and chains, are at the surface rather than in the depths when the surface-water temperature is lower. Clearly, then, if one wishes to trap or observe the longer chains, the water temperature is an important factor.

As far as motion is concerned, Michael postulates that when the chain has few members the solitary or mother form is able to drag the chain about, but as the number and size of individuals in the chain increase their combined propulsive force soon predominates and the "mother" is dragged about by the lengthening chain. Thus the analogy might be made that at first the dog wags the tail, but as the tail grows, the tail begins to wag the dog!

Another point of interest is exactly how the individuals in a chain are physically organized, since this bears on the diameter of the chains, as well as the possible appearance of alternating dark and yellow colored bands, perceived by Indian Ocean sea-serpent observers and to be discussed later.

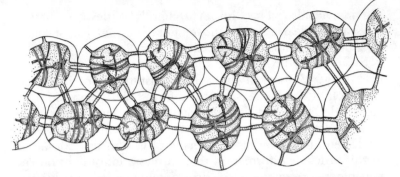

81. Portion of a salp chain showing the relationship of individual animals to each other as viewed from the top. Each individual of *Salpa democratica* is connected to all nearest neighbors, permitting the formation of very long chains, sometimes in excess of 25 meters (80 feet).

The stolon undergoes more or less regular periods of active segmentation and rest so that the aggregate salpae are developed in sets or blocks, all individuals in a single block being of approximately the same size and in the same stage of development. No evidence is at hand that the stolon ever exhausts its capacity for producing them, and segmentation probably continues until terminated by the death of the solitary salpa.

Thus we can understand how very long chains are built up and how blocks of individuals alternating through phases of rest and reproduction might produce a series of banded appearances in the chain. The chains are made up of two rows and were accurately described as early as 1893 by W. K. Brooks.

As can be seen in Illustration 81, the actual diameter of the chain is approximately twice that of the length of each individual, so that a chain made up of 12-centimeter (5-inch) individuals would be about 24 centimeters (10 inches) in diameter. The longer chains were broken up by the early methods of collecting—trawls and the like—so that the early workers in the field were unaware of the great lengths salp chains might reach.

It is not my intention to sift through the complete roster of sea-serpent reports to determine exactly which observations might be explained by the salps. A few cases by way of illustration will suffice. The sea-serpent observations of most relevance are those reported from the warmer seas and oceans, especially the Indian Ocean, because our salp candidates for sea-serpent roles are more commonly, although not by any means exclusively, found in these waters.

Only reports that describe the creature as elongated, snake-like throughout its length, are possible candidates for our explanation. Whether or not the observer described vertical or horizontal flexure (bending) or both is not important, since the organized colonial structure and the long chains of individuals flex in any direction. Of course, as should be apparent to the reader, a clearly differentiated head and tail with appendages would definitely rule out our salps.

The first case I wish to present to the reader is No. 146, as listed by A. C. Oudemans in his book *The Great Sea-Serpent*, published in 1892. The observation was made from the deck of the ship *Nestor*, while the vessel was between Malacca and Penang, and was vouched for by both the ship's captain, John K. Webster, and the ship's surgeon, James Anderson, who made an affidavit before Mr. Donald Spence, acting law secretary of the British Supreme Court, as follows:

> On September 11, at 10:30 A.M., fifteen miles north-west of North Sand Lighthouse, in the Malacca Straits, the weather being fine and sea the smooth, the captain saw an object which had been pointed out by the third officer as "a shoal!" Surprised at finding a shoal in such a well-known track, I watched the object, and found that it was in motion, keeping up the same speed with the ship, and retaining about the same distance as first seen. The shape of the creature I would compare to that of a gigantic frog. The head, of a pale yellowish color, was about twenty feet in length, and six feet of the crown were above the water. I tried in vain to make out the eyes and mouth; the mouth may, however, have been below water. The head was immediately connected with the body, without any indication of a neck. The body was about forty-five or fifty feet long, and of an oval shape, perfectly smooth, but there may have been a slight ridge

along the spine. The back rose some five feet above the surface. An immense tail, fully one hundred and fifty feet in length, rose a few inches above the water. This tail I saw distinctly from its junction with the body to its extremity; it seemed cylindrical, with a very slight taper, and I estimate its diameter at four feet. The body and tail were marked with alternate bands of stripes, black and pale yellow in colour. The stripes were distinct to the very extremity of the tail. I cannot say whether the tail terminated in a fin or not. The creature possessed no fins or paddles so far as we could perceive. I cannot say if it had legs. It appeared to progress by means of an undulatory motion of the tail in a vertical plane (that is, up and down).

Mr. Anderson, the surgeon, confirmed the captain's account in all essential respects. He regarded the creature as an enormous marine salamander.

It was apparently of a gelatinous (that is, flabby) substance. Though keeping up with us, at the rate of nearly ten knots an hour, its movements seemed lethargic. I saw no legs or fins, and am certain that the creature did not blow or spout in the manner of a whale. I should not compare it for a moment to a snake. The only creatures it could be compared with are the newt or frog tribe.

Oudemans, a well-known, even famous zoologist, then proceeded to discuss a variety of rather labored explanations, none of which were at all adequate. In 1892, when Oudemans wrote, the longest reported salp was 2 meters (7 feet) long, so that he was unaware of the giants we now know. Allowing for the usual mixture of observer inaccuracy and personal interpretations, one finds that the report represents a rather good layman's description of what must surely have been a giant salp, possibly an unknown species or variety.

On the positive side we note the absence of appendages, no fins, no distinct tail or head features, cylindrical cross section, no regions corresponding to a neck, the gelatinous or flabby description of the tissue, the lethargic motion, in keeping with the jet-propelled salp cylinders, the pale yellow color, the overall proportions of diameter of about 1 ¼ meters (4 feet) to a length of about 60 meters (200 feet) overstated, and the slight taper. A giant salp cylinder accounts for a number of difficulties, the most obvious being the observed propulsion of a cylindrical animal without fins or paddles and the absence of features such as eyes, mouth, and other specific features throughout, and the lethargic, undulatory progression.

There are, to be sure, some discrepancies, but in my judgment none of them are serious. As has been noted, the longest salp "chain" recorded is somewhat in excess of 25 meters (80 feet), less than half of the length reported. I have found no reference to clearly banded forms where yellow and brown or black alternate, although the pale-yellow color is typical of older salps.

The impression left by the observers that the forward portion was the head region 6 meters (20 feet) long is curious, but makes much more sense if regarded as a somewhat enlarged closed end of a salp tube than an elongated head. The estimated speed of 10 knots per hour (18.5 kilometers per hour or 11.5 miles per hour) is high and is probably inaccurate. To describe anything moving at such a speed as lethargic certainly is contradictory. In fairness it should be noted that the speed was estimated by comparison with the ship, which, without a reference point, can be grossly in error. Even a stationary object with wavelets breaking over it may appear to move at speed under the right conditions.

Of interest in relation to the foregoing report and also a good candidate for a salp explanation is Oudemans' episode No. 147, which also comes from the Indian Ocean. Since it is brief, I report it in full:

1877 May 21—In Mr. Andrew Wilson's Leisure Time Studies we read in a note (p. 111):

"An instance of a large sea-snake being seen in its native seas is afforded by the report of the master of the barque *Georgina* from Rangoon, which (as reported in the newspapers of September 4, 1877) put into Falmouth for orders on the 1st September. On May 21, 1877, in latitude 2°N and longitude 90° 53′ E, a large serpent about forty or fifty feet long, grey and yellow in colour, and ten or eleven inches thick, was seen by the crew. It was visible for twenty

minutes, during which time it crossed the bow, and ultimately disappeared under the port-quarter."

The dimensions are clearly those of the visible part of the
animal. The colour being stated as grey and yellow makes me
conclude that the animal had swum for a long time with its
body in a straight line, without diving, and that the part exposed
to the sunbeams had dried up.

Mr. Andrew Wilson adds: "There can be little doubt that this
sea-serpent was simply a largely developed marine snake."

The report ends with Oudemans agreeing that a large sea
snake was probably what was seen. With this one cannot
agree! There never was a sea snake of such size, even half the
size reported. Clearly the observed creature is of the same
type as described in the previous report. Unfortunately, a
paucity of detail makes a certain conclusion impossible. The
coloration is as in the previous report and would not be
incompatible with certain species of banded sea snakes. However, this idea can most certainly be ruled out on grounds
other than size. The length of 12 meters (39 feet) to 15 meters
(50 feet) with a diameter of only 25 centimeters (10 to 11
inches) are proportions far too slender for any sea snake, the
ratio of length to diameter being around 10 to 1, rather than
the 40 to 60 to 1 reported. The creature may have been a salp
cylinder or chain, most probably the latter.

To set these two accounts in perspective and to underscore
the difficulties of sorting out data such as these, we will
consider one other report, also from warm waters (the China
Sea) documented by Bernard Heuvelmans in his book *In the
Wake of the Sea-Serpents*.

According to Heuvelmans the report was made by A. G. L.
Jourdan in a letter to *La Nature* (Paris, No. 2,697, December
12, 1925), commenting on other earlier published material on
sea serpents. The descriptive part reads:

When we had reached the meridian of a little island called "Isle
of Serpents" [25 miles northwest of Port Arthur] which will
be found on any large-scale map, but was too far off for us to
see from where we were, I was surprised to see on the surface
of the water, hardly immersed, at the very close distance of

about 30 yards, an animal looking like a 10-foot snake, with a maximum diameter of 7 to 8 inches, decreasing toward the tail, the body regularly annulated from one end to the other, alternately light yellow and black, the length of each ring being 4½ to 6 inches. The rather small head was immediately followed by a swelling about 12 to 14 inches in diameter, as thick as the body which followed it, and with 4 feet, 2 each side, recalling the shape of a turtle, but without a shell, striped in yellow and black and with an annulated tail about 10 feet long. I could not see whether this body was round like a snake's, or, as I supposed, slightly flattened.

The animal seemed able to move only slowly, for despite the approach of the ship it was tossed by her wash and disappeared in her wake; a few moments later I saw two other snakes of similar appearance but with the yellow rings darker in colour; on none of them did I see appendages like those mentioned in *La Nature:* As they were futher away from the ship than the first one I could not see any other details.

This is a very curious report and seems at first glance improbable and unexplainable. The story rings true, however, and appears to be a fair and accurate description of what was observed. The question, of course, is: What are we dealing with—salp, sea snake, or something unknown? First let us tie up one or two loose ends. Jourdan does not make it clear whether or not the second two animals also had the peculiar enlarged head-neck features. It seems reasonable to infer, however, that they did not, since he states that he could not make out any details except the alternate yellow and black banding because they were observed at a greater distance.

There is no reason whatsoever not to identify these animals as two specimens of *Hydrophis spiralis* or yellow sea snake, most probably younger individuals, since he remarks that the colored rings were darker, and typically older specimens of this snake tend to lighten with age. The size of about 3 meters (10 feet) is also correct, since this is one of the largest species, reaching 2.75 meters (9 feet) in length.

Was the first creature also a sea snake or possibly a salp cylinder? In spite of the similarity of coloring to the first two cases, which we have tagged as salp chains or cylinders, the salp idea does not seem to be a satisfactory explanation for the 3-meter (10-foot)-long creature observed. One wonders, however, why Jourdan did not clearly identify the creature as a sea snake instead of saying that he had seen "an animal looking like a 10-foot snake." Perhaps the reason was the strange enlarged part of body immediately behind the head, which raised some doubt in his mind. Except for this feature one would not hesitate to label the animal a yellow sea snake, the identity already assigned to the other two creatures he observed. Now can we explain the enlarged portion? The "snake" was somewhat less than vigorous, suggesting that it was in some kind of physical trouble. One immediately thinks of some sort of abnormal pathology, tumor or the like. However, the curious four protuberances located as four legs are too suggestive to ignore. The most probable explanation is that the snake literally "bit off more than it could chew." It must have swallowed a small quadruped (four-footed animal). Perhaps close to shore a swimming rodent fell afoul of the reptile, which now was lodged in its throat, where it suffocated or was killed by the snake venom, producing a state of muscular rigor that resulted in stiff extended limbs more or less locking the creature tightly in the snake's throat. These snakes regularly swallow fish, especially eels, of a diameter equal to their own. They gradually work their jaws over the prey until the entire length of fish or eel is engulfed. However, in the case described, the snake got into trouble because of the prey's four legs, which in a paralyzed state served to anchor the prey in place, probably to the considerable if not fatal discomfort of the snake.

Long salp cylinders are not the only invertebrates that have undoubtedly contributed to the sea-serpent roster. The other backboneless animals that shall concern us belong to a small phylum of marine creatures known as ctenophores, believed to be derived from ancestral coelenterates, which include corals, jellyfish, sea anemones, and the like. The common name for these ctenophores is comb jelly, but only one group is of interest in our sea-serpent context. The animals in this group are referred to as venus girdles, including *Cestum* and *Velamen*.

82. The Venus girdle, *Cestus pectenalis*.

The animals are much elongated and laterally flattened, quite transparent so that they look somewhat like a transparent plastic belt. Actually one should say widened rather than elongated, since their width is what has increased rather than length. The animals hang motionless in the water and are almost invisible except for the upper portion, which consists of an upper and lower row of comb plates, which have a beautiful golden-green color. Older animals become violet with greenish-blue fluorescence. When disturbed they swim away with undulating snakelike movements. The maximum length reported is 1.5 meters (5 feet), which may well lead the reader to wonder what these relatively small creatures could possibly have to do with reported "sea serpents" generally described as 10 to 20 meters (30 to 60 feet) in length. The answer lies in an event so incredible that it certainly would not be accepted by the scientific community were it not for the impeccable credentials of observers reporting it. This event was reported in the New York *Times* on August 20, 1963. It occurred at a place off the coast of Sandy Hook, New Jersey. This spot in the Atlantic Ocean is the favorite dumping ground for industrial acids, and for some still unexplained reason is extremely attractive to all kinds of marine life, which literally teems in the area. Fishermen refer to the area as the "mud hole." Because of this concentration of animal life the area is also infested by dangerous sharks.

A research team consisting of scientists and frogmen under the direction of Dr. Lionel A. Walford, director of the United States Fish and Wildlife Research Center operated by the Department of the Interior at Sandy Hook, were working in the area from the 20-meter (65-foot) research vessel *Challenger*. While two frogmen were being lowered into the water in a sharkproof iron "bird cage," Walford and his team of scientists observed the incredible! There close by, undulating along like the fabled sea serpent, was an almost transparent 12-meter (40-foot)-long creature about 12 centimeters (5 inches) wide by 20 centimeters (7 to 8 inches) deep. To quote Walford, "I didn't see it at first, because I was busy with our project, but when the thing was pointed out to me there it was. It was somewhat difficult to see because it was transparent. But I finally made a tentative identification of it as what is known as a Venus Girdle, a jellylike creature.

"However, upon examining my scientific references, I soon and surprisingly determined that the Venus Girdle does not grow longer than a few feet. And no amount of research I could do provided me with a proper identification of this very strange creature." Subsequent efforts to observe and photograph the creature were unsuccessful.

Well, there you have it! Imagine if laymen or ordinary seamen had reported sighting an almost transparent 12-meter (40-foot) sea serpent swimming sinuously along, what the response would have been. Impossible! Fraud! Delusion! Hoax! Too much alcoholic refreshment!

But because competent observers were able to label the creature in spite of its unheard-of size, we now know that 12-meter (40-foot) almost transparent "sea serpents" are a reality.

X

United States Lake Monsters

Unidentified monstrous animals in the United States! At face value, that is an absurd idea indeed. Except in a goblin world, to which I do not subscribe, there are no substantiated water monsters in the popular sense in American lakes. What cannot be disputed, however, is that reports of observations of unidentified aquatic or semi-aquatic animals have been and are being made with some regularity. These reports go back to the earliest settlers and even beyond via Indian legends.

What are these reports and what is the real basis for some of those for which we have considerable data? In the pages that follow we will analyze some selected reports and whenever possible provide what I believe to be the correct explanation.

The reports selected are not a statistical sample, but rather have been chosen to illustrate the variety of explanations that play a part in these matters. They range from outright hoaxes to known animals well outside of the normal range of their geographical habitat, to a very few possible still unknown species or varieties of perfectly normal animals, not monsters in any sense. One must be careful how one uses the word "unknown," since in the widest sense any creature, no matter how familiar to science, may be unknown to a particular observer. A true unknown as I wish to define the term means "unknown to science," to the community of scholars and scientists broadly known as zoologists. New kinds of animals are continuously being discovered; recently a new species of shark and a new species of whale have gotten some publicity. This is perhaps not so surprising when we consider the vast volume of the earth's oceans that have not yet been explored by man. However, when we talk about much smaller fresh-water lakes in the United States, the proposition does indeed become highly improbable.

Let us proceed then to investigate some of these reports of so-called lake and river monsters.

Arkansas heads the list as a prolific source of "monster" reports. A variety of unlikely creatures, both terrestrial and aquatic, have been reported from this state. The White River Monster, or the White River Matter, if you prefer, is interesting because, as will emerge, we are apparently dealing with a real animal.

The story begins in July 1937, although claims for earlier observations surfaced after the intense publicity generated in that year. The original observations occurred just below Newport, Arkansas, in a deep part of the White River, a large tributary of the Mississippi. An affidavit was signed by a farmer, Bramblett Bateman.

The descriptive portion of Bateman's affidavit reads as follows:

> I, Bramblett Bateman, state under oath that on or about the first of July 1937, I was standing on the bank of White River about one o'clock and something appeared in the river, about 375 feet from where I was standing, somewhere near the east bank of said river. I saw something appear on the surface of the water. From the best I could tell, from the distance, it would be about 12 feet long and 4 or 5 feet wide. I did not see either head nor tail but it slowly rose to the surface and stayed in this position some five minutes. It did not move up or down the river at this particular time but afterward on different occasions I have seen it move up and down the river, but I never have,

at any time, been able to determine the full length or size of said monster.

Some two weeks ago, from this date, September 22, 1937, I saw the same thing upstream about 200 yards from where it made its first appearance. On the last date that I saw the monster it was in the current of the river. Before it was always seen in the eddy. There is no question in my mind whatever but what this monster remains in this stretch of water as was first seen.

A brief background on Mr. Bateman, obviously to establish him as a solid citizen, follows, including the names of others who according to Bateman have made similar observations. He writes that he knows of at least twenty-five others who would also give affidavits if asked.

Three other affidavits were actually made, one by Bateman's wife, another by J. M. Gawf, and a third by Z. B. Reid. Mrs. Bateman stated that while she had not actually seen the monster, she twice had seen "water boil up across the river about two feet high." Mr. J. M. Gawf, a merchant planter and stock raiser, also reported seeing water boil up about two feet high.

The affidavit of Z. B. Reid, deputy sheriff and law-enforcement officer of Jackson County, Arkansas, is more enlightening:

AFFIDAVIT OF Z. B. REID

I, Z. B. Reid, deputy sheriff and law-enforcement officer of Jackson County, Arkansas, make the following sworn statement:

On or about the last Saturday of June 1937, Bramblett Bateman called at the sheriff's office and asked if we had a high-powered rifle and explained that he wanted it to kill a monster he had seen in White River. I secured a rifle and on the following day, Sunday, in the company of Joe McCartney, another deputy, and Henry Harper went down to the river, about 4 o'clock, and waited until 6 o'clock. We had seen nothing and were getting in the car to go back to town when a little negro said something was coming up. We ran back to the bank and there was a lot of foam and bubbles coming up in a circle about 30 feet in diameter some 300 feet from where we were standing. It did not come up there but appeared about 300 feet upstream. It looked like a large sturgeon or cat fish. It went down in about two minutes. Joe McCartney started to shoot but the gun he carried was not loaded.

There is no doubt in my mind that it was something alive but I do not know what it was. We waited another hour but it did not appear again.

You have my permission to use this for publication.

Signed: Z. B. *Reid*

As attested by numerous newspaper reports, by the end of July 1937 the White River Monster was catapulted into national prominence.

On July 9 a Mrs. Ethel Smith of Little Rock stated she had seen the monster thirteen years earlier, which would be 1924, while she was on a vacation with her husband and children. She described the episode: "The old highway ran right along the riverbank. My husband had stopped for some fishing when the children began yelling about the submarine in the river. It was late in the afternoon and the thing stayed on top of the water about five or ten minutes. It was making a loud blowing noise but never did show its head or tail. It was a terrible-looking thing with dingy gray crusted hide. It frightened me badly."

A George Mann, identified as a White River fisherman, stated he had seen a similar monster at the same location twenty-two years before, or in about 1915.

Observations were too numerous to record here, but a few zoologically important details should be noted. The creature definitely made sounds, quite loud at times, sounding like a cross between a cow's moo and a horse's neigh. The appearance of the creature is always preceded by the appearance of a foamy ring of bubbles, which spread out with the subsequent surfacing of the creature.

These characteristics are most significant and should result in at least a tentative identification. Let us, however, continue with the remaining evidence before we proceed to our identification.

A professional diver, Charles E. Brown of the U. S. Engineers, arrived at Newport about July 20, 1937, determined to make a diving exploration of the river armed with a harpoon. Brown actually made several dives at depths of 15 to 18 meters (50 to 60 feet) but drew a blank.

There the matter rested till the summer of 1971, thirty-four years later. Again the creature or creatures were reported at least seven times to the Newport *Daily Independent*.

The first report was made to Mike Masterson, news editor of the Newport *Daily Independent*. The caller, a prominent citizen, identified himself to Masterson, but wished to remain anonymous.

The episode occurred on June 17, while the observer stood on the bank of the White River south of Newport. Descriptive phrases were "a creature the size of a boxcar thrashing"; "the length of three or four pickup trucks," at least two yards across; "it didn't really have scales"; "but from where I was standing on the shore, about 150 feet away, it looked as if the thing was peeling all over, but it was a smooth type of skin or flesh." The object was first noticed when the water "began to boil up about two or three feet high, then this huge form rolled up and over."

"I was scared . . . when I saw that thing rise up out of the river," he said. "I didn't see his head, but I didn't have to; his body was enough to scare me bad."

The next episode was reported six days later by Ernest Denks of Newport, on June 23. The actual observation was made a week or two earlier. Denks estimated that the animal, gray, real long, with a long, pointed bone protruding from its forehead, would weigh about 450 kilograms (1,000 pounds). He described the creature he had seen as more resembling an animal than a fish.

The next sighting was made by Cloyce Warren, an employee of the White River Lumber Company, with two fishing companions. Not only did they observe the creature, but they were also able to take a photograph. The episode occurred while Warren and his two companions were fishing from a boat just south of the White River bridge. They first were startled by a giant column of water erupting 60 meters (200 feet) from their boat. Warren stated:

83. Newsprint photograph of the White River Monster taken by Cloyce Warren, published by the Newport Daily Independent, Wednesday, June 30, 1971. Warren made the picture with a Polaroid Swinger camera on Monday, June 28, 1971, south of the White River bridge, Newport, Arkansas.

> I didn't know what was happening. This giant form rose to the surface and began moving in the middle of the river away from the boat. It was very long and gray colored. The creature was on the surface of the water only a few seconds. We had taken a little Polaroid Swinger camera with us to take pictures of the fish we caught. I grabbed the camera and managed to get a picture right before it submerged. It appeared to have a spiny backbone that stretched for 30 or more feet. It was hard to make out exactly what the front portion looked like, but it was awful large.

According to Warren the animal made no noise except for the violent splashing and large number of bubbles that surrounded it.

Other pictures were taken by Gary Addington and his stepfather, Lloyd Hamilton, during another episode, when a 3-to-4-meter (10-to-12-foot)-long spiny-backed creature was observed in a deep section of the river near Jacksonport. The pictures were ruined in development by the Newport *Daily Independent* because they were developed as black-and-white film, although they were made with color film.

On July 5 a new aspect was injected into the monster matter. Tracks measuring 35 centimeters by 20 centimeters wide (14 by 8 inches) were discovered on Towhead Island. Plaster casts were made by law-enforcement officers under the direction of Sheriff Ralph Henderson of Jackson County. According to these observers the tracks had three toes with claws on each. There were large pads on the heels and toes with a spur extending at an angle from the heel. After the initial report other witnesses stated that such tracks had been observed during the past two years but nothing had been made of it.

Subsequent investigations of the island revealed another set of prints leading from and back to the water. Small trees were pulled over and a large section of grass bent down as if something had been lying in the area. The obvious conclusion was that tracks and disturbances were made by something very large.

The week of July 21 added another dimension to the by now notorious monster matter. A woodsman and trapper, Ollie Ritcherson, in company with Joey Dupree, a lad of 13, decided to explore by boat in the area where the monster had been observed, especially around Towhead Island, where tracks had been found. While cruising close to the island they collided with and were lifted boat and all on the back of a large animal, which was never, however, clearly observed. The youngster verified that the boat was lifted upward out of the water.

The last sighting for 1971 was made by Jim Gates, a resident of Newport. He described an object about as long as a car, thrashing about for 15 minutes. Gates stated he fished regularly near Jacksonport, 2 miles from Newport, and that after fishing for about 20 minutes late Tuesday afternoon, August 24, something rose suddenly and began thrashing about, bubbling and making tremendous waves. Little detail was visible, as the range was about 180 meters (200 yards), in the middle of the river. He described the color as dark.

One additional sighting was reported the following year, June 5, 1972. The observation was made near Jacksonport Park by R. C. McClauglen of Lincoln, Nebraska. He and his family saw a "giant form rise to the surface of the White River." They watched the thrashing creature for 5 minutes before it submerged. "It was very long and grayish in color. I'd estimate its length at between 60 and 75 feet and I couldn't begin to estimate how much it must have weighed." He added the object appeared to have some type of head and spiny backbone.

The culmination to the White River Monster was that enough serious citizens petitioned the Newport City Board of Directors to declare that portion of White River adjacent to Jacksonport State Park a "White River Monster Refuge and Sanctuary." This idea received wide support resulting in the passage of a resolution to that effect by the Arkansas Senate in 1973. This resolution made it illegal to "molest, kill, trample, or harm the White River Monster while he is in the retreat."

We will now summarize the relevant zoological data that, the reader will see, provide a virtually positive identification of the animal involved.

Monster identikit

BEHAVIOR: When at the surface thrashes about; prior to surfacing water wells up, bubbles spreading in a ring.

SIZE ESTIMATES: 3 to 4 meters (10 to 12 feet) long; 4 meters (12 feet) by 1 to 1½ meters (4 to 5 feet) wide; size of a boxcar (18 meters [60 feet]); length of 3 or 4 pickup trucks, by 2 meters (2 yards) wide; 9 meters (30 feet) long; 18 to 23 meters (60 to 75 feet) long.

WEIGHT ESTIMATES: Very great; 1,000 pounds.

SKIN: Color unanimous agreement gray, except one observer described the color as "dark." No scales; more resembling an animal than a fish. Skin peeling all over, but smooth skin or flesh; dingy-gray crusted hide.

SOUND: Frequently makes sounds, often very loud. In one case a family was kept awake at night by the blowing of the creature; cross between a cow's moo and a horse's neigh.

HABITAT: in river eddies, occasionally in current; in deeper parts of river; in the vicinity of Towhead Island; on land as established by tracks.

HEAD: Usually not seen clearly. When seen had a long, pointed "bone" protruding from forehead.

TRACKS: 35 by 20 centimeters (14 by 8 inches) with evidence of large pads on heels and toes with a spur extending at an angle from the heel; 3 toes with claws on each digit. Large body involved since small trees pushed over; grass bent down as though something were lying down.

A few comments about the data are now in order. Except for size there is a remarkable consistency among the different witnesses over a long time. There can be no doubt that a real animal or animals had been observed.

Size range length varied from 3 meters to 23 meters (10 feet to 75 feet). Since the head and tail were hardly ever observed, the lower limit of 3 meters (10 feet) obviously understates the length. I ask the reader to take my word for the observation that untrained observers estimating size of unknown objects in water range from exactly right to threefold to fivefold too great. This is especially true when the observer has no object of known size with which to make comparison. It is generally not appreciated to what extent we rely on comparison to make size estimates.

We can reasonably suppose that the largest estimates may be overstated by as much as a factor of 5, so that the most probable greatest length of the object would be 6 meters (20 feet), with a minimum of 4 to 5 meters (15 feet), allowing for the unobserved tail and head.

Weight estimates are even more difficult, so that the single estimate of 450 kilograms (1,000 pounds) must be regarded as purely guesswork.

The White River case is a clear-cut instance of a known aquatic animal observed outside of its normal habitat or range and therefore unidentified by the observers unfamiliar with the type. The animal in question clearly was a large male elephant seal, either *Mirounga leonina* (southern species) or *Mirounga angustirostris* (northern species).

From the following description of this animal it will become clear to the reader that this is indeed the kind of animal that has been exciting the population around Newport, Arkansas, from time to time.

Seals are aquatic mammals normally existing in marine conditions rather than in fresh water. However, it is well established that occasionally individuals of a variety of species do enter fresh-water rivers or even lakes. One species of ringed seal, *Pusa sibirica*, is completely adapted to the fresh water of Lake Baikal in Siberia.

While elephant seals are extremely gregarious when on land, at sea they become more solitary creatures, especially the old males, and they are known to wander widely. Even on land individuals have been found 65 kilometers (40 miles) or more from shore. The southern species is very widely spread over a circumpolar area, while the northern form is found mainly along the Mexican and Southern California coast. It is quite conceivable that occasionally a wandering individual finds itself in the mouth of the Mississippi, which it follows, finally appearing in the White River, a large branch of the Mississippi.

The largest of all seals, male elephant seals, may reach lengths of 7 meters (22 feet) and weights of 3600 kilograms (8,000 pounds). The skin is blue-gray to gray, lighter on the underbelly. The northern species is gray when freshly molted but turns more yellowish-brown over time. The skin and hair slough off in patches annually between May and July, which

84. Southern elephant seal, *Mirounga leonina*; large male with female and pup.

of course explains the reported "peeling skin" observations of the White River Monster.

These animals are called elephant seals not only because of their bulk, but because the males have an inflatable proboscis or trunk, which is largest in the northern variety and may hang down in front of the mouth 25 centimeters (1 foot) or more. This structure accounts for the observation of a long, pointed bone protruding from the forehead of the "monster."

Elephant seals are carnivorous, feeding mainly on fish, cuttlefish, and other cephalopods at considerable depths. The preference for feeding on fish at greater depths explains why the White River Monster was more often than not observed surfacing in the deeper parts of the river and why the fishing was reported as poor while the monster was in the area. The mode of surfacing, air bubbles, and water disturbances are all consistent with elephant seal behavior.

The animals are very vocal on occasion; large bulls can be heard over distances of 1 to 2 kilometers (½ mile) or more. A single bull in the White River would have no difficulty keeping a family awake during the night, when stimulated to sound off for one reason or another.

The only other aspect of the monster data to account for is the tracks and disturbed vegetation, the latter needing no comment since a 3,600-kilogram (8,000-pound) bulk dragging over the beach certainly produces the effects described.

The front flippers of elephant seals have five digits, as with all seals; however, pads are well developed to deal with the massive bulk, and the first and fifth toe rays are long, with nails or claws on each digit. The webbing between the digits is much less weight-bearing, and the three-toed appearance results from greater pressure on the more pronounced forward three digits, with the fifth producing a spurlike mark.

From the foregoing the reader can hardly fail to be convinced that one or more elephant seals wandering into the White River are indeed the White River Monster. It would appear that these animals have occasionally made even further excursions inland, since we have very similar reports from Alkali Lake, Nebraska, which would also be accessible from the Mississippi River, especially when we remember that elephant seals are known to move over land as much as 65 kilometers (40 miles) when so inclined.

I will not burden the reader with further extensive reports from this area, but describe only one episode experienced by J. A. Johnson and printed in the New York *Times* and other papers on July 25, 1923. The observation was made on the shore of Alkali Lake near May Springs, Nebraska. Johnson and two companions had come to the lake to camp and hunt. They arose early in preparation for the duck flights, walking along the shore of the lake, when suddenly, coming around a slight rise in the ground, they came upon this animal, nearly three fourths out of the shallow water near the shore. They were less than 18 meters (20 yards) from him.

The animal was probably forty feet long, including the tail and the head, when raised in alarm as when he saw us. In general appearance the animal was not unlike an alligator, except that the head was stubbier, and there seemed to be a projection like a horn between the eyes and nostrils. The animal was built much more heavily throughout than an alligator. Its color seemed a dull gray or brown.

There was a very distinctive and somewhat unpleasant odor noticeable for several moments after the beast had vanished into the water. We stood for several minutes after the animal had gone, hardly knowing what to do or say, when we noticed several hundred feet out from shore a considerable commotion in the water.

Sure enough the animal came to the surface, floated there a moment and then lashed the water with its tail, suddenly dived and we saw no more of him.

The Alkali Lake sea elephant (monster) needs no further comment.

To keep out contrasts sharp, the next case on our docket has quite a different explanation.

On the evening of July 13, 1855, a group of "honest, temperate and industrious" men and boys who were out fishing on Silver Lake in Wyoming County, New York, sighted an 18-meter (60-foot)-long monster that allegedly chased them to shore.

After this first incident others reported seeing something in the lake. The object was described as a serpent of 18 to 30 meters (60 to 100 feet), shiny, dark green with yellow spots, and having flaming red eyes and a mouth and huge fins.

The village at the tip of the lake, known as Perry, became the center of great interest, thousands of persons visiting the area in the hope of seeing the strange creature. Expeditions to investigate the phenomenon were uniformly unsuccessful.

Two years later the explanation for the observations was discovered accidentally, as the result of a fire on December 19, 1857, when Walker House, a local hotel in Perry, burned down. In the debris left by the fire were found the remains of the Silver Lake Monster. The perpetrators of the hoax, Truman S. Gillett and A. B. Walker, owner of Walker House, confessed that they had built the monster out of waterproof canvas, paint, and wire. The monster was made to surface periodically by forcing air via a hose into the monster, which was then towed about by means of ropes. We can surmise that Walker's hotel did a booming business for the two years prior to the fire, which resulted in the exposé.

What generates the tradition of strange creatures in certain lakes and rivers, when later investigations show that in fact there are no strange creatures or ever have been? The reasons vary, of course, but more often than not the primary sources are Indian tales and legends. This is not to suggest that these legends have no objective bases; rather, what Indian legend may describe as "monster" may in reality have quite a different explanation.

One of the most interesting cases concerns two small lakes in northern Indiana: Lake Manitou (Devil's Lake) near Rochester, and Bass Lake, which may also have been known as Cedar Lake. There seems to be some confusion, since the lake currently known as Cedar Lake is quite different, located just south of the city of Hammond. The bases for a monster tradition at these lakes were the legends of the Potawatomi, who were shamefully removed from the area in 1838, two years after their land had been purchased by the Indian agent, Colonel Abel C. Pepper, at one dollar per acre.

The religious tradition of the Indians included great awe for the shores and waters of the lakes, upon which they would never encamp. Allegedly the Indian word for one or both lakes was "Mani-i-tou-hen," meaning Lake of the Devil's Bones. A gigantic creature inhabited the lake, which was held in great terror. Few if any Indians would dare to venture out onto the lake in a canoe, nor would they fish or bathe in its waters.

The clue to how this tradition evolved lies in the Devil's Bones, which undoubtedly are the fairly widespread remains of mastodon bones found throughout the area, including the shores of the lakes in question. The massive bones of these elephantine monsters, unfamiliar to the Indians as living forms, must have inspired the savages with religious awe and fear. What would be more logical than that they were the bones of lake monsters that had died over the years? This belief in the lake monsters was transmitted to the settlers and serves as the psychological background for later circumstances and events to take on the character of monster observations such as the following (c. 1828):

I have been informed that Austin W. Morris, who completed the survey of the lake for the erection of the mills, said that several of his flag-men, while assisting in its survey had become alarmed and made to shore, declaring that they had seen a monster in the water—and for a while it was difficult for him to get a man to carry the red flag. Whether they really saw anything terrible in the water, or their fears were merely the result of an excited imagination, after hearing the Indian legends, Mr. Morris never pretended to say.

Another report includes a statement that a line of the length of 40 fathoms (240 feet) was dropped without effect. Actually the maximum depth of Lake Manitou is no more than 15 meters (50 feet).

Another report alleges that when the Pottawattamie Mills (a corn mill and blacksmith shop) were constructed at the outlet of the lake, the monster was seen by workmen under the supervision of General Milroy.

Fishermen named Robinson were fishing in the lake, when they beheld with surprise the even surface of the water ruffled by something swimming rapidly, and which they suppose must have measured 60 feet. The Robinsons are respectable men, whose fears are not easily excited; yet such was the terror which this nondescript caused, that they made a hastry retreat to the shore, much alarmed. Since this circumstance took place, and but a few days since, Mr. Lindsey, who is well known here, was riding near the margin of the lake, when he saw, at the distance of 200 feet from him, some animal raise its head 3 or 4 feet above the surface of the water. He felt the security of the shore, and viewed the mysterious creature many minutes; when it disappeared and reappeared three times in succession. The head he described as being about 3 feet across the frontal bone, and having something of the contour of a "beef's head," but the neck tapering, and having the character of a serpent; color dingy, with large bright yellow spots. It turned its head from side to side with an easy motion, in apparent survey of the surrounding objects. Mr. L. is entitled to credibility. So convinced are many of the existence of the monster that some gentlemen in town have proposed an expedition to the lake, and by the aid of rafts to make an effort to capture the mysterious being which is a terror to the superstitious, but which becomes an object of interest to science, the naturalist, and philosopher.

The above report was in the last of three reports published in the *Telegraph* of Logansport, Indiana, July 21, 1838, and signed "A Visitor to the Lake." According to Donald Smalley, who published an article entitled "The Logansport *Telegraph* and the Monster of the Indian Lakes" in 1946, the articles were probably written by John B. Dillon, one of the editors of the *Telegraph* at the time.

The general tone and vagueness of the reports, in some cases second- and thirdhand, and the concomitant circumstances, in contrast to the White River data, all should suggest to the reader that there are not and never have been unidentified aquatic monsters or animals in these northern Indiana lakes.

In North Carolina, where the Valley River joins the Hiwassee, is a place known to the Cherokee Indians as Tlanusiyi (the Leech Place). John Parris of the Asheville *Citizen-Times* wrote on January 10, 1971, as follows:

CHEROKEES HAVE OWN LOCH NESS MONSTER

MURPHY—Most folks know about the Loch Ness Monster, but few have ever heard of the Great Leech of Valley River.

And yet the story of the Great Leech was old when the tale of the Loch Ness Monster was new.

Since time out of memory the spot where the Valley River joins the Hiwassee has been known to the Cherokee Indians as Tlanusiyi, the Leech Place.

Here a ledge of rock runs across the stream. The Indians used to use it as a sort of bridge.

On the south side there was an Indian trail that ascended a high bank, from which those traversing it could look down into the water.

One day, a group of Cherokee braves going along the trail

saw a great red object, fully as large as a house, lying on the rock ledge in the middle of the stream below them.

They halted in awe and stood wondering what it could be. And as they watched, the great mass began to unroll and they saw it was alive.

They watched it stretch itself out along the rock until it looked like a great leech with red and white stripes along its body.

It rolled up into a ball and again stretched out at full length.

At last it crawled down the rock and disappeared into the deep water.

The water began to boil and foam, and a great column of white spray was thrown into the air.

The Cherokee braves turned and ran back up the trail.

The column of water came down like a waterspout on the very spot where they had been standing. Only their alertness had kept them from being swept off the trail and into the stream.

But others who traveled the trail were not so fortunate.

Many an Indian was carried into the stream in this manner.

Later their bodies were found lying upon the bank with the ears and nose eaten off.

In time, folks steered clear of the trail. They refused to cross the ledge anymore because of the Great Leech.

But there was one brave who laughed at the story.

He said he was not afraid of anything in Valley River.

"I will show you," he said.

So one day he painted his face, like he was going on the warpath or to a great ritual, and put on his finest buckskins.

Then he headed toward the river. Folks from the village followed at a distance to see what would happen.

Down the trail went the brave and out upon the ledge of rock, singing:

> "I'll tie red leech skins
> On my legs for garters.
> I'll tie red leech skins
> On my legs for garters."

But before he was halfway across, the water began to boil into white foam and a great wave rose and swept over the rock and carried him down, and he was never seen again.

Just before the Great Removal of the Cherokees to Oklahoma in 1835, two Indian women went out upon the ledge to fish.

Their friends warned them of the danger, but one woman who had a baby on her back said:

"There are fish there and I'm going to have some. I'm tired of eating fat meat."

She laid the child down on the rock and was preparing her fishing line when the water suddenly rose and swept over the ledge.

The mother saw it just in time, grabbed the child, and ran up the trail to safety.

The Great Leech is still there.

For when people look down they see something moving about on the bottom.

And although they cannot distinguish its shape because of the ripples on the water, they know it is the Great Leech.

Some say there is an underground waterway across to the Nottely River, not far above the mouth, and sometimes the Great Leech goes over there and makes the water boil as it used to at the rock ledge.

That place also is called Tlanusiyi.

One more example of Indian legend water monster, this time from Wisconsin, will suffice to give a representative sampling of this type of monster-generating lore. According to legend, a destructive water monster inhabits Lake Koshkoning. The legend establishes the atmosphere in which the relatively ordinary occurrences are interpreted with "goblin world" mentality.

Carp fishermen relate how their seine engaged a very large water animal which completely wrecked its meshes. It may have been a huge pickerel, but they thought otherwise from the way it twisted and tore the stout seine. . . .

A farmer living on the west side of this big lake was quite sure that this same animal devoured several of his pigs which were feeding offshore. Others saw a strange water animal they could not identify off the mouth of Koshkoning Creek.

The above quotes from an article entitled "Sea Serpents, Wisconsin Occurrences of These Weird Water Monsters" by Charles E. Brown, published by the Wisconsin Folklore Society, illustrate the basis for a monster atmosphere, so that

ordinary events, because of psychological bias, may be interpreted as something unrealistic and marvelous.

Lest I leave the impression with the reader that this is always
the case, I will describe the real "monsters" occasionally
reported from farmers' ponds and other bodies of fresh water.

On Wednesday, July 12, 1967, several midwestern newspapers printed an article entitled "Farmer Battles Pond 'Monsters.' " The article describes the experience of a farmer from
Dewitt, Missouri. "Farmer Robert P. Stark insists he has
'monsters' in his farm pond—no matter what long name the
scientists have for them. He says the jellylike organisms are
eating his fish."

The "monster" was identified by fisheries biologist William
Plieger, but Stark was not happy with the information. He
stated, "I don't care what the guy says, I doubt if anybody
knows anything for sure. Why, I seen one of the monsters out
there looked to me like it would weigh 700, maybe 800 pounds."

Now, the farmer's statements contained both fact and error.
First, the animals he described are common and widely
distributed in bodies of fresh water, both stagnant and fresh,
but are rarely seen in as conspicuous a large mass as he
correctly described. The animals, known as *Pectinatella magnifica*, are tiny colonial creatures that secrete a common
gelatinous mass that is usually small, a few centimeters or
inches in diameter, attached to a twig, a rock, or a plant in a
pond, stream, or lake.

In early spring, depending on the climate, the *Pectinatella*
begin to grow and secrete jelly when water temperature rises
to 16 to 19° C (61 to 66° F). The jelly is transparent, 99.7 per
cent water, with a layer of animals embedded in the outer
surface, all facing outward in the same direction, which may
give a brown color running to reds and greens. In this form
the creatures escape notice except by zoologists and nature
students.

Occasionally, when conditions are just right, they form large
masses, 1 meter to 2 meters (1 yard to 2 yards) in diameter,
forming huge blobs. The adults cannot move about, but feed
by ingesting microscopic organisms that are present in their

85. Aquatic colony of *Pectinatella magnifica* growing on a small waterlogged tree branch. Under the right conditions, these colonies may grow to large size, 2, to 3 meters (6 to 9 feet) in diameter, weighing up to 350 kilograms (800 pounds).

surroundings. They cannot eat fish, even the smallest of which are many times the size of an individual in the larger colony. Normally these creatures present no hazard to man, although they may clog sewers and drainage pipes.

In the summer of 1928 they grew in these great numbers, forming large masses, in a lake formed by damming a river near Independence, Iowa. Late in summer, especially after heavy rains, the jellylike masses began floating down the river, clogging the sluice gates of a hydroelectric plant newly constructed at the dam. For a period of weeks it was necessary for a team of men to constantly clear away the masses of *Pectinatella*.

The similarity of this rapid growth and appearance to the proverbial Hollywood science fiction "blob," which grows without restraint and eats everything in sight, certainly is suggestive to anyone unfamiliar with the creatures.

What exactly are these animals? The farmer thought that no one really knew. Actually he was partially correct, in that their exact affinities are unclear. They belong to a group of animals known as moss animals or "ectoprocts," meaning with external anus, and they do have a true body cavity, which distinguishes them from other animals with a superficially similar appearance. The best we can say is that they represent one of several lines of evolution derived from primitive one-celled animals long ago in the pre-Cambrian. Of living forms their closest relatives appear to be a group of solitary marine worms known as *Phoronida*, and one assumes that our fresh-water "moss animals" were also derived from some ancient marine forms, although there is no fossil record to support this conclusion.

Up to now we have concluded that reports of U.S. lake monsters are either due to Indian legends, hoaxes, or known life forms unfamiliar to the observers. Are there any cases where none of these explanations are probable and that we may indeed be up against a true unknown?

Possibly the best such case involves Lake Champlain in Vermont. Again Gary S. Mangiacopra has done a yeoman's job in collecting and sorting out all available data, and I will be leaning heavily on the information he has so generously shared with me.

Compared to the lakes we have so far discussed, Lake Champlain is very large, over 150 kilometers (100 miles) long, very narrow at its southernmost tip, gradually widening to a maximum of 21 kilometers (13 miles). It is quite deep in parts, up to 125 meters (400 feet). Most of the lake is in New York State, although the northernmost tip, which drains into the St. Lawrence, is in Canada.

A great deal has been written about the Lake Champlain monsters, but little serious work except that of Gary Mangiacopra and Joe Zarzynski has been done. This is understandable, since aquatic investigations in large, deep lakes are time-consuming and expensive and require high technology. Mangiacopra and Zarzynski have gathered the available data, including tracking down eyewitnesses so as to obtain firsthand reports.

This case is of particular interest to me because of the similarities to and differences from the phenomena in Loch Ness, Scotland. There the first recorded observation was made by St. Columba sometime before A.D. 565. In the case of Lake Champlain, the first observation was made in 1609 by the explorer Samuel de Champlain, for whom the lake is named. He observed a 6-meter-long (20-foot-long) snakelike creature with a horselike head. Mangiacopra and Zarzynski have collected reports that span the period between July 22, 1819, and the present. The persistence of the phenomena over time argues for an objective basis for these observations.

Of some twenty-seven reports two have been dismissed as probable hoaxes and six as known animals, leaving nineteen unexplained. We will not bore the reader with the complete details of each report, but confine ourselves to an identification of the creatures. The reader should be aware that we are assuming on the basis of the evidence that a real animal is involved. Certainly there is a body of opinion that holds that there is no substance to these observations. To individuals holding this view, what follows is of course nonsense and they need read no farther.

I will proceed first to note especially significant aspects as reported and then to summarize overall features, size, shape, color, and the like.

One of the earliest reports, by a party of six on August 30, 1878, from a small yacht, includes references to "two large folds just back of the head projecting above the water, and at some distance, say 50 feet or more behind, two or more folds at what was apparently the tail."

On May 20, 1960, a Mr. and Mrs. Patch stopped along the lake near the town of Albany for a picnic. These observers definitely report "vertical humps" ⅔ meter (2 feet) in the air, indicating vertical flexure, in contrast to the horizontal flexure of eels and snakes. The Patches were interviewed by Zarzynski.

On May 17, 1920, a group of friends and relatives including a Mrs. Grace Lee, while fishing near the town of Isle la Motte, reported observing a snake or eel-like animal 4½ to 6 meters (15 to 20 feet) long. Mangiacopra corresponded with Mrs. Lee, who provided details of the observation, some of them contradictory. The head was periodically elevated above the water, eyes and nostrils were noted in position regarded as usual by laymen. The mouth was closed and did not reach beyond the eyes. This latter feature would be important; however, since the viewing was from a distance of 100 meters (300 feet) or so and the mouth was not observed to open, the actual extent of the mouth gape cannot be reliably inferred. There is general agreement that vertical humps or flexure was observed, but Mrs. Lee also states that the animal swam in a wriggling, sideways manner at a slow rate of speed (less than 10 kilometers per hour [6 miles per hour]).

Another sighting made in July of 1973 refers to a gray dorsal fin. The last sightings recorded by Mangiacopra occurred in 1975.

The features based on the overall consensus consist of a head not much differentiated from the neck, eyes not large, nostrils; body snakelike, elongated, flexing vertically; overall length 4 to 30 meters (10 to 90 feet); diameter 25 to 60 centimeters (1 foot to the diameter of a barrel); color dark, gray to black or greenish black, skin texture smooth, no scales, tail pointed, flattened when observed.

Taken all together, the above features are very much like those we attributed to the primitive whales known as *Basilosaurus*, suggested as a possible explanation for the creatures observed along the British Columbia coast in Chapter II. In fact, Mangiacopra has suggested that a smaller variety adapted to fresh water may be responsible for the Lake Champlain monster sightings.

The two "folds" behind the head may well represent the front appendages, while the tail "folds" described may be the tail flukes, flattened top to bottom. The pointed tail observation may occur when only one of the flukes is seen out of the water at an oblique angle.

The Lake Champlain monster appears to be both persistent and relatively consistent so that a fully mounted investigation would be worthwhile.

The reports that have been analyzed in this chapter are only a small fraction of the recorded data. Anyone interested enough to take the time could turn up dozens of additional incidents. The following list certainly is not exhaustive, but can be a starting point for anyone interested in trying some zoological sleuthing or in some cases explaining a mystery that may not turn out to have a zoological aspect at all.

The list that follows indicates the name of the lake, a nearby town or city, and the date, often approximate, for the most recent monster report. In some cases active research is in progress, but in most cases these are virgin territory.

> Alaska: Illiamna Lake, September 7, 1975
> Arkansas: Conway, Lake Conway, July 21, 1974
> California: Elizabeth Lake, May 1890
>   Lafayette, Lafayette Lake, October 30, 1975
> Connecticut: Danbury, Lake Kenosha, November 11, 1891
> Florida: Jacksonville, St. Johns River, June 12, 1975
> Idaho: McCall, Payette Lake, 1952
> Illinois: Du Quoin, Stump or Flat Pond, July 14, 1968
> Kentucky: Harrington Lake, recent?
> Kentucky Lake, recent?
> Montana: Hamilton, Lake Chelan, November 19, 1892
>   Polson, Flathead Lake, September 1974
>   Currently being investigated by
>   Tim Church
>   603 Overlook Way No. 4
>   Missoula, Mont. 59801
> New Jersey: Trenton, Old Mill Pond, March 1, 1975
> Utah: Logan, Bear Lake, June 19, 1946
> Wisconsin: Madison, Lake Mendota, 1917
>   Madison, Lake Monona, June 12, 1897
>   Edwards Park, Lake Waubesa, 1922?
>   Lake Keonsa, ?

Lake Wingra, ?
Rock Lake, August 31, 1882
Red Cedar Lake, 1941
Waukesha, Pewaukee Lake, 1890s
Oconomowoc Lake, 1890s
Sheboygan, Elkhart Lake, ?
Lake Geneva, around 1900?
Delavan Lake, around 1900?
Lake Michigan, June 25, 1976
   Makinac Straits and Lake Huron,
   near Cheboygan, Michigan
Evanston, Lake Michigan, August 8, 1867
Milwaukee, Jones Island, 1905?

XI

Canadian Lake Monsters

The Naitaka are real animals. That is my opinion after reviewing the available evidence. Most readers probably have never heard of Naitaka, Na-ha-ha-itkh, N'ha-a-ith, or N'hahtik, but have heard of the Canadian Okanagan Lake Monster, popularly known as Ogopogo. The term "Ogopogo" is of recent origin, whereas the Indian name Naitaka and its variations go back hundreds of years. "Ogopogo" was the appellation invented by Rotarian William Brimblecombe in 1926 and used in his "Ogopogo Song," a parody of a popular English tune. The press picked up the term and it has been in vogue ever since.

I hope to lead the reader to the conclusion that there is a serious side to this nonsense and that there is in reality a small population of aquatic fish-eating animals residing in Lake Okanagan and perhaps a few other Canadian lakes. And I will suggest what these creatures most probably are.

After fifteen years researching Loch Ness and its so-called monsters, I was struck by the remarkable parallels in both cases. Until recently, prior to studying the Lake Okanagan data carefully, I had glibly assumed, admittedly with some reason, that we were dealing with the same kind of animal. Now, as will become clear as we go along, there is some difficulty in maintaining that view. Let us back up, however,

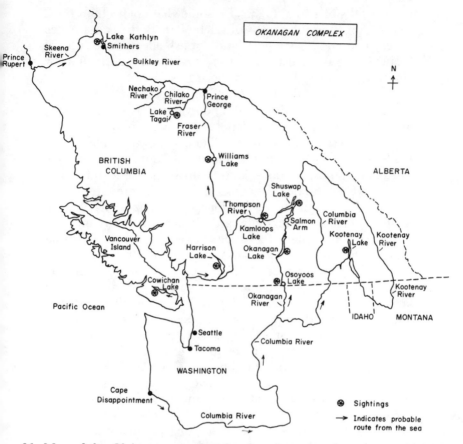

86. Map of the Okanagan complex showing the connecting system of lakes and rivers linking sightings of Naitaka-like animals to each other and the sea. The probable path of the animals is indicated by arrows, leading from the sea along the British Columbian coast.

and start at the beginning. Lake Okanagan, like Loch Ness, is cold and deep, some 125 kilometers (79 miles) long by 3 kilometers (2 miles) wide, with the greatest depth at some 250 meters (800 feet). Compare Loch Ness: 38 kilometers (24 miles) by 0.6 kilometers (1 mile) by 215 meters (700 feet). Okanagan never freezes over in winter and has a constant temperature in its depths of 1 to 2° C (34° F), somewhat colder than the 4 to 5° C (42° F) in the depths of Loch Ness. Both lakes are well oxygenated and have a population of fish adequate to support a small colony of fish predators, maintained ultimately by connections through rivers to the sea.

As to the evidence for something unusual in these lakes, there is a marked difference. The evidence from Okanagan without exception is soft, anecdotal, hardly the proper material for rigorous scientific analysis. Those who are familiar with Loch Ness know that in addition to anecdotal data we have still photographs, motion-picture film sequences, and repro-ducible sonar (underwater sound) data. There are a few purported photographs of the Ogopogo phemonena, but all of the available photographs are pictures of disturbances in the water, rather than of any actual object. It may well be that these disturbances were caused by some kind of aquatic creature, but experience at Loch Ness has taught us that all kinds of natural phenomena are responsible for many honest but mistaken observations. So we will discount these pictures and also the one-minute color-film sequence made by Arthur Folden, a sawmill worker, in August of 1968. According to Mary Moon, the author of the book *Ogopogo*, Arthur Folden and his film have both disappeared. The controversy and criticism of the film appear to have been the major factors responsible for Arthur Folden's withdrawal from the public eye. However, a careful reading of descriptions of what the film showed convinces me that nothing of consequence has been lost, since the film appears to have also been a record of a disturbance, rather than of the creature or creatures proper. One cannot, of course, be certain that a thorough, professional analysis might not have yielded some valuable information.

The anecdotal evidence begins, as is so often the case, with Indian legends. These date back at least to the latter part of the seventeenth century. There are a variety of these, explain-ing from the Indian viewpoint some aspect or other of the lake demon or monster. In most cases these legends are miraculous in content and provide few clues as to the nature of any possible unusual animals in the lake. There are at least three

87. Petroglyph of the Naitaka from
Lake Okanagan.

crude pictographs on rocks around the lake, now in an
extremely poor state of preservation, which may be related to
an alleged lake monster. The relationship is tenuous and can
be inferred only from the nature and location of the pictographs
themselves. Mary Moon describes one as depicting a horselike
left profile with horns or upstanding ears, one hump, and a
forked tail. Associated with this drawing is another one showing
a creature "stealing" away through the weeds. Aside from the
impression of a serpentlike configuration, including appendages that might be interpreted as flippers, the forked-tail aspect
is very interesting and crucial for our analysis, as will emerge
later.

Over the years between 1700 and the present, almost two
hundred reports or observations of the Ogopogo are on record.
It would be a boring and nonproductive exercise to review all
of these; rather we will confine our attention to those that
have descriptive content that aid in building up a picture of
the creatures. However, before I do that, I ought to state
briefly why I think real animals are involved, and address the
idea that a hoax or fraud may be responsible for the sightings.

When sightings of purported phenomena are related to a
particular geographic locality and persist over a period of
several hundred years, one can hardly dismiss them as ongoing

hoaxes, illusion, or human idiosyncrasies or psychological aberrations. It would literally take generations of affluent nitwits with unlimited funds and technology far in advance of their time plus a phenomenal public-relations and security capability to establish and maintain such a hoax. In other words, it is simply not possible. An occasional caper or trick to test public gullibility or to fool the "expert"—yes, but not almost two hundred sightings over two hundred or more years.

The reader may agree up to this point, but could there be a fantastic yet trivial explanation? Certainly this possibility must be kept in mind when investigating a cryptozoological mystery. A good example was the report by natives of a seasonal many-humped monster in an African lake, which upon investigation turned out to be two or more male crocodiles pursuing a female during the mating season. Similarly, a small number of sea-serpent reports describing a series of vertical loops with a small fin on each loop most probably result from observing a string of dolphins (Illustration 78).

In the case of the Okanagan phenomena there does not appear to be such a deceptive explanation. By focusing on the most descriptive anecdotal evidence, a picture of the Okanagan creature can be built up that ought to result in identification if a known animal type, living or extinct, is involved.

A most important observation was made by Mr. and Mrs. Leslie L. Kerry of South Kelowna and Mr. and Mrs. W. F. Watson of Montreal and their children. The episode occurred at 7 P.M. on July 2, 1949, just as Mr. Kerry was taking his friends, the Watson family, out in his boat. Note that the observation was made by several people at close range, 30 meters (100 feet), which is optimal.

The animal was lying low in the water, showing about 9 meters (30 feet), diameter of one part of the snakelike body being 20 to 30 centimeters (8 to 12 inches). There appears to be some confusion as to whether the circumference or diameter was specified. Mary Moon states, "between eight and twelve inches around," which contradicts other reports. Diameter seems the best interpretation. In any case anecdotal estimates of size are just guesses, varying widely in accuracy.

No appendages were observed, but the tail was observed and definitely described as "forked." The forked or bilobate tail feature is extremely important and was described as going up and down. This kind of configuration and motion is restricted to certain aquatic mammals—cetacea (whales), sirenians (sea cows), and possibly certain pinnipeds (seals).

According to Mary Moon, Kerry wanted to get a camera from the house, but did not want to miss seeing the head if it came up, as it was then presumably submerged for feeding. Kerry chose not to run for a camera but asked Watson to row the boat closer to get a better view. Watson rowed only slightly closer, fearing to scare his children, also in the boat. Periodically the group observed vertical undulations, at least three each about 1.5 meters (5 feet) in length. Frequently the entire body sank beneath the surface.

Up to this point the animal was observed at close range not for a fleeting moment but for five to ten minutes. Initially Mrs. Kerry was up at the house, but she came down in response to her husband's call. She viewed the animal briefly and ran back for binoculars, also telephoning her neighbors, Dr. Stanley and Mrs. Joyce Underhill, who also came out to the beach with binoculars.

By now the creature had been in view at least fifteen minutes. The Underhills also observed the creature through binoculars, but at a greater distance, since the water had become choppy and the creature had moved off into deeper water, where it was seen to dive and disappear, but shortly surfaced again swimming and creating a wake. The Underhills thought they saw fish jumping in the vicinity of the swimming animal. Underhill described the body as smooth and black with undulations about 2 meters (7 feet) long with no estimate of thickness as the undulations or coils protruded no more than 30 centimeters (1 foot) above the surface. He further suggested that more than one animal was involved, since the separation between some coils was in his judgment too great for all to belong to the same individual. There are a number of additional reports that also describe at least two separate creatures appearing simultaneously. Whether or not Underhill was right we do not know, except that if the phenomenon in Lake Okanagan is animal in nature, a small, stable population rather than a single individual must certainly obtain.

The next report, although brief, is very important and dates from 1967, a year when only two sighting reports were recorded. The sighting was made by Mr. and Mrs. John Durrant, residents of White Rock, British Columbia, from shore at Naramata, a small town at the southern tip of Lake Okanagan. The object was viewed at a range of about 185 meters (200 yards) on a calm, sunny day early in the afternoon. They observed an 8-meter (25-foot) humped, serpentlike animal that left a wake as it moved. Binoculars were used during part of the eight-second sighting. According to Mary Moon the animal was trying to get at a school of fish but submerged when a motorboat approached. Fifteen other people, nearby cannery employees, also observed the same creature.

The importance of this sighting is that the animal was observed to "spout water" or "blow." I will quote Mrs. Durrant on this point. "It had a head like a bucket and *was spouting water* [my emphasis]. It was something more than a big fish. I just don't know what you would call it. It was very weird. We've seen whales and seals and things, but it was nothing like that. This was something different." Another piece in the identity jigsaw puzzle!

Another important factor we need to consider is how amphibious are these animals—that is, are they completely aquatic or do they also come out on land, and if so, how frequently? In the case of the Loch Ness animals, eighteen land sightings have been reported, which is a significantly larger proportion than in the case of Ogopogo. I know of only two, which are also reported by Mary Moon. In both cases the reports were made by young children, which may raise doubts in the minds of some. The Indian legends also leave the impression that the creatures do come out on land, although rarely. One legend on a more sanguinary note has it that certain rocks on a small island in Lake Okanagan between Penticton and Sunnyside represent the place where the Naitaka devours its prey, leaving piles of bleached bones.

Getting back to our two land-sighting reports, the first is very vague, recorded by Mary Moon on page 80 of her book *Ogopogo*. It states that Ernest A. Lording's daughter at the age of eight saw an enormous something on the beach at the mouth of Mission Creek. She and the little friend who was with her at the time both screamed and became hysterical. Mr. Lording himself has observed Ogopogo many times. Precious little on which to base any conclusion.

The second report, page 56 of *Ogopogo*, comes from Audrey Gellatly, daughter of Mr. and Mrs. David Gellatly. Now Mrs. John Weinard of Kamloops, she was only a child in 1935 when she took a walk northward along the lake from the pilothouse on Gellatly Point, where she lived with her parents. She came to the place where the yacht club is now, where Powers Creek empties into Okanagan Lake, when a "log" that had been lying on the sandy point suddenly slithered into the water. Frightened, the child ran the half mile home.

Further data that bear on possible amphibious behavior concern the matter of footprints. A number of reports of strange footprints have been attributed to the Naitaka. The descriptions vary from "cup shaped," 15 centimeters (6 inches) across, with a pad foot and 8 toes, to an irregularly shaped configuration, 46 centimeters (18 inches) by 30 centimeters (12 inches). The latter were discovered around a wharf in a 1-meter (3-foot) depth of water. Although the "prints" were 15 centimeters (6 inches) in depth, some of the irregularity might be due to water action. Jack J. Fuhr, around whose wharf the prints were found, stated that the sand was firm so that the prints must have been made by something with considerable body weight.

The trouble with footprints is that anyone can fake them easily. Further, to assume that they were made by Naitaka is pure conjecture and supposition—certainly possible but without even a circumstantial link to the two cases cited of direct land sightings.

Another case reported by Moon has a little bit for eveyone. "The late Miss Candace McDougald (who was for many years the postmistress of Peachland) and a friend saw Ogopogo at six on a morning several years ago. It seems that Ogopogo was partly out of the water and was surveying Peachland. She said that they had found tracks in the sand of the beach. Unfortunately, she did not dare tell anyone about this until long after the incident. Local gossips around Peachland say the tracks were three-toed . . . like the dinosaur footprints in front of the provincial museum in Victoria." From eight toes to the proverbial three toes! It need hardly be stated that the foregoing leaves a very great deal to be desired as evidence, and the best we can do with it is keep an open mind toward the possibility that the Naitaka has at most a limited amphibious capability. I will not tax the reader with any more of two hundred eyewitness descriptions, but rather proceed to build a word picture of the Naitaka and its habits. If the reader recalls Chapters II and X, a unique identification should be obvious.

The Naitaka live in very cold, fresh water that is inhabited by a large fish population, including the Kokanee salmon. There is a connection to the sea over a somewhat tortuous route.

The animals when at the surface usually show vertical flexure—that is, one to five vertical humps or coils, occasionally more (but probably more than one individual is involved in those cases). Observers are unanimous and specific that the undulations are not horizontal like a snake or eel.

Propulsion appears to depend on the up-and-down movement of a powerful forked tail. The impression is given of at least one pair of forelimbs, variously interpreted as fins, flippers, or legs. Hind limbs have never been observed, although observers have indirectly inferred these from water disturbances toward the rear of the animal. That the animal can at times swim at great speeds, at least up to 40 kilometers per hour (25 miles per hour), is clearly established. Greater speeds have been reported, but we know from experience that speed estimates over water are usually high. A water skier moving at 30 kilometers per hour (20 miles per hour) seems to be literally flying. Nevertheless, fairly high speeds have been established by the ability of the animals to keep pace with occasional power boats moving at known speeds.

The creatures are almost completely aquatic, although rare occasional excursions onto beach areas cannot be ruled out. As a consequence reproduction must be achieved by live births in the water. Small versions of the adults have been reported and are presumably juveniles. There is no evidence of reproduction along the shore in the form of eggs, or observations onshore, in spite of two or three tenuous reports of unexplained tracks.

The animals look most like a log, elongated, serpentine, no thickened body centrally, about 12 meters (40 feet) long, although a range of smaller sizes has been reported and a few larger, up to say 20 meters (70 feet). The head tapers toward the snout and is somewhat flattened top to bottom. Comparison is most often made to the head of a horse, sheep, or alligator. Eyes are definitely reported large enough to be clearly noted. Very occasionally a pair of protuberances referred to as "ears" or "horns" have been noted. Nostrils have not been reported as such, but "blowing" has been observed, although rarely.

The skin is described as dark green to green-black or brown to black and dark brown. Occasionally the color is given as gray to blue-black or even a golden brown. Most often the skin is smooth with no scales, although part of the body must possess a few plates, scales, or similar structures observed by close-up viewers and compared to the lateral scutes of sturgeon. Most of the back is smooth, although a portion is saw-toothed, ragged-edged, or serrated. Sparse hair or hair-bristle structures are reported around the head, and in a few cases a mane or comblike structure has been observed at the back of the neck. The food appears to be fish, since a number of people have observed behavior that can best be attributed to an active fish predator.

In reviewing the two hundred or more descriptive reports I was struck by repetitive consistency of the descriptions, almost to the point of boredom. The characteristics as outlined fit one and only one known creature, either living or as deduced from the fossil record. The fit is so remarkably good that there can be hardly any doubt that the Naitakas are a small population of primitive whales (cetaceans) belonging to

the group known as archeoceti, specifically *Basilosaurus cetoides*, or a closely related form. We have already suggested
that the marine animals observed along the British Columbian
coast are of this nature and that the fresh-water creatures in
Lake Champlain are similar, as suggested by Mangiacopra.

Next I will briefly outline the relevant characteristics of
Basilosaurus or "zeuglodons" as established in the zoological
literature so that the reader may see for himself just how
remarkably well the data correspond with the Naitakas. Since
only fossilized skeletal remains have up to now been available
for study, behavior and the nature of soft parts have had to
be inferred from the fossils themselves, associated artifacts,
localities and nature of deposits, and from living forms of
cetaceans, which are represented by two main groups: the
Baleen whales and the toothed whales, which include porpoises
and dolphins. Usually whales are thought of as being exclusively marine, and for the larger modern species this is certainly
true. However, it does not follow that there should not be or
have not been fresh-water forms of more primitive types. As
a matter of fact, the four major groups of aquatic mammals
all have fresh-water forms, the cetaceans being no exception.
It seems probable that adaptation to life in the water proceeds
through a fresh-water phase, since all known aquatic mammals
are derived from land-dwelling forms.

Secondary adaptation of marine forms to fresh water also
occurs. A case in point are the river dolphins, which include
the Ganges (*Platonista gangetica*), Chinese (*Lipotes vexillifer*),
Amazon (*Inia geoffrensis*), and La Plata (*Stendelphis blain-
vellei*) varieties. The smaller toothed whales are classified as
"dolphins" more or less without regard to their actual relationships. The Chinese river dolphin is somewhat misnamed
since it is found only in one place, Lake Tung-Ting in Hunan
Province, central China. Some of the larger whales will swim
into rivers. A white whale, *Delphinopterus leucas*, entered the
Rhine River of Germany in the spring of 1966 and spent an
entire month there. The animal became quite an attraction
during its fresh-water sojourn. Even the common porpoises
occasionally travel up rivers, feeding on fish. Other species of

porpoises and dolphins live in brackish water along coasts and in river deltas.

Fresh water could certainly be a suitable environment for a primitive whale, and being warm-blooded it would have no difficulty with the cold 1° to 2° C (34° F) water in the depths of Lake Okanagan. The reader undoubtedly is aware that whales are quite at home among the ice floes of the Arctic and Antarctic oceans.

All whales flex vertically and propel themselves by up-and-down movement of the powerful tail flukes. This characteristic, so well established for the Naitakas, almost restricts our choice to marine mammals. The single pair of forclimbs or paddles of whales also are consistent with observations at Lake Okanagan. The top swimming speeds recorded for whales, up to 50 kilometers per hour (30 miles per hour) in the case of the large finback whale, are remarkable. Many species are easily able to keep pace with modern seagoing vessels. Again the reported swimming speeds of the Naitakas match the known performance of whales.

Modern whales are completely aquatic, giving birth to their offspring in the water. They are not able to function on land, and when beached, the larger—because of their great bulk—experience breathing difficulties, which often result in death by asphyxiation. The reader will recall that the evidence for very limited excursions of Naitaka on beaches and rocks of Lake Okanagan is extremely weak. Even if correct, there is no serious objection to supposing that a primitive serpentine whale, with only ¹/₆ to ¹/₇ the bulk of a sperm whale of comparable length, would not be able to slither on and off beaches. In addition, the front flippers might leave tracks, as have been reported.

The general appearance of *Basilosaurus* tallies almost exactly with the loglike descriptions of the Naitakas. Of all marine mammals, with the exception of certain sea cows, the Dugongs, and Steller's sea cow, only the whales possess horizontally oriented forked tails.

The shape of the head tapering toward the snout, flattened top to bottom, is exactly what one finds in the skull of

Basilosaurus. The nostrils had already gone through half of their migration to the top of the head as found in modern whales, so that the observation of "blowing" of the Naitaka is perfectly consistent. In fact, whales are the only aquatic animals that "blow." "Blowing" occurs after deep dives when air within the animal has been highly compressed at great depth. As the animal surfaces the pressure is released suddenly and the expanding air escaping from the blowhole expands rapidly. The expansion of the gas produces rapid cooling so that moisture in the exhaled air condenses, giving the appearance of a water spout. Naitakas would not be observed to "blow" regularly, but only after a deep dive, which would of course not be possible except in the deeper parts of Lake Okanagan.

No one, of course, knows what the skin color of *Basilosaurus* was, but the colors attributed to the Naitakas are certainly compatible with those found in living whales. The observation that part of the back contour of the Okanagan creatures are smooth and other parts serrated or saw-toothed is perfectly consistent with the condition in some modern whales and may well have been a characteristic of the *Basilosaurus*. The humpback whale, with its smooth back, which gradually develops into serrated protuberances as the tail is approached, is most suggestive.

An even more convincing piece of evidence is the hairless, smooth-skin texture, except that at close quarters "scales" or "plates" are observed on part of the body of the Naitaka. One is hard pressed to find animals that have such characteristics, but again *Basilosaurus* fits the bill exactly. Just such partial exoskeletal bony plates have been found in association with the *Basilosauridae* skeletons proper. The inference that they possessed these structures is strengthened by the fact that certain dolphins still possess evidence of such "plates" in a rudimentary form.

The sparse hair or bristles around the head region are common in many types of whales, as are a variety of protuberances. We cannot of course be sure as to the nature of the "horns" or "ears" reported occasionally on the head of Naitaka until a close examination is possible. The "mane" along the back reported in a few cases but not in others might reflect sexual dimorphism (secondary sexual characteristics present in one sex but not the other—for example, male lion's mane, none on the lioness, or in the case of some deer, antlers on the bucks, none or much smaller versions on the does).

Last, the available food supply of Lake Okanagan in the form of fish is a most suitable and common diet for many whales.

I believe most readers will now agree that short of comparing an actual Naitaka specimen, a better correspondence of characteristics could hardly be desired. At this point a few words regarding the possible identity of the Loch Ness animals are in order, because of the great similarities between Lake Okanagan and Loch Ness and the unidentified animals present in each body of water. It is very tempting to suggest that not only are Naitakas, British Columbian Caddies, and the Lake Champlain animals *Basilosauridae*, but to include the Loch Ness animals as well. However, at least one underwater photograph and the reports of a number of reliable close-up observations of the Loch Ness animals indicate that these animals possess a relatively thin, long head-neck attached to a thickened body. Such descriptions hardly, if ever, have been reported from Lake Okanagan, and remain the single major reason for dismissing *Basilosaurus* as the identity of the Loch Ness animals. The elongated neck and thicker body data at Loch Ness could be incorrect, but it would be improper to reject the data without cause.

Nevertheless, a note of caution seems appropriate. Perhaps I was too hasty in dismissing cetaceans as candidates for the Loch Ness Monster. I have tried to inject objectivity into the Loch Ness Monster identification process by constructing a table listing the characteristics of the animals on the one hand and comparing the major groups of animals by scoring positively those features that are possessed by the animals. For example, if a particular animal possessed ten of twenty descriptive features of the monster, the animal would be rated 50 per cent. The larger the percentage the better the possible candidate fits the description. It will be instructive to compare the Naitakas and the *Basilosauridae* with the Loch Ness animals. When this is done both Naitakas and *Basilosauridae* score about 78 per cent. It is hardly surprising that both give the same value, since they are so similar. But what is significant is that they should score so high; compare 56 per cent for seals, 47 per cent for sea cows, 69 per cent for *Plesiosaurus*, 88 per cent for primitive amphibians, 78 per cent for eels, and 59 per cent for invertebrates (gastropods, sea slugs, and the like).

There is one other nagging possibility, which must be considered. As has been noted, the extinct land mammals known as creodonts from which the *Basilosauridae* have evolved had a variety of head-neck configuration, some with somewhat elongated necks. The neck vertebrae in *Basilosauridae* were not shortened as much nor fused, as in modern whales. The shortening of the neck and fusion of neck vertebrae in whales has been a gradual evolutionary process over a period of perhaps seventy-five million years or more. It may well be that the Naitakas and the Loch Ness animals are a form even more primitive than the known examples of *Basilosauridae*, which may have had a more elongated and differentiated neck configuration. Also hind limbs, paddles, or feet might be less rudimentary, and might still be functional, although hind limbs are not well documented in any case. If we make this assumption, the Loch Ness score for such primitive whales would be no less than 84 per cent, which is about as much as one can expect from data of this kind.

The last point to be made is that during our researches at Loch Ness we recorded unidentified animate sounds that came in pulse trains, similar although not identical to the echo-locating sounds emitted by certain species of whales. It seems more reasonable to attribute such sounds to primitive whales than to any other kinds of animals.

To this day the real identity of the Loch Ness animals remains a mystery. Further research is continuing and perhaps a definitive answer will be arrived at in the not too distant future.

In analogy to the popular name Ogopogo, similar creatures reported from Lake Manitoba, Winnipegosis, and Dauphin have been named Manipogo and Winnipogo. The reports are far fewer, dating from 1908, and more sketchy, although during the 1950s and 1960s there were far too many to ignore. At least one scientist, Professor James A. McLeod, head of the Department of Zoology at the University of Manitoba, has taken a serious interest in the matter. Beginning in 1960, Professor McLeod led a number of investigative teams including divers to search Lake Manitoba. He believed that there was something unusual in the lake, but his main purpose was to look for remains. He based his approach at least in part on the fact that a district resident, Oscar Frederickson, discovered an unusual bone in the 1930s. The location where the alleged bone was discovered was along the north shore of Lake Winnipegosis 32 kilometers (20 miles) from Burrow's Landing. Even though McLeod was guided by Frederickson, the search was unsuccessful.

In spite of this result, if an actual bone were in hand it could certainly be identified by paleontologists and zoologists. Unfortunately this was not the case, as the alleged original had been destroyed by fire and only a model of the original was available. The model was about 15 centimeters (6 inches) by 7 centimeters (3 inches) in diameter and obviously represented or was intended to represent a spinal vertebra. Even if there were no fraud involved, the model was of no evidential value. One cannot, for example, determine from the model whether the original was fossilized or "green." In spite of the inadequacy of such evidence, this report, coupled with the "monster" sighting reports from the area, was sufficiently intriguing to move Professor McLeod to investigate further.

The descriptive features of the reports, such as they are, are identical to those from Lake Okanagan, so that we must conclude that if there is any substance to them, they refer to animals identical to those in Lake Okanagan. One curious added feature of the "Manipogo" is the reported cry of the creature, "a bellow like a goods train whistle," and again, "an unearthly cry." The very few references to the sounds made by the Naitaka describe a sucking sound rather than a cry.

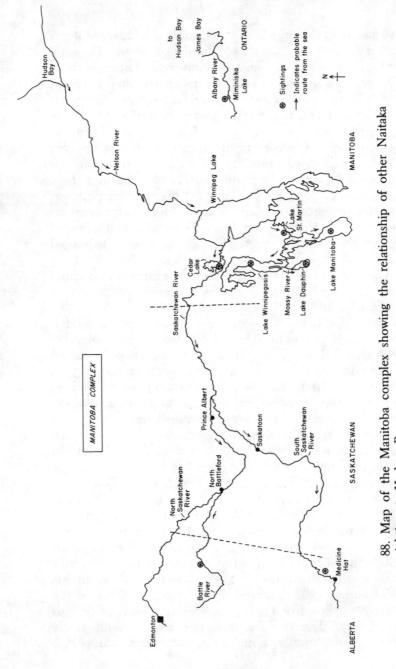

88. Map of the Manitoba complex showing the relationship of other Naitaka sightings to Hudson Bay.

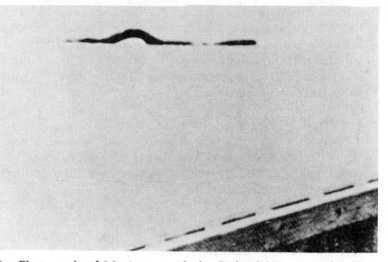

89. Photograph of Manipogo made by Richard Vincent and John Konefell on August 12, 1962, at Lake Manitoba, Canada.

This apparent difference is probably not significant, as the latter might result from air intake, while the "cry" may represent a rare bona fide vocalization, perhaps not improbable for a very primitive whale.

Although the anecdotal data for the Manipogo are not as abundant as for the Naitakas, the photographic evidence is better, since there is one photograph of Manipogo, which if genuine does show part of an animal that corresponds to the verbal and written descriptions.

During the month of August 1962 fishermen were reporting sightings of Manipogo. On August 12, Richard Vincent and John Konefell photographed the creature. Vincent and Konefell were out fishing, with an unnamed American television commentator, when the first successful photograph was taken. They stated, "We first spotted the object to the left of our boat about 300 yards away. After swinging into the direction it was heading we saw what we believed to be a large black snake or eel . . . which was swimming with a ripple action . . . it was about a foot in girth, and about 12 feet of the monster was above water. No head was visible." Peter Costello, in discussing this episode in his book *In Search of Lake Monsters*, observes, I believe correctly, that as the gunwale of their boat appears in the photograph, their estimate that the object was 45 meters (50 yards) to 70 meters (75 yards) away seems accurate enough. Though their boat had a 10-horsepower outboard engine, they had to give up trying to catch up with it and so the animal escaped.

Numerous reports of similar observations from lakes across all of Canada approximately between 50° and 60° N latitude continue to be made. I have tabulated and analyzed these reports with absolutely astonishing results.

First it should be noted that much of Canada is a virtual network of interconnecting lakes and rivers, which form natural subnetworks. If we plot the location of sightings on a map showing lakes and rivers, a coherent pattern is immediately apparent, which is easily explained if we assume that the Naitakas or Naitaka-like animals enter fresh water from the sea via rivers and streams. By now we have concluded that "Caddy" is identical to the Naitaka so that we begin in the Vancouver-Victoria area, where these animals are frequently sighted. There is also a report from Lake Cowichan, located approximately in the center of the southern tip of Vancouver Island. The animals apparently swim into the mouth of the nearby Fraser River, until they reach the point where the Harrison River joins the Fraser. Some continue up the Fraser River, while others follow the Harrison River to Lake Harrison, where sightings are reported. Most appear to turn east into the Thompson River, although some continue north up the Fraser to Williams Lake, and Lake Tagai via the Nechako and Chilako rivers. The Thompson River leads directly to Kamloops Lake, where sightings are in evidence. From there some Naitakas continue on to Shuswap Lake via the South Thompson River, to be sighted again. The Shuswap Lake complex includes Salmon Arm and various connections to Lake Okanagan via the Salmon River, Fortune Creek, Deep Creek, and others. Not all of these connections are complete at all times, although recent but now extinct glacial lakes existed over the area. Even now the largest excursions over land are less than 1 kilometer (½ mile). With at least a limited amphibious capability such small distances probably present no problem to the movement of the creatures. In any case, there is a complete waterway via the Salmon River and a very extensive secondary route into Okanagan from the south. As established by other sighting reports, the Naitakas also enter Lake Okanagan from the sea via the Columbia River, entering at Cape Disappointment, U.S.A. They proceed up the Columbia into the Okanagan River into Lake Osoyoos, where sightings are recorded, and on into Lake Okanagan. A few do not enter the Okanagan River but remain in the Columbia, entering Kootenay Lake via the Kootenay River. It may be that a few continue on via Trout Lake, which brings them far enough north for access to Shuswap Lake from the east. It seems that such a clear correlation between sightings and geophysical features establishes beyond doubt that real animals are involved. Unfortunately no one has bothered to study this aspect of the phenomenon.

Other complexes of lakes and river systems can be similarly documented. The Manitoba complex, including Lake Manitoba, Lake Dauphin, and Lake Winnipegosis, the South Saskatchewan River, and the Battle River, connecting to Hudson Bay via Lake Winnipeg, is as extensive as the Okanagan system. Aside from the lakes, sightings have been reported from both rivers. The Albany River, which connects Lake Meminisha to Hudson Bay, is also implicated, since sightings have been reported from the lake.

The other complex, St. Lawrence (Ontario–Quebec), appears to involve the St. Lawrence as an access from the sea, and sightings have been reported from Aylmer Lake, Lake Simcoe, Lake Duchesne, Muskrat Lake, and Lake Champlain, discussed in the previous chapter.

Three other lakes with monster traditions are Lake Utopia, Lake Kathlyn (formerly called Chicken Lake), and Lake Pohenegamook. Lake Utopia cannot be included in the other complexes so far discussed. The lake is located in the most southern part of New Brunswick, near St. George. It is

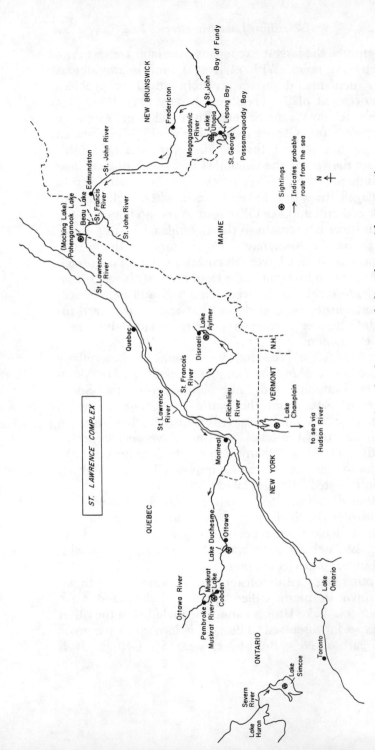

90. Map of the St. Lawrence complex of sightings, including those with connections to the Bay of Fundy.

connected to the sea via the Magaguadavic River, Passama-quoddy Bay, and the Bay of Fundy. To the east exists another possible access route via Lepang Bay, which extends to within less than 1½ kilometers (1 mile) of the lake.

References to a monster in these lakes are, as usual, found in Indian legends. The first recorded observation was reported by A. Seith Adams in 1967. Lumbermen employed at a sawmill on the lake repeatedly observed a creature 9 meters (30 feet) long splashing about in the lake. As a consequence, unsuc-cessful attempts were made to catch the creature with giant baited hooks. The early residents in the area correctly supposed that the creature entered the lake from the Bay of Fundy. Allegedly a slimy track of a huge beast had been traced from the bay to the lake thirty years earlier. Over the years others reported very odd mud slicks—from the lake to the ocean in spring and fall, which led to the assumption that the creature only inhabited the lake during the summer. The trail appeared to support the view that a heavy body had been in transit. Some even alleged that claw marks were observed. The appearance of the creature as described tallies with those of the Naitakas and must have been the same species.

The last recorded sighting was made by Mrs. Fred McKillop. One beautiful spring day while the "men folks" went fishing, Mrs. McKillop, left at home on the shore of the lake, was enjoying the view and the fine weather. She reports, "It (the lake) was beautiful. It was as clear as glass and there wasn't a ripple on it.

"Suddenly while I watched the water began to boil and churn, and make waves which came in and broke on the shore. Then a huge creature of some sort emerged from the water; at least its head did and part of its body. It looked like a huge black rock, but it moved and churned in the water."

Mrs. McKillop's observation was confirmed by some fish-ermen who witnessed the same event from another vantage point at some distance.

Since that time not a single additional observation has been reported. It is believed by some, not unreasonably, that the building of the Trans-Canada Highway has cut off the access from the sea, since it passes between the lake and the bays.

91. The Monster of Lake Utopia by Kroupa.

No good photographic evidence is available, although a sketch made by B. Kroupa based on observations made in 1872 is part of the Webster Collection at the New Brunswick Museum, St. John, New Brunswick. Actually the drawing need not be modified greatly to provide a very creditable picture of *Basilosaurus*.

During training flights, the Royal Canadian Air Force, based nearby, made routine aerial photographs of the lake and adjacent areas. Interestingly, some of the shots of the lake show a long shadow moving below the surface. While these photographs would not convince skeptics, they are at least suggestive. There the matter rests, possibly with no hope of solution if the lake access is indeed blocked for these creatures.

Northeast along the coast of New Brunswick about 60 kilometers (38 miles) from Lake Utopia one comes to the mouth of the St. John River. This river has its origin well above the tip of the state of Maine, in the southern part of Quebec. Close to the Maine border is Lake Pohenegamook, connected to the St. John River by the St. Francis River. It appears that Naitakas have entered this river system, since sightings have been reported as recently as November of 1977.

The Indian name for the creatures is Ponik, and sightings have been reported for many years. The most recent Ponik sightings have been investigated by a professional scientist,

Dr. Vadim Vladykov, a marine biologist and director of the Quebec Department of Game and Fisheries. Vladykov became involved because the Quebec provincial government was getting so many reports that they commissioned him to investigate. The descriptive details are identical to those of the Naitakas. Vladykov has concluded, "There definitely is a strange, large animal living in Lake Pohenegamook."

Some attempts of varying degrees of competence have been made to identify the creature. The investigations ranged from efforts by amateur divers to the deployment of sonar devices, under the direction of Bob Murray, a professional diver. Sonar devices were reported to have picked up a large object 8 meters (25 feet) long in the lake's depths. Since the lake is relatively small—10 kilometers (6 miles) long, although quite deep, up to 90 meters (300 feet)—it would not be as formidable an undertaking to search as the large lakes, such as Lake Okanagan, Lake Manitoba, or Lake Champlain, although it seems likely that the animal or animals might leave the lake via the St. Francis River if conditions should become unfavorable.

The last lake we will consider is Lake Kathlyn, located at about 127° W longitude, 55° N latitude, near Smithers in British Columbia, but not really a part of the Okanagan complex. Its monsters probably arrived via the Skeena River, which has its mouth about halfway up the British Columbian coast at Prince Rupert. At Hazelton the Bulkley River branches from the Skeena and continues south until slightly above Smithers, where the connection to Lake Kathlyn is made. The Indian legend about the Kathlyn monster was printed in the Vancouver *Sun* on February 17, 1934, written by an attorney, L. S. McGill, a resident of Smithers.

> Centuries ago, before the first white man came to what is now British Columbia, Indians lived in the Bulkley River valley, which they called Wut-sin-kwa, in peace and plenty. The rivers teemed with salmon; berries and fruits were everywhere; deer and other wild game and many birds abounded in the woods and no one went hungry.
>
> The great chief had one lovely child, a daughter whom he hoped would succeed him when he passed on. But one day she was fishing in Lake Kathlyn with her dearest girl chum, when

out of the depths rose a monster larger than the greatest war canoe that ever came up the Skeena River from the coast.

At the front it looked like a beast and from the back it resembled a serpent. It rushed at the two terrified girls, seized the Indian princess, swallowed her and dived into the lake again.

Bent on revenge, the Indians held a great council of war. Tribes came from far and near to discuss plans for attacking and killing the monster. Finally, someone thought of a good plan. The Indians first gathered hundreds of large stones from the foot of Hudson Bay Mountain which towered above the lake. They placed the rocks close to the water's edge. Then they cut down trees and dragged logs and brush to the lakeshore and burned them on top of the large stones. The lake was soon surrounded by a great ring of fire and the stones became red hot. All at the same time, the Indians pushed the rocks into the water, which began to boil.

The monster was boiled to death and his huge corpse rose to the surface. When the fires were out and the water had cooled sufficiently, the Indians made a raft and went out to bring the body to shore. In its stomach, they found their dead princess and they gave her a grand funeral.

The miraculous parts of the legend are of course obvious, but the descriptive part is not far from the mark. *Basilosaurus* certainly fits the description. "At the front it looked like a beast and from the back it resembled a serpent."

It seems quite fitting to close our discussion with the Indians, the original observers of these creatures long thought to be extinct. Regardless of how reasonable the hypothesis I have presented, it must be kept in mind that it is only a hypothesis. The next step will have to be the isolation of an actual specimen to establish whether or not the Naitakas are really primitive whales, archeoceti related to the *Basilosauridae*.

The data so far assembled permit certain conclusions and suggest likely avenues of research. Since the path of egress from the sea can be plotted, the inhabitants along these river-like chains could be interviewed, with the probable result that perhaps hundreds if not thousands of heretofore unreported observations might come to light. These might aid in rounding out the descriptive details of the creatures. Such data might also be useful in finding a situation most favorable for isolating a specimen for study. A small lake at the headwaters of one of the river systems might be ideal. Most importantly, the working hypothesis that the creatures are primitive whales provides a basis for formulating investigative techniques with high probabilities of success.

XII

The Monstrous Plants

Plants that eat meat: a bizarre contradiction to most of our experience; after all, everyone knows that man and animals eat plants, not the reverse. Meat-eating (carnivorous) plants have held a fascination for many people, including botanists and zoologists, ever since Charles Darwin became interested in these unusual plants and wrote a definitive description of the major varieties.

Some years ago, after reading Darwin's book, I acquired six or seven species, which I cultivated for some time with considerable interest. These kinds of plants not only capture animals, by passive or active means, but also actually digest the animals' protein and assimilate it for their own nourishment. Most species of insectivorous plants trap and eat insects, although some trap small fish, crustaceans, worms, larvae, and even small mammals.

You may wonder why these plants have developed this propensity for animal food. The answer is that by doing so they are able to thrive in nitrogen- (nitrate-) and phosphorus-poor soil where ordinary plants are not able to survive; the insectivorous plants' crucial food requirements are supplied or supplemented by digested animal tissue.

The Venus flytrap, *Dionaea muscipula*, is most spectacular, with its pronged valvelike trap, which springs shut in the wink of an eye when the trigger hairs on the leaf are touched, trapping the insect or pressing down on the bit of hamburger placed there by the horticulturist.

The most complete work on these plants since Darwin is *The Carnivorous Plants* by a professor of botany, Francis Ernest Lloyd, and published in 1942. In his Introduction he makes a most interesting statement regarding his table of known carnivorous plants, including 450 species divided in 15 genera and 6 families. In speaking of this list he notes certain species that had been thought to be carnivorous, but were found later not to be so. Then he writes, "The 'man-eating tree of Madagascar' must at present also be excluded, since the evidence of its existence is elusive."

Can one believe that a man-eating tree is a serious possibility? It certainly appears that Professor Lloyd had considered the matter. Further, in his Preface he summarizes some of the evidence, including references to rather lurid Sunday supplement reports.

This reference led me to embark on research to find out more about the matter. Once I got going, I found references enough, but much of the material was obscure, out of print, and hard to come by. After considerable effort I was able to sort it out to my satisfaction.

I found the best approach was to list as many references as possible in chronological order and then work backward in time to check each one. The story here will be told in forward order.

As far as the Western world is concerned the story begins in 1878. A German traveler in Madagascar by the name of Carle (or perhaps "Karl") Liche was reported to have written a letter to a Polish savant, Dr. Omelius Fredlowski, describing Liche's eyewitness experience of human sacrifice to a man-eating tree. The letter reads:

The Mkodos, of Madagascar, are a very primitive race, going entirely naked, having only faint vestiges of tribal relations, and no religion beyond that of the awful reverence which they pay to the sacred tree. They dwell entirely in caves hollowed out of the limestone rocks in their hills, and are one of the smallest races, the men seldom exceeding fifty-six inches in height. At the bottom of the valley (I had no barometer, but should not think it over four hundred feet above the level of the sea), and near its eastern extremity, we came to a deep tarnlike lake about a mile in diameter, the sluggish oily water of which overflowed into a tortuous reedy canal that went unwillingly into the recesses of a black forest composed of jungle below and palms above. A path diverging from its southern side struck boldly for the heart of the forbidding and seemingly impenetrable forest. Hendrick led the way along this path, I following closely, and behind me a curious rabble of Mkodos, men, women and children. Suddenly all the natives began to cry "Tepe! Tepe!" and Hendricks, stopping short, said, "Look!" The sluggish canallike stream here wound slowly by, and in a bare spot in its bend was the most singular of trees. I have called it "Crinoida," because when its leaves are in action it bears a striking resemblance to that well-known fossil the crinoid lily-stone or St. Cuthbert's head. It was now at rest, however, and I will try to describe it to you. If you can imagine a pineapple eight feet high and thick in proportion resting upon its base and denuded of leaves, you will have a good idea of the trunk of the tree, which, however, was not the color of an anana, but a dark dingy brown, and apparently as hard as iron. From the apex of this truncated cone (at least two feet in diameter) eight leaves hung sheer to the ground, like doors swung back on their hinges. These leaves, which were joined at the top of the tree at regular intervals, were about eleven or twelve feet long, and shaped very much like the leaves of the American agave or century plant. They were two feet through at their thickest point and three feet wide, tapering to a sharp point that looked like a cow's horn, very convex on the outer (but now under) surface, and on the under (now upper) surface slightly concave. This concave face was thickly set with strong thorny hooks like those on the head of the teazle. These leaves hanging thus limp and lifeless, dead green in color, had in appearance the massive strength of oak fibre. The apex of the cone was a round white concave figure like a smaller plate set within a larger one. This was not a flower but a receptacle, and there exuded into it a clear treacly liquid, honey sweet, and possessed of violent intoxicating and soporific properties. From underneath the rim (so to speak) of the undermost plate a series of long hairy green tendrils stretched out in every direction towards the horizon. These were seven or eight feet long, and tapered from four inches to a half inch in diameter, yet they stretched out stiffly as iron rods. Above these (from between the upper and under cup) six white almost transparent palpi reared themselves toward the sky, twirling and twisting with a marvelous incessant motion, yet constantly reaching upwards. Thin as reeds and frail as quills, apparently they were yet five or six feet tall, and were so constantly and vigorously in motion, with such a subtle, sinuous, silent throbbing against the air, that they made me shudder in spite of myself, with their suggestion of serpents flayed, yet dancing upon their tails. The description I am giving you now is partly made up from a subsequent careful inspection of the plant. My observations on this occasion were suddenly interrupted by the natives, who had been shrieking around the tree with their shrill voices, and chanting what Hendrick told me were propitiatory hymns to the great tree devil. With still wilder shrieks and chants they now surrounded one of the women and urged her with the points of their javelins, until slowly, and with despairing face, she climbed up the stalk of the tree and stood on the summit of the cone, the palpi swirling all about her. "Tsik! Tsik!" (Drink! Drink!) cried the men. Stooping, she drank of the viscid fluid in the cup, rising instantly again, with wild frenzy in her face and convulsive cords in her limbs. But she did not jump down, as she seemed to intend to do. Oh no! The atrocious cannibal tree that had been so inert and dead came to sudden savage life. The slender delicate palpi, with the fury of starved serpents, quivered a moment over her head, then as if instinct with demoniac intelligence fastened upon her in sudden coils round and round her neck and arms; then while her awful screams and yet more awful laughter rose wildly to be instantly strangled down again into a gurgling moan, the tendrils one after another, like green serpents, with brutal energy and infernal rapidity, rose, retracted themselves, and wrapped her about in fold after fold, ever tightening with cruel swiftness and the savage tenacity of anacondas fastening upon their prey. It was the barbarity of the Laocoön without its beauty—this strange horrible murder. And now the great leaves slowly rose and stiffly, like the arms of a derrick, erected themselves in the air, approached one another and closed about the dead and hampered victim with the silent force of a hydraulic press and the ruthless purpose of a thumb screw. A moment more, and while I could see the bases of these great levers pressing more tightly towards each other, from their interstices there trickled down the stalk of the tree great streams of the viscid honeylike fluid mingled horribly with the blood and oozing viscera of the victim. At sight of this the savage hordes around me, yelling madly, bounded forward, crowded to the tree, clasped it, and with cups, leaves, hands and tongues each one obtained enough of the liquor to send him mad and frantic. Then ensued a grotesque and indescribably hideous orgy, from which even while its convulsive madness was turning rapidly into delirium and insensibility, Hendrick dragged me hurriedly away into the recesses of the forest, hiding me from the dangerous brutes. May I never see such a sight again.

The retracted leaves of the great tree kept their upright position during ten days, then when I came one morning they were prone again, the tendrils stretched, the palpi floating, and nothing but a white skull at the foot of the tree to remind me of the sacrifice that had taken place there. I climbed into a neighboring tree, and saw that all trace of the victim had disappeared and the cup was again supplied with the viscid fluid.

This letter was allegedly published in several European scientific journals and in popular-circulation magazines and newspapers. Some specific publications were: Graefe and Walther's magazine of Karlsruhe, Germany, a popular magazine, no date, but supposedly between 1878 and 1880; the Madras *Mail* between 1878 and 1882; the New York *World*, 1880; the South Australian *Register*, no date, but presumably shortly after 1880; and in the *Antanarivo Annual and Madagascar Magazine* for the year 1881, a local magazine published and printed by missionaries in Madagascar.

A Dr. R. G. Jay of Willungo, Australia, was stated to have read the account at a soirée at the Willunga Institute. In 1887 Dr. Conrad Keller published a book entitled *Reisebilder aus Ostafrika und Madagasar* (Travel Sketches from East Africa and Madagascar), the Contents of the book describing Keller's visits to Madagascar, 1881–82 and 1886. It was published in installments in Swiss newspapers.

Willy Ley, our late romantic zoologist, discovered the Keller material, and I quote him as follows: "He (Keller) stated that something fantastic had been added to the actually marvelous flora of Madagascar in an alleged letter written 'by a traveler Carl Liche whom I don't know' to 'a certain Dr. Fredlowski' which was published 'in a journal said to appear in Karlsruhe which I could not obtain.' Because 'the German original' could not be found Dr. Keller translated the letter from the *Antanarivo Annual and Madagascar Magazine* for the year 1881 (already mentioned), which he stated was a small local magazine published and printed by the missionaries."

Next we find a reference to the Madagascan man-eating tree in "Science Jottings" by Dr. Andrew Wilson in the *Illustrated* London *News* of September 24, 1892, page 403, and the reference to publication of Liche's letter in the Madras *Mail* (already mentioned). After 1892, discussion of the horrible tree appears to have abated.

We next find the subject surfacing in 1920 in the "American Weekly," a Sunday supplement of wide circulation, syndicated to a large number of American newspapers. The article was published over the name of Dr. B. H. William, with the subheading "The Distinguished American Botanist" in the September 26, 1920, issue, page 6. Traveler Karl Liche has become "Dr. Karl Leche, the noted German explorer and scientist." The popular magazine published by Graefe and Walther in Karlsruhe has become *Carlsruhe Scientific Journal* and the original contents of the Liche letter is given, with many added details, mostly lurid and sensational. A picture of an alleged Mkodo warrior is shown, including an artist's sketch of a naked blonde in the embrace of the horrendous plant. Additional, more mundane information about real carnivorous plants rounds out the article.

During this time Chase Salmon Osborn, LL.D., and governor of Michigan, 1911–13, read or heard about the alleged vegetable horror of Madagascar. His interest kindled, and being a world traveler, he traveled to Madagascar to see if he could track down the monster. Returning from his visit, he wrote a book about his visit that was entitled *Madagascar, Land of the Man-eating Tree*, published in 1924. It is clear from the list of books he consulted that he had done a lot of homework. He reprinted the Liche letter as originally pub-

92. Artist's conception of a victim being sacrificed to a man-eating plant. As published in the "American Weekly" of September 26, 1920.

lished, *sans* Sunday supplement embellishments, and gives additional earlier references that have already been cited in chronological order.

Our popular "American Weekly" of October 9, 1924, ran an article on Osborn and his search, toned down slightly, with a new drawing of a damsel in the clutches of the monster. This must have produced considerable mileage, since a third article, entitled "Escaped from the Embrace of the Man-eating Tree," appeared on January 4, 1925, purporting to be the report of W. C. Bryant, exploring in the island jungle of the Philippines. It was a quite conventional drawing of a tree now, with one or two boughs growing through skulls, with great explorer with native guide recoiling in horror.

The reaction by botanists to these articles was mostly of rage, resulting in a spate of violently critical letters, articles,

93. A second artist's version, in the "American Weekly" of October 19, 1924.

and comments. Willard N. Clute closed his article in the *American Botanist* in 1925 after summarizing the Sunday supplement stories, "The wild tales in the Sunday papers would not be worth attention were it not for the fact that they impress the unbotanical public with an erroneous idea of plants and in many cases deprive the readers of a sane attitude toward science and the outdoor world. Field and forest do not teem with poisonous plants and animals. They are far more peaceful and harmless than the streets of any city. If there is such a plant as those we have been describing we hereby offer ten thousand dollars for a living specimen. There are one or two people we want to introduce it to, and then we are going to make our fortune, and get the funds needed to make this

94. The third "American Weekly" effort, January 4, 1925.

magazine bigger, by exhibiting the thing, properly caged, at $1.00 a head."

In contrast to this caustic professional reaction, another professional, Sophia Prior, wrote Field Museum of Natural History pamphlet No. 23, entitled *Carnivorous Plants and the Man-eating Tree*. Ms. Prior proceeds to give the reader a balanced description of the known carnivorous plants, turning to Sunday supplement material from page 7 to the end of the pamphlet at page 19 plus a bibliography. Although she listed Osborn's book in her bibliography, she published the Sunday supplement version of Liche's letter and even in her discussion refers to *Dr.* Carle Liche and states that part of the account appeared in the *Carlsruhe Scientific Journal*, ignoring both Osborn and the original text of the Liche letter.

Finally, Willy Ley investigated the matter, doing a great deal of research. He published his views in 1955 by devoting Chapter 7 to it in *Salamanders and Other Wonders* and again in 1962 in Chapter 17 of his *Exotic Zoology* to the man-eating tree.

Let us now attempt to determine whether Dr. Ley's conclusions were warranted. We can approach this material from two viewpoints, both of which are worthwhile. First we can go over Ley's analysis, extending his work and adding our own; and we can dissect the Liche letter with botanical and zoological scalpel.

Ley writes correctly that according to Sophia Prior the Liche letter was first published in the *Carlsruhe Scientific Journal*. Then comes a surprise, for Ley writes, "This information is copied from Osborn, who added that the magazine was published by 'Graefe and Walther in Karlsruhe.' Osborn added further that the letter also was published in 'several European scientific publications' and was first published in America by the New York *World* in 1880.' Copies of newspapers three quarters of a century old are hard to come by, so I did not check the *World*." He then states how scientific magazines are another story and details his unsuccessful search for the *Carlsruhe Scientific Journal*.

His statement that the *Carlsruhe Scientific Journal* came from Osborn is astonishing indeed, for it came from the "American Weekly," not Osborn. The relevant text by Osborn reads as follows: "The most lurid and dramatic description of the man-eating tree of Madagascar I have seen was written by a traveller named Carle Liche [no *Dr.*] in a letter to Dr. Omelius Fredlowski, a Pole. This letter was published in several European scientific publications, was given popular circulation in Graefe and Walther's magazine of Karlsruhe [note no mention of a *Carlsruhe Scientific Journal*], and was published in America by the New York *World* in 1880. Then it pursued its conquest of interest around the world and appeared in the South Australian *Register*. Dr. R. G. Jay, of Willungo, Australia, read this account at a soirée at the Willungo Institute." He continues, "So much for the character of the reception given to this long-forgotten report of the arboreal monster. One of the first inquiries I made in Madagascar was about this tree. Of all the tales I heard none was better than the description in Liche's letter, and also Liche seemed to be better informed as to detail and to possess enough character to make his report impressive." The Liche letter then follows. Osborn further states that he traveled the thousand mile-length of Madagascar and across it many times but was not actually able to see the tree. But from all the peoples he met, including Hovas, Sakalanas, Sihanakas, Betsileos, and others, he heard stories and myths about it. He found that most missionaries did not believe the tree existed but that they were not united in this opinion. Osborn expresses the wonder of some missionaries as to how the belief about the devil tree could be so widespread and not have any basis in fact.

So in at least one important point Ley was wrong. Ley now decided to check the period 1878 to 1924 for independent references to the man-eating tree. There was, of course, the "American Weekly" article of 1920. Ley details the works he consulted, drawing a complete blank, till almost the last book on his list, which was *Reisebilder aus Ostafrika und Madagaskar* (Travel Sketches from East Africa and Madagascar) by Dr. Conrad Keller, published in Leipzig in 1887. Keller had been to Madagascar twice, once in 1881–82, just after the Carle Liche letter, and again in 1886. Among other things Keller mentioned the man-eating tree and Carle Liche, as has already been noted.

Willy Ley, usually a very meticulous researcher, probably concluded wrongly that the *Antanarivo* article in 1881 was actually the first publication. Be that as it may, he had in his hands the reference by Sophia Prior to "Science Jottings" in the *Illustrated* London *News* of September 24, 1892. I checked this reference and found it indeed referred to the Liche letter. I was not so successful with the *World* of 1880 published in New York. I obtained the microfilm of the entire year of this newspaper, which was carefully scanned page by page for me by Scott Sprinzen, a professional librarian, without success. At least the "Science Jottings" in the 1892 *Illustrated* London *News* established that our Michigan governor had *not* invented the whole thing, corroborating Willy Ley's discovery of the Keller reference.

Apparently by now Ley was so disenchanted with Osborn

because of his failure to find the *Carlsruhe Scientific Journal*, incorrectly attributed to Osborn, that he did not believe Osborn when he stated that the man-eating-tree tradition was widespread in Madagascar both among the natives and the missionaries. Ley could find no references to the myth by missionaries, nor to the tribe "Mkodos."

I attacked the matter of the myth first. I checked titles listed by Ley, Prior, and others and was able to find at least one clear-cut reference to the legend by a missionary, leading me to accept Osborn's statements that there was such a tradition.

The corroboration was recorded in *Madagascar and France*, written by the Reverend George A. Shaw, F.Z.S., stationed at the London Mission, Tamatave, Madagascar, and published by the American Tract Society of New York covering the period 1880–84. Shaw's book describes the island, its people, its resources, its development, and the then current political upheaval involving France.

On page 398 he wrote as follows: "Many of the curiosities of vegetable life are found in the island, and the romance of the early travellers has added many extraordinary forms, unknown except in the imagination of the writers. Such is the man-eating tree, which was said to be able to entangle in its fibrous, tendril-like leaves human beings, whom it crushed to death and devoured. No such plant exists, but it is doubtless the romancers' magnified description of the insectivorous plants, which are not uncommon."

Further research established that the idea of man-eating trees or plants that required human nourishment was not confined to Madagascar, but was quite widespread throughout the Indian Ocean area and even included India.

A collection of poems from India includes the following:

Story by Lalla-ji, the Priest

He loved the Plant with a keen delight,
    A passionate fervour, strange to see,
Tended it ardently, day and night,
    Yet never a flower lit up the tree.

The leaves were succulent, thick, and green,
   And, sessile, out of the snakelike stem
Rose spinelike fingers, alert and keen,
   To catch at aught that molested them.

But though they nurtured it day and night,
   With love and labour, the child and he
Were never granted the longed-for sight
   Of a flower crowning the twisted tree.

Until one evening a wayworn Priest
   Stopped for the night in the Temple shade
And shared the fare of their simple feast
   Under the vines and the jasmin laid.

He, later, wandering round the flowers
   Paused awhile by the blossomless tree.
The man said, "May it be fault of ours,
   That never its buds my eyes may see?

"Aslip it came from the further East
   Many a sunlit summer ago."
"It grows in our jungles," said the Priest,
   "Men see it rarely; but this I know,

"The jungle people worship it; say
   They bury a child around its roots—
Bury it living;—the only way
   To crimson glory of flowers and fruits."

He spoke in whispers; his furtive glance
   Probing the depths of the garden shade.
The man came closer, with eyes askance,
   The child beside them shivered, afraid.

A cold wind drifted about the three,
   Jarring the spines with a hungry sound,
The spines that grew on the snakelike tree
   And guarded its roots beneath the ground.
. . . .

> After the fall of the summer rain
> The plant was glorious, redly gay,
> Blood-red with blossom. Never again
> Men saw the child in the Temple play.

This rather chilling piece presents certain features similar to those attributed to Liche's man-eating tree.

Charles M. Skinner in his book *Myths and Legends of Flowers, Trees, Fruits, and Plants* provides us with another interesting legend. He writes: "We may dismiss as mythical the travelled tale of a Venus flytrap which was magnified into quite another matter before Captain Arkright was through with it, for such tales grow larger the farther they go from their beginning. It was in 1581 that the valiant explorer learned of an atoll in the South Pacific that one might not visit, save on peril of his life, for this coral ring enclosed a group of islets on one of which the Death Flower grew; hence it was named El Banoor, or Island of Death. This flower was so large that a man might enter it—a cave of color and perfume—but if he did so it was the last of him, for lulled by its strange fragrance, he reclined on its lower petals and fell into the sleep from which there is no waking. Then, as if to guard his slumber, the flower slowly folded its petals about him. The fragrance increased and burning acid was distilled from its calyx, but of all hurt the victim was unconscious, and so passing into death through splendid dreams, he gave his body to the plant for food."

Where or from what basis might such a tale originate? There exists as a matter of fact a monstrous flower—monstrous in size, that is—1 meter (3 feet) or more in diameter, which almost fits the description of the death flower. It is the parasitic plant known as *Rafflesia arnoldii*, which grows on the root of another plant, the vine *Tetrastigma*, in the jungles of Sumatra. This giant flower, much like a washtub, consists of thick petals, flesh-colored and speckled with cream-colored spots. At the center of the petals is a large bowl or nectary filled with 6 or 7 liters (6 quarts) of water. In the basin the true flowers, quite

95. *Rafflesia arnoldii*, perhaps the world's largest flower, reaching a diameter of 1 meter (3 feet).

small, give the impression of torture devices. The plant, however, does not derive its nourishment from the bodies of dead humans, but from the root of its host.

This giant was discovered in 1818 when Dr. Joseph Arnold, in the company of Sir Stamford and Lady Raffles, patrons of the Royal Society, penetrated the jungles of Sumatra to the Mann River at Pulo Lebbar. Flies were described as hovering over the bowl and much elephant excrement was present around the flower. The significance of this latter observation is not clear, although according to botanist W. A. Emboden it was later suggested that the flowers were pollinated by elephants; not substantiated, of course!

Reports of monstrous flesh-eating plants are not exclusively a product of the African-Indian Ocean region. South America also provides its fair share. Some of the more interesting were recorded in "Science Jottings," the column in the *Illustrated*

London News, by Dr. Andrew Wilson, already mentioned. He reported the following in the August 27, 1892, issue:

It appears that a naturalist, a Mr. Dunstan by name, was botanising in one of the swamps surrounding the Nicaragua Lake. The account goes on to relate that "while hunting for specimens he heard his dog cry out, as if in agony, from a distance. Running to the spot whence the animal's cries came, Mr. Dunstan found him enveloped in a perfect network of what seemed to be a fine, ropelike tissue of roots and fibres. The plant or vine seemed composed entirely of bare-interlacing stems, resembling more than anything else the branches of a weeping willow denuded of its foliage, but of a dark, nearly black hue, and covered with a thick, viscid gum that exuded from the pores. Drawing his knife, Mr. Dunstan attempted to cut the poor beast free, but it was with the very greatest difficulty that he managed to sever the fleshy muscular fibres (*sic*) of the plant. When the dog was extricated from the coils of the plant, Mr. Dunstan saw to his horror that its body was bloodstained, while the skin appeared to be actually sucked or puckered in spots, and the animal staggered as if from exhaustion. In cutting the vine the twigs curled like living, sinuous fingers about Mr. Dunstan's hand, and it required no slight force to free the member from their clinging grasp, which left the flesh red and blistered. The tree, it seems, is well known to the natives, who relate many stories of its death-dealing powers. Its appetite is voracious and insatiable, and in five minutes it will suck the nourishment from a large lump of meat, rejecting the carcass (*sic*) as a spider does that of a used-up fly." This is a very circumstantial account of the incident, but in such tales it is, of course, absurd "to leave such a matter to a doubt." If correct, it is very clear we have yet to add a very notable example to the list of plants which demand an animal dietary as a condition of their existence; and our sundews, Venus flytraps, and pitcher plants will then have to "pale their ineffectual fires" before the big devourer of the Nicaragua swamps.

In the September 24, 1892, issue, Dr. Wilson reports further: "The 'snake-tree' is described in a newspaper paragraph as found on an outlying spur of the Sierra Madre, in Mexico. It has movable branches (by which I suppose, is meant sensitive branches), of a 'slimy, snaky appearance,' which seized a bird that incautiously alighted on them, the bird being drawn down till the traveller lost sight of it. Where did the bird go to? Latterly it fell to the ground, flattened out, the earth being covered with bones and feathers, the débris, no doubt, of former captures. The adventurous traveller touched one of the branches of the tree. It closed upon his hand with such force as to tear the skin when he wrenched it away. He then fed the tree with chickens, and the tree absorbed their blood by means of the suckers (like those of the octopus) with which its branches were covered."

Undoubtedly additional reports such as these could be uncovered if a search of periodicals and literature were made.

We can with some confidence conclude that the idea of a large tree or plant devouring large animals, including man, is fairly widespread, and that Ley was wrong on this point.

Ley pursued another aspect of the Liche letter, which was the reference to the primitive tribe called Mkodos. In all references consulted none contained the word "Mkodos" in any context whatsoever. I followed Ley's procedure with exactly the same result, except that I consulted additional works, lists of Madagascan words, and lists of tribal groups. The major groupings mentioned by Osborn as having the tradition of course turned up over and over again. However, being in a university community, represented by experts in almost every field, I consulted some of the specialists in African studies, after a particularly futile attempt to obtain information from the Malagasy Consulate in Washington, D.C.

I learned that *m* was a common enough prefix for many African words and that perhaps the stem Kodo, plural Kodos, was the key. Back to the references under *k*. No luck with this approach either, except a reference to a group known as Kodos in the vicinity of the Upper Nile River, clearly not the alleged Madagascan tree worshipers.

One expert thought that "Mkodo" might be a general local derogatory term for "primitives," "bush niggers," and the like, rather than the name of a specific tribal group.

At this point I was ready to give up, but decided to read Liche's letter once more. He described these people as practically at a Stone Age level, but also as of small stature, rarely taller than 1.4 meters (56 inches), almost pygmies. Back to the references. Quickly it became clear that as far as the present native population was concerned there were no groups known to be diminutive.

The two volumes entitled *Madagascar* by Captain Samuel Pasfield Oliver published in 1886 proved most helpful. In Chapter X "Ethnology," page 34, I found the following:

"Pigmy race. Quimos or Kimos. M.M. Commerson and De Maudeave, the latter of whom was governor of Fort Dauphin from 1768 to 1770, have left circumstantial accounts of a pigmy race of people who were said to inhabit the southern centre of Madagascar, in 22° S lat., about 180 miles northwest of Fort Dauphin. These Quimos or Kimos are said to have been of lighter colour than the majority of the Malagasy, to have had woolly hair and very long arms. They are also reported to have been very bold in defending their own territory, and to excel in handicraft, and to be of an ingenious and active disposition, with pastoral habits." Further checking established that the Kimos were almost as elusive as the Mkodos or Kodos, since their existence has never been corroborated.

On the positive side they were the only people of small stature ever to be described in Madagascar; they lived in about the right area (southeastern part of Madagascar), and their name "Kimos" could conceivably be a variation of "Kodos." However, they were hardly described as primitive, as Liche had painted the Kodos. Well, that is where the matter stands. Almost one hundred years after the "fact" we probably will never be able to come to a certain conclusion.

We can, however, consider critically the plausibility of a horrendous vegetable having characteristics attributed to it by Liche on purely botanical or zoological grounds. First let us consider size. The alleged tree is described as something like a 2.5-meter (8-foot)-high pineapple, with 8 leaves regularly arranged around a 60-centimeter (2-foot) apex, dangling to the ground, some 3 to 4 meters (11 to 12 feet) long, quite thick at the base, 60 centimeters (2 feet), and about 1 meter (3 feet)

96. *Welwitschia mirabilia*, a bizarre giant found growing in the desert plains of western tropical Africa.

wide, tapering to a sharp point, concave on the inner surface, studded with strong, thorny hooks. At the apex was a double receptacle filled with clear liquid having properties allegedly attractive to potential prey.

This configuration immediately reminds one of *Welwitschia mirabilis*, given a 2.5-meter (8-foot)-long pineapple or cycadlike stem plus a few hooks or thorns for good measure. This bizarre plant is grotesque indeed, found only in western tropical African deserts, and has a 2-meter (6-foot)-wide reservoir with leaves extending 5.5 meters (18 feet) around the apex. The plant is certainly not carnivorous, and the reservoir serves to collect rain under arid desert conditions, no thorny hooks are present, and no part of the plant is capable of movement. Nevertheless, it is conceivable that it may have fired someone's fertile imagination.

Well and good, but are there any true carnivorous plants of

a size comparable to the Liche description? The answer is a decided negative if we consider total bulk or mass. The largest carnivorous plants are those falling into the category of "pitcher plants." These plants *are* found in Madagascar, although the largest are reported from Borneo. *Nepenthes rajah* develops pitchers with openings 30 centimeters (1 foot) across holding 3½ liters (7 pints) of liquid in which rodents, birds, and other small animals can drown. Other species climb trees, possessing vines or stalks 6 meters (20 feet) tall, but have nowhere near the bulk of Liche's man-eater.

Some pitcher plants have pitchers lined with scalelike cells covered with glandular hairs that excrete a sweet honeylike juice, which entices animals into the pitcher. This latter feature is one also attributed to the Madagascar man-eater.

Next Liche describes long, hairy green tendrils, 2 to 2½ meters (7 to 8 feet) long, tapered from 10 centimeters (4 inches) to 1 centimeter (0.5 inch) in diameter, protruding stiffly as iron rods from beneath the lower, outer lip of the reservoir. Above these, between the lower, outer lip and the inner, upper lip, six white palpi reared upward, writhing in constant motion. These structures were thin as reeds but about 2 meter (6 feet) tall. According to Liche's description of the reactions of this plant to its victim, the hairy green tendrils as well as the large leaves were motile and capable of helping to imprison, hold, and crush its victim.

It is always risky to state categorically that something is impossible, but this combination of attributes certainly would be a good candidate. No known plant possesses any structure that is in constant rapid motion, as the palpi Liche described, nor do any plant structures truly have the octopus tentacle grasping capability ascribed both to the palpi and the tendrils.

The small sundew, *Drosera rotundifolia*, has thin stalks radiating from a central point with the leaf on each stalk lying flat on the ground. These leaves are covered with tiny gland-bearing tentacles, which secrete a digestive fluid. If touched by an object they bend toward the center of the leaf, causing the entrapment of the object.

The Venus flytrap, *Dionaea muscipula*, with its toothed

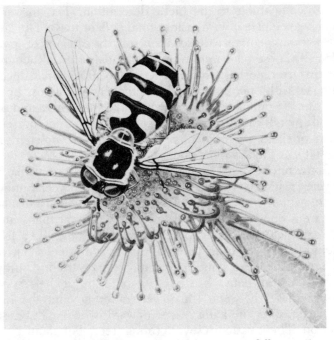

97. The sundew, *Drosera rotundifolia*, successfully trapping a hover fly, *Syrphus ribesii*.

bilobed leaf, which springs shut when triggered by a victim, comes closest in analogy to the great leaves that Liche stated sprang upward to trap and crush the human victim.

We note that Liche's tree incorporated not one, but five or six of the special adaptations found singly in carnivorous plants. Clearly such a set of redundancies are a never-never-land combination that could not reasonably be the result of effective evolutionary adaptation. Nor could the adaptation to humans as a food source be possible, since even primitive man, including man's closest relatives, the apes, are far too intelligent to permit themselves to be trapped regularly for plant food. On the other hand, if it were adapted to trap the relatively small primitive primates of Madagascar, known as lemurs, the possibility of accommodating humans would hardly exist. Liche suggests that birds might be the normal prey for the plant, but the same objection holds.

At this point we are led to agree with Willy Ley's main conclusion, that no man-eating plant as described by Liche ever existed. Ley was wrong, however, in maintaining that there were no myths or legends about a man-eating tree. It seems conceivable to me that Carle Liche, if he ever existed, combined observations of a variety of plant characteristics from various exotic plants, both noncarnivorous and carnivorous types, to embellish and describe a native legend, making himself the eyewitness reporter.

It may well be that there existed or still exists an unknown relatively large carnivorous plant that has one or two of the adaptations described for trapping birds or other smaller arboreal creatures. There are still large forest areas, especially in the southeastern and south-central portions of Madagascar, that would be interesting to explore.

Era	Period	Began million years ago	Length in million years	Development of Life
CENOZOIC	Quaternary	3	3	The Pleistocene and recent periods. Widespread dominance of mamma Evolution of the homonid line leading to *Homo erectus* about 500,000 years ago.
	Tertiary	70	67	Paleocene to Pliocene. Ancestral horses, pigs, cattle and primates appe at the dawn of the Age of Mammals. Flowering plants reach full develo ment.
MESOZOIC	Cretaceous	135	65	Great dinosaurs, ammonites and primitive fish extinct during the late Cretaceous. Flowering plants develop. Mammals and primitive birds more numerous.
	Jurassic	180	45	The Age of Reptiles: many and varied reptile forms dominant in a forest-swamp-plain environment. First winged reptiles and primitive birds evolve.
	Triassic	225	45	Worldwide desert conditions with seasonal rainfall creating deltas and salt lakes. First primitive mammals. Period of great diversity of reptile groups.
PALEOZOIC	Permian	270	45	Climax of Carboniferous mountain building period. Rich marine and freshwater life. Modern insects (bugs, beetles) appear. Rise of the rep
	Carboniferous	350	80	Lycopods and tree ferns dominant on land. First appearance of gymn sperms. Winged insects evolve along with spiders and land scorpions. First reptiles appear.
	Devonian	400	50	Remarkable evolution of fishes invading freshwater environments and giving rise to the first airbreathing amphibians. Insects numerous on la
	Silurian	440	40	Seaweeds abundant in shallow seas giving rise to the first land plants. Freshwater and estuarine deposits hold fossils of jawed fish and sea-scorpions.
	Ordovician	500	60	Mild climate over much of the earth. Corals, sponges, cephalopods an trilobites abundant in reduced oceans. First fish-like vertebrates appe in North America.
	Cambrian	600	100	First appearance of abundant fossil remains. Trilobites, echinoderms, graptolites and foraminifera common in shallow seas covering much earth's surface.
PROTEROZOIC / ARCHEOZOIC	Pre-Cambrian (Not divided into periods)	4600	4000	Evidence of primitive invertebrates—bacteria, sponges and worms. Earliest traces of life are algae and bacteria dated at over 3000 millior years old.

Bibliography

INTRODUCTION

Colbert, Edwin H. "Was the Extinct Giraffe (*Sivatherium*) Known to the Early Sumerians?" *American Anthropologist*, Vol. 38, pp. 605–8, 1936.

Dagg, Anne Innis, and Foster, J. Bristol. *The Giraffe*. New York: Van Nostrand Reinhold Co., 1976.

Johnston, Sir Henry H. *The Okapi: The Newly Discovered Beast Living in Central Africa*. Annual Report of the Board of Regents of the Smithsonian Institution, pp. 660–66. Washington, D.C.: U.S. Government Printing Office, 1901.

Leakey, L. S. B. "Does the Chalicothere—Contemporary of the Okapi—Still Survive?" *Illustrated London News*, Vol. 97, No. 2,532, pp. 730–33, 750, Nov. 2, 1935.

Maurice, Albert. *H. M. Stanley—Unpublished Letters*. London and Edinburgh: W. R. Chambers Ltd., 1955.

Spinage, C. A. *The Book of the Giraffe*. Boston: Houghton Mifflin Company, 1968.

Stanley, Henry M. *In Darkest Africa*, Vols. I and II. New York: Charles Scribner's Sons, 1890.

———. *My Dark Companions and Three Strange Stories*. New York: Charles Scribner's Sons, 1893.

Stanley, Richard, and Neame, Alan (eds.). *The Exploration Diaries of H. M. Stanley*. London: William Kimber, 1961.

CHAPTER I

Bell, Margaret E. *Touched with Fire*. New York: William Morrow & Company, 1960.

Ford, Corey. *Where the Sea Breaks Its Back*. Boston and Toronto: Little, Brown & Company, 1966.

Golder, F. A. *Bering's Voyages* (in two volumes). New York: American Geographical Society, 1925.

Masterson, James R., and Brower, Helen. *Bering's Successors*, 1745–1780. Seattle: University of Washington Press, 1948.

Nordenskjöld, A. E. *The Voyage of the* Vega. New York: Macmillan and Company, 1886.

Stejneger, Leonhard. "Contributions to the History of the Commander Islands. No. 2. Investigations Relating to the Date of the Extermination of Steller's Sea-Cow," *Proceedings of the United States National Museum*, Vol. VIII, pp. 181–89. Washington, D.C.: U. S. Government Printing Office, 1884.

————. *Georg Wilhelm Steller*. Cambridge, Mass.: Harvard University Press, 1936.

Steller, G. W. *De Bestiis Marinis. Novi Commentarii Academiae Scientiarum Imperialis Petropolitanae*, Vol. 2, pp. 289–398, with Pls. 15 and 16. St. Petersburg: 1751.

Tilesius, W. G. *Die Wallfische*, pp. 709–52. Isis (Oken's): 1835.

CHAPTER II

Heuvelmans, Bernard. *In the Wake of the Sea-Serpents*. New York: Hill and Wang, 1968.

Kellogg, Remington. *A Review of the Archaeoceti*. Washington, D.C.: Carnegie Institution of Washington, 1936.

King, Judith E. *Seals of the World*. London: Trustees of the British Museum (Natural History), 1964.

Leblond, Paul H., and Sibert, John. *Observations of Large Unidentified Marine Animals in British Columbia and Adjacent Waters*. Manuscript Report No. 28, June 1973. Vancouver: Institute of Oceanography, University of British Columbia.

New York *Times*. " 'Sea Serpent' Appears off Vancouver Island," Feb. 11, 1934.

Scammon, Charles M. *The Marine Mammals of the North-Western Coast of North America*. San Francisco: John H. Carmany and Company, 1974.

Scheffer, Victor B. *Seals, Sea Lions and Walruses*. Stanford, Calif.: Stanford University Press, 1958.

CHAPTER III

Benjamin, George J. "Diving into the Blue Holes of the Bahamas," *National Geographic*, Vol. 138, No. 3, Sept. 1970.

Haley, Delphine. "Saga of Steller's Sea Cow," *Natural History*, Vol. LXXXVII, No. 9, Nov. 1978.

Heuvelmans, Bernard. *In the Wake of the Sea-Serpents*. New York: Hill & Wang, 1968.

Mangiacopra, Gary S. "*Octopus giganteus* Verrill: A New Species of Cephalopod," *Of Sea and Shore*, Spring 1975, pp. 3–10. Port Gamble, WA.

———. "The Great Ones," *Of Sea and Shore*, Summer 1976, pp. 51–52. Port Gamble, WA.

Verrill, A. E. "A Gigantic Cephalopod on the Florida Coast," *American Journal of Science*, 4th series, Vol. III, No. CLII (No. 13), p. 79, Jan. 1879.

———. "Additional Information Concerning the Giant Cephalopod of Florida," *American Journal of Science*, 4th series, Vol. III, No. CLIII (No. 14), pp. 162–63, Feb. 1897.

———. "Gigantic Octopus," New York *Herald*, 2nd ed., No. 22,049, 4th sec., p. 13, Jan. 3, 1897.

———. "The Florida Monster," *Science*, Vol. V, No. 114, p. 392, Mar. 5, 1897.

———. "The Florida Sea Monster," *The American Naturalist*, Vol. XXXI, pp. 304–7, 1897.

———. "The Supposed Great Octopus of Florida—Certainly not a Cephalopod," *American Journal of Science*, 4th series, Vol. III, No. CLIII (No. 16), p. 355, Apr. 1897.

———. "What Is This Creature?," New York *Herald*, No. 22, 5th sec., p. 112, Mar. 7, 1897.

Wood, F. G., and Gennaro, Joseph F., Jr. "An Octopus Trilogy," *Natural History*, Vol. LXXX, No. 3, p. 14, Mar. 1971.

Wright, Bruce. "The Lusca of Andros," *The Atlantic Advocate*, June 1967.

CHAPTER IV

Augusta, Josef, and Burian, Zdeněk. *Prehistoric Reptiles and Birds*, London: Paul Hamlyn, 1961.

Desmond, Adrian J. *The Hot-blooded Dinosaurs*. New York: The Dial Press/James Wade, 1976.

Gilmore, W. Charles. "A Nearly Complete Articulated Skeleton of Camarasaurus, a Saurischian Dinosaur from the Dinosaur National Monument, Utah," *Memoirs of the Carnegie Museum*, Vol. 10, No. 3, pp. 347–84, Dec. 1922–June 1925.

Gregory, William K. "Restoration of *Camarasaurus* and Life Model," *Proceedings of the National Academy of Sciences*, Vol. 6, p. 16, 1920.

Grzimek, H. C. Bernhard (ed.-in-chief). Grzimek's Animal Life Encyclopedia, Vol. 6, *Reptiles*. New York: Van Nostrand Reinhold Company, 1968.

Heuvelmans, Bernard. *Les Derniers Dragons d'Afrique*, 1st volume of a series entitled *Bêtes Ignorées du Monde*. Paris: Plon, 1978.

――――. *On the Track of Unknown Animals*. New York: Hill and Wang, 1959.

Horn, Alfred Aloysius. *Trader Horn* (ed. by Ethelreda Lewis). New York: Simon and Schuster, 1927.

Kondo, Herbert, Editor. The Illustrated Encyclopedia of the Animal Kingdom. Danbury, Conn.: Danbury Press, 1970.

Melland, F. H. *In Witchbound Africa*. London: Seeley, Service & Company, 1923.

Osborn, Henry F., and Mook, Charles C. "*Camarasaurus, Amphicoelias*, and other Sauropods of *Cope*," *Memoirs of the American Museum of Natural History*, Vol. III, Part 3, pp. 251–387, Jan. 1921.

――――. "Characters and Restoration of the Sauropod Genus *Camarasaurus Cope*," *Proceedings of the American Philosophical Society*, Vol. LVIII, pp. 386–96, 1969.

――――. "Reconstruction of the Skeleton of the Sauropod Dinosaur *Camarasaurus Cope*," *Proceedings of the National Academy of Sciences*, Vol. 6, p. 15, 1920.

Seeley, S. H. G. *Dragons of the Air*. New York: D. Appleton & Company, 1901.

Smith, J. L. B. *Old Fourlegs: The Story of the Coelacanth*. London: Longmans, Green & Company, Ltd., 1956.

Sundberg, Jan-Ove. "The Monster of Sraheens Lough," *Info Journal*, No. 22, Mar. 1977, International Fortean Organization.

CHAPTER V

Burden, W. Douglas. *Dragon Lizards of Komodo*. New York: G. P. Putnam's Sons, 1927.

Grzimek, H. C. Bernhard (ed.-in-chief). Grzimek's Animal Life Encyclopedia, Vol. 6. *Reptiles*. New York: Van Nostrand Reinhold Company, 1975.

Izzard, Ralph. *The Hunt for the Buru*. London: Hodder and Stoughton, 1951.

Kondo, Herbert (ed.). The Illustrated Encyclopedia of the Animal Kingdom. Danbury, Conn.: Danbury Press, 1970.

Ouwens, P. A. "On a Large *Varanus* Species from the Island of

Komodo," *Bulletin du Jardin Botanique de Buitenzorz*, Deuxième serie No. VI, 1912.

von Fürer-Haimendorf, Christopher. "The Valley of the Unknown," *Illustrated* London *News*, No. 3,149, Vol. 121, pp. 526–30, Nov. 8, 1947.

CHAPTER VI

Augusta, Josef, and Burian, Zdenĕk. *The Age of Monsters*. London: Paul Hamlyn, 1966.

Buick, T. Lindsay. *The Moa-Hunters of New Zealand*. New Plymouth, N.Z.: Thomas Avery and Sons Ltd., 1937.

———. *The Mystery of the Moa*. New Plymouth, N.Z.: Thomas Avery and Sons Ltd., 1931.

Greenway, James C., Jr. *Extinct and Vanishing Birds of the World*. New York: Dover Publications, Inc., 1967.

Hachisuka, Masauji. *The Dodo and Kindred Birds*. London: H. F. & G. Witherby Ltd., 1953.

Heilman, Gerhard. *The Origin of Birds*. New York: D. Appleton and Company, 1927.

Heuvelmans, Bernard. *On the Track of Unknown Animals*. New York: Hill and Wang, 1959.

Ley, Willy. *Exotic Zoology*. New York: Viking Press, 1962.

Rothschild, Walter. *Extinct Birds*. London: Hutchinson & Company, 1907.

CHAPTER VII

Barnes, Robert D. *Invertebrate Zoology*. Philadelphia: W. B. Saunders Company, 1966.

Eights, James. "Description of a New Crustacean Animal Found on the Shores of the South Shetland Islands, with Remarks on their Natural History. Art. IV; Description of a New Animal belonging to the Crustacea, Discovered in Antarctic Seas. Art. XV," *Transactions of the Albany Institute*, Vol. II, 1833–52.

Geological-Geophysical Atlas of the Indian Ocean. Moscow: Academy of Science of USSR, 1975.

Heezen, Bruce C., and Hollister, Charles D. *The Face of the Deep*. New York: Oxford University Press, 1971.

Levi-Setti, Riccardo. *Trilobites*. Chicago: University of Chicago Press, 1975.

Ley, Willy. *Exotic Zoology*. New York: Viking Press, 1962.
————. *The Lungfish, the Dodo, and the Unicorn*. New York: Viking Press, 1948.
Linklater, Eric. *The Voyage of the* Challenger. Garden City, N.Y.: Doubleday & Company, 1972.
Moore, Raymond C. (ed.). *A Treatise on Invertebrate Paleontology*. Lawrence: University of Kansas Press and the Geological Society of America, 1959 (Part O) and 1955 (Part P).
Moore, Raymond C.; Lalicker, Cecil G.; and Fischer, Alfred G. *Invertebrate Fossils*. New York: McGraw-Hill, 1952.

CHAPTER VIII

Botting, Douglas. *Humboldt and the Cosmos*. New York: Harper & Row, 1973.
Chatwin, Bruce. *In Patagonia*. New York: Summit Books, 1977.
Costello, Peter. *In Search of Lake Monsters*. New York: Coward, McCann & Geoghegan, 1974.
De Terra, Helmut. *Humboldt*. New York: Alfred A. Knopf, 1955.
Dinsdale, Tim. *The Leviathans*. London: Routledge & Kegan Paul, 1966.
Fawcett, Colonel P. H. *Exploration Fawcett*. Arranged by Brian Fawcett. London: Arrow Books, 1968.
Fleming, Peter. *Brazilian Adventure*. New York: Charles Scribner's Sons, 1934.
Foster, Robert J. *General Geology*. Columbus, O.: Charles E. Merrill Publishing Company, 1969.
Heuvelmans, Bernard. *On the Track of Unknown Animals*. New York: Hill & Wang, 1959.
Smith, Anthony. *Mato Grosso*. New York: E. P. Dutton, 1971.
von Hagen, Victor Wolfgang. *South America Called Them*. New York: Alfred A. Knopf, 1945.

CHAPTER IX

Barnes, Robert D. *Invertebrate Zoology*. Philadelphia: W. B. Saunders Company, 1966.
Berrill, N. J. *The Tunicata*. London: Ray Society, Bernard Quaritch, 1950.
Bigelow, Henry B. "Medusae from the Maldive Islands," *Bulletin of the Museum of Comparative Zoology at Harvard College*, Vol. XXXIX, No. 9, April 1904.

Brooks, W. K. "The Genus Salpa," *Memoirs Biological Laboratory, Johns Hopkins*, Vol. 2, 1893.

Heuvelmans, Bernard. *In the Wake of the Sea-Serpents*. New York: Hill & Wang, 1968.

Lohmann, Hans, and Neuman, Günther. "Tunicata," in *Handbuch der Zoologie*, Vol. 5, Part II. Berlin: Walter De Gruyter & Company, 1956.

Mayer, Alfred Goldsborough, *Ctenophores of the Atlantic Coast of North America*. Washington, D.C.: Carnegie Institute of Washington, 1912.

Michael, Ellis L. "Differentials in Behavior of the Two Generations of *Salpa Democratica* Relative to the Temperature of the Sea," *University of California Publications in Zoology*, Vol. 18, No. 12, pp. 239–98, 1918.

Oudemans, A. C. *The Great Sea-Serpent*. Published by the author. London: Luzac & Co., 1892.

Parker, T. Jeffery, and Haswell, William A. *A Textbook of Zoology*. New York: Macmillan & Company, 1964.

Thompson, Harold. *Pelagic Tunicates of Australia*. Melbourne: Commonwealth Council for Scientific and Industrial Research, 1948.

CHAPTER X

WHITE RIVER MONSTER
Newspaper articles:
  Arkansas *Democrat*, Little Rock, Ark.
    Feb. 16, 1973
    May 26, 1974
  Arkansas *Gazette*, Little Rock, Ark.
    May 12, 1924
    June 19, 1971
    June 23, 1971
    June 25, 1971
    July 1, 1971
    July 7, 1971
    July 9, 1971
    July 28, 1971
    July 2, 1972
    Feb. 25, 1973
    Apr. 19, 1973
    May 12, 1973

Commercial Appeal, Little Rock, Ark.

   July 7, 1937
   July 9, 1937
   July 22, 1937
   July 24, 1937

Log Cabin Democrat, Conway, Ark.

   Feb. 16, 1973

Newport *Daily Independent*, Newport, Ark.

   June 18, 1971
   June 21, 1971
   June 24, 1971
   June 28, 1971
   June 30, 1971
   July 6, 1971
   July 28, 1971
   Aug. 16, 1971
   June 6, 1972
   June 7, 1972

Northwest Arkansas *Times*, Fayetteville, Ark.

   July 10, 1972

Nonnewspaper citations:

Federal Writers' Project: Celebrating the Third Annual Rice and
   Cotton Festival Oct. 7, 8, and 9, Newport, Ark., Jackson
   County, "Home of the White River Monster," Sponsored
   by the Newport Chamber of Commerce. Little Rock, Ark.
   1937.

Pursuit, Vol. 4, No. 4, pp. 89–95, Oct. 1971.

ALKALI LAKE MONSTER, ARKANSAS

New York *Times*, New York, N.Y.

   July 25, 1923
   July 27, 1923
   Aug. 5, 1923

"Sea Monster Reported in Nebraska Lake," *Frontier Times*,
   June–July 1975. Courtesy Nebraska State Historical Society,
   Lincoln, Neb.

SILVER LAKE MONSTER, NEW YORK

Sherman *Democrat*, Sherman, Tex.

   June 25, 1976

LAKE MANITOU MONSTER, INDIANA

Smalley, Donald. "The Logansport *Telegraph* and the Monster
   of the Indiana Lakes," *Indiana Historical Society Publications*, Vol. II, 1946.

VALLEY RIVER MONSTER, NORTH CAROLINA
  Asheville *Citizen-Times*, Asheville, N.C., Jan. 10, 1971.
LAKE KOSHKONONY MONSTER, WISCONSIN
  Brown, Charles E. *Sea Serpents—Wisconsin Occurrences of These
    Weird Water Monsters*. Madison: Wisconsin Folklore Society,
    1942.
WISCONSIN LAKE MONSTERS
  Wisconsin *State Journal*, Madison, Wis.
    June 28, 1883
    June 12, 1897
FARMER'S POND MONSTER
  Arkansas *Gazette*, Little Rock, Ark.
    July 12, 1967
  The Brunswicker, Brunswick, Mo.
    July 13, 1967
  Grand Rapids *Press*, Grand Rapids, Mich.
    July 12, 1967
LAKE CHAMPLAIN MONSTER
  Newspaper articles:
  Burlington *Free Press*, Burlington, Vt.
    "The Lake Champlain Sea Serpent," Nov. 7, 1879
    "Lake Champlain's Serpent," July 16, 1886
    "Lake Champlain's Sea Serpent," May 16, 1887
    "Lake Champlain Sea Serpent," July 11, 1887
  Hartford *Courant*, Hartford, Conn.
    "Sea Serpent Again," July 11, 1887
  New York *Times*, New York, N.Y.
    "A Vermont Sea Serpent," Nov. 10, 1879
    "Milk and Lemonade Serpent," July 11, 1887
    "Legendary Sea-Serpent Rears Head Once More," Aug. 18,
      1929
  Plattsburgh *Republican*, Plattsburgh, N.Y.
    "Cape Ann Serpent on Lake Champlain," July 26, 1819
    "Is There a Lake Champlain Sea Serpent, After All?," Sept.
      28, 1878
    "Lake Champlain Mysteries," Dec. 11, 1886
    "The Champlain Sea Serpent," May 21, 1887
    "The Champlain Sea Serpent," July 16, 1887
    "How Are the Mighty Fallen," Mar. 2, 1895
    "The Champlain Sea Serpent Has Arrived," Aug. 5, 1899
  Plattsburgh *Sentinel*, Plattsburgh, N.Y.

"A Lake Monster," May 16, 1879
"The Lake Serpent Again," Sept. 19, 1879
"The Lake Champlain Monster Seen Again," May 27, 1887
"Champlain's Sea Serpent," Aug. 15, 1887
Sunday Times Union, Albany, N.Y.
"Champlain Monster," Nov. 23, 1975
Swanton *Courier*, Swanton, N.Y.
"The Lake Champlain Sea Serpent," July 31, 1886
Nonnewspaper citations:
Mangiacopra, Gary S. "Lake Champlain: America's Loch Ness,"
    Of Sea and Shore, Spring 1978 (Part I), Summer 1978 (Part
    II). Port Gamble, WA.
Vermont Life, Montpelier, Vt.
"Champlain Ace in the Hole," Summer 1959
"Monster Time Again," Spring 1962
"The Champlain Monster," Summer 1970

CHAPTER XI

Buckland, Frank. *Story of the Ogopogo*. Okanagan Historical Society,
    1943.
Costello, Peter. *In Search of Lake Monsters*. New York: Coward,
    McCann & Geoghegan, 1974.
Grzimek, H. C. Bernhard (ed.-in-chief). Grzimek's Animal Life
    Encyclopedia, Vol. 11, *Mammals*. New York: Van Nostrand Rein-
    hold Company, 1975.
Lyons, Chess. *Milestones in Ogopogoland*. Victoria, B.C.: M. Page,
    1957.
McLean, Roy Patterson. "Ogopogo: His Story," Kelowna *Daily
    Courier*, 1952. Based on files of the Kelowna *Daily Courier*.
Moon, Mary. *Ogopogo*. Vancouver, B.C.: J. J. Douglas Ltd., 1967.

CHAPTER XII

Cooke, M. C. *Freaks and Marvels of Plant Life*. New York: Society
    for Promoting Christian Knowledge, E. J. B. Young & Company,
    1882.
Copland, Samuel. *A History of the Island of Madagascar*. Westport,
    Conn.: Greenwood Press, 1970.
Darwin, Charles. *Insectivorous Plants*. London: John Murray, 1888.
Ellis, Rev. William. *Three Visits to Madagascar*. London: John
    Murray, 1858.

Emboden, William A. *Bizarre Plants*. New York: Macmillan, 1974.

"Escaped from the Embrace of the Man-eating Tree," "American Weekly," Jan. 4, 1925, p. 6. Based on a report by W. C. Bryant, of Bryant, Miss.

Hope, Laurence. *Complete Love Lyrics*. New York: Garden City, 1940.

Keller, Conrad. *Reisebilder aus Ostafrika und Madagaskar*. Leipzig, 1887.

Ley, Willy. *Exotic Zoology*. New York: Viking Press, 1962.

———. *Salamanders and Other Wonders*. New York: Viking Press, 1955.

Lloyd, Francis Ernest. *The Carnivorous Plants*. New York: Dover, 1976.

"Mystery of the Man-eating Tree of Madagascar," "American Weekly," Oct. 19, 1942, p. 6. Based on a report by Chase Salmon Osborn, former governor of Michigan.

Oliver, Samuel Pasfield. *Madagascar*. New York: Macmillan, 1886.

Osborn, Chase Salmon. *Madagascar, Land of the Man-eating Tree*. New York: Republic Publishing Company, 1924.

Prior, Sophia. *Carnivorous Plants and "The Man-eating Tree,"* Botany Leaflet No. 23. Chicago: Field Museum of Natural History, 1939.

Shaw, George A. *Madagascar and France*. New York: American Tract Society, 1884.

Skinner, Charles M. *Myths and Legends of Flowers, Trees, Fruits, and Plants*. Philadelphia: J. B. Lippincott, 1911.

Williams, Dr. B. H. "Sacrificed to a Man-eating Plant," "American Weekly," Sept. 26, 1920, p. 6.

Wilson, Andrew. "Science Jottings," *Illustrated* London *News*, Aug. 27, 1892, p. 279; Sept. 24, 1892, p. 403.

Index